Governing International Commons

The Amazon rainforest is a vital carbon reservoir and climate regulator, and yet global demands on its natural resources are leading to irreversible environmental damage, impacting the planet's water cycle, climate, and food security. How to balance the interests of the eight Amazon basin states with these global environmental concerns, and the ancestral rights of the over 400 indigenous peoples that live there?

Building on fieldwork in Peru, Brazil, and Ecuador, this book provides a novel multi-scalar and multi-sectoral analysis of the Amazon. In doing so, it argues that the current governance of the Amazon exhibits the policy failures of polycentricity, with different authorities developing localized environmental initiatives with weak coordination. It sets out a policy paradigm shift to plurinational governance that incorporates indigenous peoples and conservation scientists in international decision-making.

This book will interest academics of environmental law, politics and governance, and policymakers and practitioners involved in global environmental governance in general and international commons and the Amazonian region in particular.

Roger Merino is Associate Professor at the Public Management School, University of the Pacific (Universidad del Pacífico), Lima, Peru. He has been research associate at the University of Georgia's Center for Integrative Conservation Research and visiting scholar at the Harvard's Institute for Global Law and Policy. He holds a PhD in Social and Policy Sciences from the University of Bath, United Kingdom, and master's degree in International Policy and Comparative Law. He has authored numerous research articles, book chapters, and a monograph on issues of political ecology, environmental governance, human rights, and international environmental law.

Transnational Environmental Law

TEL

Transnational Environmental Law (TEL) is a series of books for the study of environmental law and governance beyond the state. It approaches legal and regulatory developments with an interest in the contribution of non-state actors and an awareness of the multi-level governance context in which contemporary environmental law unfolds. TEL has a broad disciplinary focus open to scholarly contributions covering a wide range of environmental issues and the evolving dynamics between environmental law and other legal disciplines. TEL strives for a new generation of environmental scholarship that will bridge geographical boundaries, scholarly styles and generations.

BOOKS IN THE SERIES

Jessika Eichler and Mario G. Aguilera, *Indigenous Environmental Rights: Towards a Holistic Regime*
Roger Merino, *Governing International Commons: From Polycentric to Plurinational Governance in the Amazon*
Annika Frosch, *Navigating the Souring Seas: The Global Experimentalist Governance of Ocean Acidification*
Agung Wardana, *Turning Defenders into Defendants: The Use of Lawfare against Environmental Activists in Southeast Asia*

Governing International Commons

From Polycentric to Plurinational Governance in the Amazon

Roger Merino
Universidad del Pacífico, Lima, Perú

TEL

CAMBRIDGE
UNIVERSITY PRESS

CAMBRIDGE
UNIVERSITY PRESS

Shaftesbury Road, Cambridge CB2 8EA, United Kingdom

One Liberty Plaza, 20th Floor, New York, NY 10006, USA

477 Williamstown Road, Port Melbourne, VIC 3207, Australia

314–321, 3rd Floor, Plot 3, Splendor Forum, Jasola District Centre, New Delhi – 110025, India

103 Penang Road, #05–06/07, Visioncrest Commercial, Singapore 238467

Cambridge University Press is part of Cambridge University Press & Assessment, a department of the University of Cambridge.

We share the University's mission to contribute to society through the pursuit of education, learning and research at the highest international levels of excellence.

www.cambridge.org
Information on this title: www.cambridge.org/9781009689045

DOI: 10.1017/9781009689076

When citing this work, please include a reference to the DOI 10.1017/9781009689076

First published 2026

A catalogue record for this publication is available from the British Library

Library of Congress Cataloging-in-Publication Data
Names: Merino, Roger author
Title: Governing international commons : from polycentric to plurinational governance in the amazon / Roger Merino, Universidad del Pacífico.
Description: Cambridge, United Kingdom ; New York, NY : Cambridge University Press, 2026. | Series: Transnational environmental law | Includes bibliographical references and index.
Identifiers: LCCN 2025037656 (print) | LCCN 2025037657 (ebook) | ISBN 9781009689045 hardback | ISBN 9781009689076 ebook
Subjects: LCSH: Environmental law – Amazon River Region | Environmental policy – Amazon River Region | Environmental justice – Amazon River Region | Environmental law, International | Common heritage of mankind (International law) | Human rights – Amazon River Region | Democracy | LCGFT: Law materials
Classification: LCC KH642.A46 M47 2026 (print) | LCC KH642.A46 (ebook) | DDC 344.81104/6–dc23/eng/20250814
LC record available at https://lccn.loc.gov/2025037656
LC ebook record available at https://lccn.loc.gov/2025037657

ISBN 978-1-009-68904-5 Hardback

To Eva

CONTENTS

FIGURES

FOREWORD

The Amazon rainforest has long stood as a symbol of the world's ecological wealth and fragility. As the largest tropical forest on Earth, it serves as a global carbon reservoir and climate regulator, providing irreplaceable ecosystem services that extend far beyond the eight basin states of Brazil, Peru, Colombia, Bolivia, Venezuela, Guyana, Suriname, and Ecuador, and the overseas French Department of French Guiana. Yet, despite its centrality to global environmental stability, the Amazon is subject to relentless pressures: the global demand for agricultural commodities, timber, minerals, gas, and oil is driving unprecedented land-use change and deforestation. These processes imperil not only biodiversity and the planet's climate, but also the rights and survival of more than 400 Indigenous peoples whose ancestral territories and cultures are interwoven with the forest.

Against this backdrop, the governance of the Amazon presents one of the most pressing transnational challenges of our time. Balancing the sovereign developmental aspirations of basin states, the legitimate claims of Indigenous nations, and the imperatives of global environmental protection is an inherently complex task. The international community has attempted to grapple with this challenge, but progress has been uneven and fragmented. The Amazonian Cooperation Treaty Organization (ACTO), the primary regional mechanism for cooperation, has struggled to play a decisive role. Meanwhile, the expansion of extractive economies continues to overshadow both environmental priorities and Indigenous rights.

Roger Merino's book, *Governing International Commons: From Polycentric to Plurinational Governance in the Amazon*, confronts these tensions head-on. Drawing on more than a decade of sustained research, it offers a critical examination of the Amazonian governance regime through the lens of polycentric governance theory. Polycentricity – understood here as a framework in which multiple authorities at different scales develop initiatives with limited central coordination – has gained considerable traction in international environmental law and governance debates. Yet, as the author convincingly demonstrates, the Amazon illustrates the shortcomings of this paradigm. Fragmented, weakly coordinated initiatives have reinforced rather than challenged the dominance of nation-states, entrenching extractive policies and marginalizing Indigenous voices.

The book's central contribution lies in articulating an alternative vision. It argues that the Amazon requires not more of the same but rather a profound reimagining of governance frameworks. Specifically, it advances the concepts of plurinational and pluriversal governance. A plurinational approach demands a redefinition of sovereignty itself, ensuring meaningful participation for Indigenous peoples in international decision-making processes. Interestingly, this reinterpretation of governance has important parallels with the understanding of polycentric governance as developed by Vincent and Elinor Ostrom, where self-governance was the foundation for polycentric governance, and a plurality of actors a natural consequence of such self-governance. A pluriversal approach, additionally, opens international forums to diverse worldviews on the human–nature relationship, allowing for more inclusive, intercultural deliberations on how shared ecological systems should be managed.

This book is a bold and timely intervention in the field of Transnational Environmental Law (TEL). It pushes the boundaries of established theoretical frameworks and calls attention to the normative and institutional transformations required to govern ecosystems that transcend national borders. By situating the Amazon at the intersection of Indigenous rights, state sovereignty, and global environmental concerns, the book deepens our understanding of how governance structures can perpetuate ecological and social harm - or, conversely, open pathways toward more equitable and sustainable futures.

The TEL series seeks to highlight works that combine rigorous scholarship with normative ambition and policy relevance. *Governing International Commons* exemplifies this aspiration. It offers vital insights not only to scholars of international and environmental law, but also to policymakers, Indigenous leaders, and civil society actors engaged in the struggle for the Amazon's future. We are delighted to include this important contribution in the TEL series.

Thijs Etty & Josephine van Zeben
Series Editors,
Transnational Environmental Law Book Series

ACKNOWLEDGMENTS

Many people, networks, and institutions have encouraged and supported my continued engagement with the political ecology and environmental governance of the Amazon rainforest. I am deeply grateful to each colleague, friend, and mentor who has accompanied me through the reflections, discussions, and writing that have shaped this book over the years.

I am especially thankful for the ongoing support of my home institution, University of the Pacific (Universidad del Pacífico, UP) in Lima, Peru. A research grant from UP enabled me to begin investigating the tensions between conservation initiatives and Indigenous territorial rights in the Peruvian Amazon. Much of the empirical content in Chapter 3 draws on findings from this project, which were also published in *Global Environmental Politics* in 2022 as "Conflicting Sovereignties: Global Conservation, Protected Areas, and Indigenous Nations in the Peruvian Amazon."

I would also like to thank the Global Development Network (GDN) for funding my research on the international governance of the Amazon. A GDN grant allowed me to conduct fieldwork at the headquarters of the Amazon Cooperation Treaty Organization (ACTO) in Brasília and the offices of the Coordinator of Indigenous Organizations of the Amazon Basin (COICA) in Quito. Under the guidance and mentorship of Professor Laura Rival from the Oxford Department of International Development, I conducted two studies through this project: "Governing International Commons: Re-examining Environmental and Sovereignty Imaginaries in the Amazon," published in *Transnational Environmental Law* (2025), and "Indigenous Sovereignties in International Governance: Envisioning a Plurinational Amazon," published in *Globalizations* (2024). Chapters 2 and 5 of this book are grounded in the theoretical and empirical developments of these articles.

My thanks also go to the Latin American Council of Social Sciences (CLACSO), which supported my research on mega-infrastructure and extractivism in the Amazon. The early working paper from this project was discussed at the University of Kassel in 2022 during my fellowship under the project "Extractivism." I shared ideas with Professor Hans-Jürgen Burchardt and colleagues there, and I am grateful for their generous feedback. The resulting article, "The Open Veins of the Amazon: Rethinking Extractivism and Infrastructure in Extractive Frontiers," was published in *The Journal of Peasant Studies* in 2024 and forms the basis of Chapter 3 of this book.

Numerous concepts and sections of this book were enriched by critical conversations with friends and peers. During my sabbatical year (2023–2024), I was a research associate at the Center for Integrative Conservation at the University of Georgia. There, I presented early drafts of Chapter 4 at the Warnell School of

Forestry and engaged with a vibrant academic community. I am thankful to Laura German and Jesse Abrams for their warm welcome and for including me in their academic initiatives. I am also grateful to Professor Moisés Arce of Tulane University for inviting me to present ideas from this book at the Earth Day Symposium "Andes Melting / Amazon Burning" in New Orleans in April 2024. Professor Américo Mendoza-Mori kindly allowed me to present the main thesis of the then-book project in his class at Harvard University. I also thank Professor Krushil Watene for encouraging me to present an early version of Chapter 6 at the international conference on Climate Justice: Transdisciplinary and Intercultural Conversations, held at the University of St Andrews in May 2024.

I am indebted to my critical legal friends from the TWAIL (Third World Approaches to International Law) movement. Over the years, our encounters at workshops, conferences, and informal gatherings have inspired many of the ideas developed in this book. I am especially thankful to Tony Anghie, Luis Eslava, Julia Dehm, Usha Natarajan, and other TWAILers for involving me in thought-provoking and meaningful projects.

I am also deeply grateful to the civil society and Indigenous organizations that have supported my research journey. Thanks to Amazon Watch, I had the opportunity to fly across the northern Peruvian Amazon to attend the 2023 Congress of Indigenous Autonomous Governments. The Forest Peoples Programme, the Institute for Legal Defense, and Law, Environment and Natural Resources have always been open and generous in responding to my inquiries. I owe special thanks to anthropologist Flica Barcklay of Peru Equidad for her continuous support and advice. I also extend my gratitude to the Indigenous leaders and officials at COICA who welcomed me into their offices, as well as to the current and former officials at ACTO and the scientists from the Science Panel for the Amazon, all of whom graciously answered my many questions.

Finally, I wish to express my eternal gratitude to my wife, Ady, and my daughter, Eva, for their unwavering patience, love, and support throughout this journey.

CHAPTER 1

Introduction

The Amazon has historically been a place of ecological imaginaries: a pristine, inhospitable, and incommensurable forest full of hidden cultural and natural treasures, and hailed as "the lung of the world," spanning vast territories of South American nations. When I flew in a small airplane over the Northern Peruvian Amazon, the view appeared to align with this image. Kilometers of a sea of greenness seemed endless, and this is only a small portion of the 5.3 million km^2 that encompasses the Amazon basin. The Amazon is indeed the largest tropical forest and the greatest biodiversity and freshwater reserve in the world (Nobre et al., 2016; Fausct et al., 2015; Picq, 2017). As a global carbon reservoir and climate regulator (Cardil et al., 2020), and a global source of food, water, and energy (Garrido et al., 2020), the Amazon benefits not only the eight basin states of Brazil, Peru, Colombia, Bolivia, Venezuela, Guyana, Suriname, and Ecuador, and the overseas department of France, French Guyana, but also the international community at large (Garcia, 2011).

However, this majestic rainforest is slowly, increasingly, and unstoppably dying. In addition to ecological and romantic imaginaries, economic imaginaries of the Amazon justify massive transnational investments in mining, hydrocarbons, infrastructure, energy, and agribusiness over the rainforest. Between 2013 and 2018, at least 3.3 million cattle slaughtered in the Brazilian Amazon – were raised inside protected areas (West et al., 2022). More than 2,800 kilometers (1,740 miles) of pipe lines run through the Amazon regions of Peru, Bolivia, Ecuador, and Colombia. Along the way, there have been more than 3,000 spills between 2012 and 2022 that have affected thousands of local and indigenous communities (Fernández, 2023). In twenty years (2001–2020), the Amazon lost 8.7 percent of its forested area (542,581 km^2) due to legal and illegal extractive activities (RAISG, 2022).

Political imaginaries of the Amazon also conceive it as a place for fulfilling developmental goals through infrastructure projects that seek commercial connectivity and modernization. Since 2004, under the "Initiative for the Integration of the Regional Infrastructure of South America" (IIRSA), the Inter-American Development Bank (IDB), and Development Bank of Latin America (CAF) have supported 335 infrastructure projects to connect the Atlantic with the Pacific, and many of these mega-projects include Amazonian areas (Betancur-Santiago and Rubiños-Cea, 2021; Agostinis and Palestini, 2021). China's Belt and Road Initiative (BRI), an ambitious global investment plan announced by President Xi Jinping in 2013, also contributed to the mega-infrastructure boom in the region. Today, China provides more sovereign financing to Latin American governments on average than either the IDB or the World Bank. Ecuador, Bolivia, and Peru have been the main recipients of infrastructure loans for energy and transportation projects directly impacting the Amazon Basin (Gallagher and Myers, 2019).

Land-use change and massive deforestation caused by extractive and infrastructure initiatives, coupled with global climate change, are deteriorating the Amazon's resilience, possibly leading to irreversible environmental damage during this century (Pereira and Viola, 2020; Garrido et al., 2020). The scientific community warns that the Amazonian forest might turn from being a carbon sink to becoming a carbon emitter, altering the water cycle, climate, and food security on the planet (Figure 1.1).

Even though the impacts of Amazonian degradation and the benefits of its protection are global, the first and most vulnerable communities affected are more

Figure 1.1 Amazon rainforest in Northern Peru. Photo by the author, 2022

than 400 Indigenous peoples living in the basin (SPA, 2021). These peoples have not only ancestrally practiced self-determination in their territories, but they have also played a critical role in the conservation of the Amazonian rainforest (Brondizio and Le Tourneau, 2016; Garnett et al., 2018). These efforts have continued over centuries despite national and global forces that have historically impacted indigenous territories and environments. After being a route to traffic Inca silver and gold across the Atlantic, the Amazon River became a focal point of the "scrambling for the Amazon," the rival claims of sovereignty by European imperial powers over Amazonian territories and populations (Hecht, 2013). New international interests in this area emerged in the postcolonial era over the development of infrastructure for nation-building and border defense; transnational rubber exploitation; oil and mining reserves discoveries; the growth of drug trafficking; and the extension of the agricultural frontier for agribusiness, producing displacement and enslavement of indigenous communities, and enclosure and degradation of their territories (Picq, 2017; Fontaine, 2006).

The environmental turn in the 1970s started a transition from "globalization in the Amazon," an idea that conceived the Amazon as a site of global extraction, to "globalization of the Amazon," since global conservation NGOs started to redefine the region as the "lungs of the world" (Palacio, 2012). But this turn has been unable to push for the building of an international regimen that includes, along with national developmental projects, ecological goals, and indigenous rights. Basin states signed the Amazonian Cooperation Treaty in July 1978 to reject the interest of the international community in taking meaningful actions to protect Amazonian ecosystems. They conceived the environmental discourses that proclaimed that Amazonian forests were global goods as an illegitimate attempt at the "internationalization of the Amazon." The Treaty intended to demonstrate that basin states could manage this region with no foreign interference that would threaten their sovereignty. In 1998, the parties created the Amazonian Cooperation Treaty Organization (ACTO) as an international organization, with headquarters in Brasilia. The ACTO agenda included commerce, infrastructure, education, health, tourism, Indigenous peoples' rights, and climate change. However, the ACTO does not have enforcement mechanisms among its member countries. It has been limited to performing diplomatic coordination and the exchange of information. Thus, rather than having a regional strategy for protecting Amazonian ecosystems and indigenous rights, each basin state enacts its own economic and environmental policy, often privileging the interests of the most powerful stakeholders at play, such as mining and oil companies, agribusiness, or construction firms.

How can the governance of the Amazon conciliate the developmental agenda of nation-states, local and global ecological concerns, and ancestral indigenous rights? What lessons might the study of Amazon governance offer to govern international commons? This book answers these questions by examining the current political imaginaries, ontologies, and international governance in the Amazon rainforest.

Based on this research journey, it formulates a theory of plurinational and pluriversal governance for governing the Amazon and other international commons.

1.1 The Polycentric Governance of the Amazon

On August 9, 2023, the presidents of the eight Amazonian governments attended a long-awaited summit in the city of Belém in Brazil. This was the fourth presidential meeting in forty-five years since the creation of the ACTO, the third had taken place fourteen years ago. In this meeting, the presidents approved the Declaration of Belém, an agreement that promises the reinforcement of ACTO, the deepening of international cooperation and coordination, and the inclusion of Indigenous peoples, among others. Despite these promises, the Declaration has been seen as "a long list of good intentions" (Fearnside, 2023). The governments agreed on general and undisputed issues, such as urging developed countries to meet their climate obligations; contributing more money to deforestation-reduction efforts; or condemning trade practices that drive deforestation produced by soy, beef, and timber industries. Although the Declaration incorporated some institutional innovations, such as the creation of an Indigenous Mechanism to reinforce indigenous presence within the organization and the creation of a Scientific Panel for supporting the formulation of international policies, disruptive actions were left aside. The proposal for creating an International Tribunal for Environmental Justice did not gain support, and no commitments were made to impose a moratorium on infrastructure development that opens rainforest to the entry of loggers, the suspension of oil licenses in the basin, or the prohibition of industrial mining along Amazonian rivers and headwaters.

The Treaty of Amazonian Cooperation could be conceived as an international regimen for the sustainable development of the region, as it seeks to ensure both, socioeconomic development and environmental protection of the Amazon rainforest. But this regimen is far less relevant than national and local extractive and environmental initiatives. This resembles the challenges of international regimes in general and the climate regimen in particular, built on the United Nations Framework Convention on Climate Change (UNFCCC) and the Kyoto Protocol. The regimen or integration model relies on institutional centralization to make multilateral decisions among nation-states (Biermann, 2014). However, observers show the limited effectiveness of multilateral treaty-making in solving transboundary problems, the slow progress of international negotiations, and the neglect of the significance of sub- and non-state actors in the management of cross-border issues (Hickmann, 2015). For these reasons, scholars turned to the concept of "global governance," as this notion seemed better suited to explain the fragmented dynamic of environmental efforts to address climate change. The initiatives advanced by bilateral negotiations, national and subnational policies, World Bank programs, and other non-state projects would be pragmatic solutions, given the difficulty of reaching global agreements (Dryzek and Pickering, 2019; Hoffmann, 2011; Keohane and Victor, 2011).

This fragmented and multilevel global environmental governance has been theorized as a regimen complex, experimental governance, and polycentric governance. The notion of regimen complex emphasizes the overlapping and intersections between policy domains that govern different aspects of environmental challenges (Zelli et al., 2020), comprising an array of regulatory elements (Keohane and Victor, 2011). It includes governance initiatives by non-state actors, such as environmental NGOs, technical experts, and business associations. The notion of "experimental climate governance" often refers to how different actors operating at and across different scales adopt trial and error approaches to problem-solving (Turnheim et al., 2018). This governance impels policy initiatives outside multilateral forums, such as the Global Covenant of Mayors for Energy and Climate and the We Mean Business Coalition. For others, experimental governance might be found in regional arrangements, such as the European Union (Sabel and Zeitlin, 2012; Zeitlin, 2015), or even in global arrangements, such as the Paris Agreement (Dryzek and Pickering, 2019), which has formalized some forms of participation of nongovernmental actors, including cities, regions, businesses, and investors, through the Non-State Actor Zone for Climate Action Portal.

Whereas regimen complex and experimental governance are descriptive notions of current global environmental dynamics, "polycentric governance" provides the theoretical framework for both approaches and develops normative claims. In the late 2000s, some perceived the proliferation of non-state initiatives as a negative development that triggered policy fragmentation and distracted international efforts (Biermann et al., 2009). The Nobel Prize-winning economist Elinor Ostrom was more pragmatic in analyzing the relationship between the various levels, units, and domains (Jordan et al., 2018). Ostrom's approach, derived from her earlier reflections on public choice theory, collective action, and neo-institutionalism, focused on the potential of local collective property to manage resource commons efficiently, instead of choosing either bureaucratic government or privatization (Sauvêtre, 2018).

On these premises, Ostrom (2010, 1998) portrayed the global environmental regimen as formed by interactions between multi-scale and independent governing authorities that create new and more dynamic forms of governing climate change. This would demonstrate that not all aspects of governance would have to be designed by nation-states in international negotiations (Jordan et al., 2018). By focusing on local practices, this model would enhance the quality of decision-making and its legitimacy (Weston and Bollier, 2013). In this framework, possible inefficiencies and redundancies at one level of governance can be compensated for by the other. Besides, in contrast to centralized governance systems, in the polycentric approach, different governance centers can move at different speeds without obstructing overall progress (Schoenefeld, 2023). Another assumption is that polycentric systems share information more easily and therefore have greater access to local knowledge and better feedback loops. This would allow the scaling up of otherwise sustainable invisible behaviors, institutional learning, and system resilience (Weston and Bollier, 2013). In sum, polycentric systems tend to enhance innovation, learning, adaptation, trustworthiness, cooperation, stakeholders' participation, and the achievement of more effective, equitable, and sustainable outcomes at multiple scales (Ostrom, 2010).

For many scholars, polycentric climate governance is already in place (Jordan et al., 2018). The Cambrian explosion (Keohane and Victor, 2011) or groundswell (Falkner, 2016) in the number of governance initiatives that emerged in the last years channelized different hybrid forms led by state (e.g., coalitions promoting carbon pricing such as the Carbon Pricing Leadership Coalition) and non-state actors (e.g., international standards developed by companies and NGOs). For Ostrom and her followers, these activities, although initially small in size and few in number, would become cumulatively additive over time. The concept is thus used to describe climate governance and prescribe better responses to the climate crisis (Dehm, 2021).

The Amazon is often portrayed as a space of polycentric governance (De Wit and Mourato, 2022; Mcgahan and Pongeluppe, 2021). In this governance, international conventions, national laws, global standards, and companies' codes of conduct address overlapped and interconnected issues, such as climate change, biodiversity, forests, trade, extractive industries, foreign direct investments, and indigenous rights (Bastos Lima et al., 2021). Thus, different authorities located at different levels, from local and national governments to international actors and organizations, shape the governance of Amazonian resources (Carattini et al., 2019; De Wit and Martins de Freitas, 2019). This is the case even after the creation of ACTO, supposedly a third party that should define common goals and arbitrate countries' behavior (Bastos Lima et al., 2021). As Chapters 2–4 show, the social and environmental outcomes, however, are far from satisfactory, and conflicts and tensions among the different actors involved in the sustainable development of the basin are constant. The study of the international governance of the Amazon provides crucial insights into the limitations of polycentric governance.

1.1.1 Polycentric Governance: Genealogy and Success

The development of polycentric governance can be traced back to the early works of Vincent and Elinor Ostrom, a couple of academics based at Indiana University, who engaged with the debate on public administration reform in American metropolitan areas in the 1950s. During this decade, governance arrangements in metropolitan areas across the United States and Europe received much criticism because of the large number of small-, medium-, and large-scale government units operating in the same area, creating a chaotic system. Ostrom et al. (1961) formulated the concept of polycentricity in their effort to understand whether the activities of the diverse array of public and private agencies providing public services were chaotic or potentially beneficial. For the Ostroms, far from being a pathological situation, this complexity could be a natural and healthy one. The Ostroms explained that the variety of relationships between governmental units, public agencies, and private businesses coexisting and functioning in a public economy can be coordinated through patterns of interorganizational arrangements (Aligica and Tarko, 2011). The underlying idea was that any group of individuals facing collective problems should first try to solve their problems themselves with their own institutional rules, rather than immediately turning to some government unit for authoritative and centralized decisions (McGinnis and Walker, 2010).

These developments were influenced by public choice theory and the classic textbook *The Calculus of Consent* (1962) by James Buchanan and Gordon Tullock (Ostrom, 2011). Vincent and Elinor Ostrom were also founding members and later chairs of the public choice society, initiated by Buchanan in 1963 (Wall, 2014). The Ostrom approach builds on three fundamentals of public choice theory: its conception of the failures of central government, its assumption of economic rationality to comprehend every problem of political organization, and its nature as a "science of government." Ultimately, they shared the idea that it is too simplistic to redress market failures by means of state interventions, since failures also abound in public administration (Sauvêtre, 2018). Unlike Mancur Olson's argument (1965) that collective action could not be attained without external constraints, for the Ostroms, self-organized actions that achieve collective benefits are possible through the ability of individuals to implement new rules. The neo-institutionalism of Vincent and Elinor Ostrom thus can be seen as an original extension of the public choice theory (Sauvêtre, 2018).

Another influence is Michael Polanyi's (1951) original formulation of the term "polycentricity" in his reflections on the functioning of scientific communities and markets. Polanyi argued that the success of science depended on its "polycentric organization" since participants enjoy the freedom to structure their research activities and make individual and personal contributions. Researchers' efforts do not usually dissipate in unproductive directions because they share a common ideal: the search for an abstract end goal (objective truth). Polanyi's key point is that such an ideal cannot be imposed on the participants by an overarching authority since progress is the outcome of a trial and error evolutionary process of many agents interacting freely. For him, the market should also be seen as a polycentric system involving a web of agents that constantly adjust their behavior to the decisions made by others. In contrast to a monocentric socialist system, the market is more apt to manage autonomously and spontaneously the high amount of information of individuals (Aligica and Tarko, 2011).

Polanyi used the term "spontaneous" as synonymous with "polycentric," being closer to Friedrich Hayek's idea of spontaneous order, which assumes that the self-interested actions of individuals will converge and thereby promote the collective good, without the need for governmental coordination (Aligica and Tarko, 2011). Vincent Ostrom (1972 in McGinnis 1999) developed these ideas, arguing that in a polycentric system, spontaneity is a function of self-organizing tendencies occurring under specific conditions at several different levels. These conditions are the freedom of entry and exit of new decision centers, the enforcement of general rules of conduct that provide the legal framework for a polycentric order, and the possibility of reformulation and revision of the basic rules that define the framework (Aligica and Tarko, 2011).

Since the Ostroms' research agenda was to identify the patterns of order existing within the apparent chaos of polycentric systems, their approach might be considered a theory of the "invisible hand" directing many aspects of social order, as foreseen by Polanyi (Aligica and Tarko, 2011). From these premises, they advanced a solid empirical research agenda (Schoenefeld, 2023). In the 1960s, the Ostroms examined how multiple public and private agencies had searched out productive ways of organizing water resources in California and how federal and local policy departments served similar neighborhoods in different metropolitan areas (Ostrom, 2010). The Ostroms demonstrated that public services can be most efficiently provided under a system of multiple and overlapping jurisdictions (McGinnis and Walker, 2010). These findings also reinforced the civic dimension of collective self-organization in the tradition of American democracy (Ostrom, 2010). For the Ostroms, the designing of the American constitution could be viewed as an experiment in polycentricity, and federalism would be the institutional form to operationalize this type of order. In this perspective, polycentricity became a necessary condition for achieving political objectives such as liberty and justice. The polycentric dispersion of decision-making capabilities would be an essential characteristic of democratic societies (Aligica and Tarko, 2011).

These early empirical studies and theoretical reflections led over time to the development of the Institutional Analysis and Development (IAD) framework within the "Workshop in Political and Policy Analysis" set up in 1973 at the University of Indiana (Sauvêtre, 2018). The IAD framework proposes three external variables (biophysical conditions, attributes of a community, and rules-in-use) to examine the diversity of institutional settings, including human interactions within markets, private firms, families, communities, legislatures, and government agencies. It provides a metatheoretical language to enable scholars to understand interactions of participants and action situations through microlevel theories deemed compatible with the framework, such as game theory, microeconomic theory, transaction cost theory, and public goods/common-pool resource (Ostrom, 2010). This framework facilitated a variety of empirical studies on common-pool resource systems around the world. Thus, decades before sustainability became a dominant discourse, the Ostroms began to investigate the conditions under which natural resources can be managed sustainably (Aligica and Tarko, 2011). They found that large irrigation systems in Nepal and forests' communal governance around the world challenge the presumption that governments always do a better job than users in organizing and protecting important resources (Ostrom, 2010). The Ostroms emphasized the myriad advantages of empowering communities to address their own collective problems, even in the poorest regions of the developing world. The most fundamental lesson drawn from this research agenda was the critical importance of local solutions to complex policy problems (McGinnis and Walker, 2010).

In this view, the challenges to govern environmentally crucial common resources, such as the forest and climate change, are similar to the provision of public goods in metropolitan areas. In the latter, the conventional assumption was that coordination problems could only be solved by centralized federal-scale solutions; in the former, the dominant assumption was that all solutions depended on the global scale. Ostrom (2010) revalorized small- and medium-scale units of governance. The focus on the rules, structures, and frameworks advanced by self-organized communities demonstrated that there is no "one size fits all" approach to managing common resources and shared environments (Stevenson, 2017; Baber and Bartlett, 2015). For Ostrom, if this is true for local environmental problems, it is also the case for global environmental problems. These developments contrasted with the monocentric model of the Kyoto Protocol, which involves legally binding international treaties with quantified emission goals (Jordan et al., 2018).

1.1.2 Challenges and Questionings on Polycentric Governance

Polycentric governance is often studied under a politically neutral position; then, it can be efficient or inefficient, just or unjust, cohesive or fragmented, depending on specific rules and actions (Thiel and Moser-Priewich, 2019). Consequently, most studies propose some reforms aimed at improving coordination, articulation, legitimacy, and effectiveness of polycentric systems. Problems of coordination (duplicity, overlapping of efforts) might be addressed through "orchestration" by leading international organizations over subnational initiatives (Lin, 2018) or by reinforcing the unified architecture of climate governance to support each echelon in achieving its climate objectives (Barichella, 2023). Problems of effectiveness are addressed by reinforcing policy evaluations of environmental initiatives (Schoenefeld, 2023; Turnheim et al., 2018; Stevenson, 2017) and adopting the model of independent climate advisory bodies and monitoring agencies, such as the system developed by the European Union (Coen et al., 2020). Issues of legitimacy would require trade offs between "input or procedural legitimacy" that fosters local collaboration, transparency, and stakeholder participation, and "output legitimacy" or the ability of governance to satisfy the public, which is difficult to assess in fragmented systems (Jordan et al., 2018). Improving legitimacy would also require expanding participation at different levels: from local programs for forest management (Fischer, 2017; Nuesiri, 2018) to diverse international environmental forums and expert assessment bodies, such as the Intergovernmental Panel on Climate Change (IPCC) and the Intergovernmental Science-Policy Platform on Biodiversity and Ecosystem Services (IPBES) (Dryzek and Pickering, 2019).

Those studies focused on coordination and effectiveness tend to approach global environmental governance from a technocratic perspective, neglecting issues of power and legitimacy in the interactions among the different state and non-state actors. The emphasis on policy evaluation disregards different power relations among the actors involved in multilateral environmental agreements and proper ways of accountability (Le Prestre, 2017). Coordination and articulation concerns neglect how contradictory economic and environmental policy regimes, influenced by powerful economic actors, co-exist at the international level, creating problems of policy coherence at the national level (Bulkeley and Newell, 2023). Those studies that address the problem of legitimacy fall short in exploring how governance is conditioned by power unbalances. For instance, in the Circumpolar North, nonstate initiatives remain slow, partial, fragmented, inconsistent, and contradictory because many firms and banks that have made climate pledges also support anti-climate protection lobbying and provide capital to carbon-intensive industries (Zubrow et al., 2019).

Moreover, all reformist approaches are ethnocentric as they rely on the ethnocentric assumptions of the polycentric framework. Collective action is understood as a result of "coordinated strategies" developed under rationality assumptions and institutional choices. For instance, Pierre Sauvêtre explains how, for Ostrom, institutional choices, such as sticking to collective ownership or moving to private property, depend on an assumed transaction costs calculus by the "villagers" instead of being embedded in indigenous thinking and governance. Even more, the way her work combined the criticism of bureaucratic government, the insistence on citizen autonomy, and the generalization of economic rationality, made it effortlessly suitable to support neoliberal development policies during the 1980s. Namely, abandoning forms of bureaucratic regulation and shifting the responsibility for financial costs onto assumed rational individuals and communities. Ethnocentrism is even more problematic concerning the worldwide implications of polycentrism. Whereas Ostrom highlighted the long-term sustainability of certain traditional forms of community management in the Third World, the use of her theory as a tool for development policy legitimized the action of international organizations to impose foreign agendas upon ancestral and already self-organized environmental management systems (Sauvêtre, 2018).

Counter-intuitively, the polycentric framework is also state-centric. Despite celebrating the plurality of authorities located at different levels in environmental governance, most of them are soft-law authorities with the capacity to enact standards, policies, and initiatives framed within the hard national and international laws of nation-states. In these systems, the "rulers" are constrained and limited under a "rule of law." Polycentric systems are, ultimately, rule of law systems (Aligica & Tarko, 2011). This is the case because polycentricity requires the background legal norms that frame the economy (Dehm, 2021). This explains why Polanyi (1951) argued that a polycentric task can be socially managed only by a system of mutual adjustments subject to general rules. The practical implications of this scheme are that only governments can enact and implement policies that set real constraints on environmental destruction (Urpelainen, 2022). Multilateral treaty-making is still critical since transnational climate initiatives use international climate agreements as a point of reference and the basis for their rules and procedures (Hickmann, 2015). Ultimately, by not questioning state power and power unbalances in international relations, polycentric governance ends up legitimizing extractivist and business-as-usual developmental policies. As suggested by Dehm (2021), attention to the "legal background" conditions of polycentric governance shows the simultaneous consolidation of forms of global authority alongside the devolution, decentralization, and pluralization of governance. For instance, REDD+ programs construct local spaces and subjects that are "attuned with global expectations," and increasingly "responsibilized" to be accountable for the realization of global imperatives. Devolution, therefore, represents not a dismantling of global authority but a reconfiguration of its forms of exercise and implementation.

Polycentric governance is finally anthropocentric because its state-centrism and ethnocentrism exclude the possibility of including non-Western conceptions and ontologies of human-nature relationships. For instance, in the Ecuadorian Amazon, local politics of self-determination and the rights of nature have had some influence on national institutions, however, higher governance levels and the global economy constrain the struggles of local communities (Etchart, 2022). Indigenous cosmologies and self-determination are integrated as participatory rights into specific programs or in "invited spaces" in international forums, with no direct incidence in decision-making.

This state-centric, anthropocentric, and ethnocentric framework is more visible in the international architecture of the Amazon. This governance is state-centric because Indigenous nations as autonomous political actors are excluded from governing this international commons; they are either stakeholders or a second-level authority over their specific territories. This governance is ethnocentric because it relies on foundational Western notions and imaginaries, such as sovereignty, nationhood, and development, excluding notions and principles derived from indigenous thinking. This governance is finally anthropocentric because it excludes the rights of nature as a non-human legal and political subject or the possibility of negotiating in the international arena, different worldviews over natural beings. Is there any alternative between polycentric and centralized governance for the Amazon?

1.2 Plurinational Governance

The Coordinator of Indigenous Organizations of the Amazon Basin (COICA, the acronym in Spanish) is one of the biggest international indigenous organizations in the world. Since 1984, it has grouped indigenous organizations from the nine Amazonian countries, including the eight nation-states and French Guyana. In the eighties, COICA participated in the discussions toward the enactment of the ILO Convention 169 and the implementation of the Treaty of Amazonian Cooperation. Since the nineties, it has participated in global forums and UN Work Groups related to the promotion of indigenous rights and global sustainability. In 2021, COICA enacted a Declaration for the celebration of its 37 years of creation, stating: "We are more than 511 indigenous peoples, including our brothers in Isolation Voluntary and Initial Contact, pre-existing, 10,000 years before the States; we are people with knowledge and wisdom, with languages and our own systems of government, we are struggle and resistance, we are Amazonia, we are COICA." COICA's affirmation of the autonomy and self-government of Indigenous peoples resembles the struggles of indigenous movements to enact plurinationalism across the region.

Plurinationalism can be understood as a state model. This conceptualization requires deciphering historical indigenous struggles for sovereignty, autonomy, and self-determination. Despite the oppressive nature of colonization, Indigenous peoples used colonial laws – mainly in the South – and treaty arrangements – mainly in the North – that recognized their character as original nations. In the post-colonial era, the new nation-states denied the historical sovereignty claims of Indigenous nations through policies of open exclusion and assimilation. Indigenous nations opposed these policies and, at the same time, used some of them strategically to struggle for more spaces of autonomy. By the middle of the last century, peasants and indigenous movements in Latin America framed their struggles for autonomy as struggles for land reform whereas, at the international level, indigenous movements appealed to the right of self-determination. The United Nations Charter and the Declaration on the Granting of Independence to Colonial Countries and Peoples (1960) recognized this right to all peoples, but Indigenous peoples couldn't benefit from it because self-determination was conceived in restrictive terms. Under the Salt Water or Blue Water thesis, only overseas colonies seeking statehood were eligible for self-determination, such as African nations (Henderson, 2007; Craven, 2010).

In the following years, international scholars criticized minimalist interpretations that attached self-determination to statehood and other conceptualizations that deflected attention from its political nature, such as a "bundle of social and cultural rights" – based on the International Covenant on Civil and Political Rights and the International Covenant on Economic, Social and Cultural Rights (Lightfoot, 2021). Indigenous movements finally achieved an explicit recognition of self-determination as a political right within the boundaries of state unity or "internal self-determination" (Craven, 2010), at the 2007 United Nations Declaration on the Rights of Indigenous Peoples (UNDRIP). The UNDRIP would support the current understanding of the notion that highlights the multiple possibilities for Indigenous–state relationships and the right of Indigenous peoples to negotiate their political status with the states where they live (Daes, 2008). For Lightfoot (2021), this supports the agenda for decolonizing self-determination away from its state-centric form to accommodate indigenous self-determination and state sovereignty without creating a discriminatory two-class system.

However, the decolonization of self-determination must also entail the decolonization of state sovereignty. This is crucial because to fully recognize indigenous self-determination, the state's sovereign power and arrangements must be transformed to make a significant space for the decision-making of Indigenous nations. The tensions between state sovereignty and the practice of indigenous sovereignty have led scholars to formulate notions such as shared or overlapped sovereignty (Clavé-Mercier, 2018), a third space of sovereignty neither fully within nor fully without the state (Bruyneel, 2007), multiple or relational sovereignty (Conversi, 2016; Wheatley, 2014), nested sovereignty (Simpson, 2014) or parallel sovereignty (Lenzerini, 2006). These notions express everyday social practices, grassroots activism, and litigation, and the use of international law to defend indigenous rights as an expression of indigenous practical sovereignty in the Global South and the Global North.

In South America, since the eighties, the quest for indigenous sovereignty became entangled with state provisions of autonomy understood as the self-government of Indigenous peoples over specific lands. Self-determination was conceived as a collective right, and autonomy was a limited territorial arrangement under the nation-state sovereignty. This framework, theoretically justified under imported ideas of multiculturalism, portrayed Indigenous nations as ethnic minorities with collective property rights in pluricultural or multiethnic societies. Since the end of the eighties, multicultural provisions in political constitutions recognized land rights, customary law, language rights, and some degree of autonomy (some territorial control and the recognition of indigenous systems of justice), whereas regulating ancestral territories as collective property lands with restricted decision-making power. Given these limitations, Indigenous peoples criticized the neoliberal multicultural state and demanded a new state form, the plurinational state, that fully recognizes their character as ancestral nations with self-determination and territorial rights.

After years of social mobilization, the Political Constitution of Ecuador of 2008 incorporated plurinationality as a foundational feature of the state. The constitution recognized strongly indigenous territorial rights, the indigenous notion of *Buen vivir* (Living well) as a societal principle to living in harmony with nature, and recognized nature as a holder of rights. The Political Constitution of Bolivia of 2009 enacted the Plurinational State of Bolivia as a new state form and provided the branches of government with a plurinational character, incorporating designated seats in Congress and the Supreme Court for indigenous representatives. In both constitutional texts, Indigenous peoples' territories are not merely lands subjected to property arrangements. Indigenous territories are part of the multilevel state governance through the creation of Indigenous First Peoples' Peasant Autonomies (Bolivia) and Indigenous Circumscriptions (Ecuador). Grassroots struggles were incorporated into an institutional process of plurinationalism from above.

1.2.1 Plurinationalism as a Political Space

Plurinationalism has also been conceptualized as a political space in which different indigenous and grassroots movements constantly negotiate their views and practices of autonomy in-relation-to and beyond the state. Plurinationalism is, in this way, a constant practice of politics from below.

In the context of Bolivia, Augsburger (2021) argues that plurinationality seeks to institutionalize in political form René Zavaleta's classical conceptualization of Bolivian society as a *formación abigarrada* (motley, disjointed social formation). Unlike Zavaleta's distrust of lo *abigarrado*, social and political actors formulated plurinationality as a positive horizon beyond the liberal nation-state emanating from different indigenous and peasant social formations. This would express a plurality of sociocultural, material, epistemological, and ontological positions that challenge the nation-state as a modern-colonial form (Radhuber and Radcliffe, 2023).

Similar ontological challenges have been found in indigenous sovereignty claims in Canada, the United States, and Australia. In contrast to the dynastic, imperial, and material origins of nation-state sovereignty, indigenous ontologies have origin stories "inextricably connected to being in and of their lands" and find expression in kinship relations, respect, responsibility, and obligation to humans and non-humans as peoples of the Earth, outside the logic of nation-states (Moreton-Robinson, 2021: 320). Therefore, whereas indigenous sovereignties imply plurality and multiple human and more-than-human agencies, Western human-centered and culturally homogenized sovereignties rely on the principle of indivisibility – there can be only one sovereignty – and sovereignty's supreme authority to create states of exception and exclude those who might risk this political system (Moreton-Robinson, 2021).

In the institutional translation of plurinational politics, different indigenous ontologies seek to be expressed in plurinational arrangements (Sempértegui and Báez, 2024). Even more, diverse indigenous and non-indigenous (mestizo, Afro-Latin) life-worlds (Rivera Cusicanqui, 2012) aim at reconfiguring resource governance to express the parallel existence and juxtaposition of multiple and overlapping societies (Radhuber and Radcliffe, 2023). In this framework, plural subjects should hold decision-making competencies and sovereign rights operating within a pluralized set of arrangements rather than a binary distinction between a single national regulatory regime containing homogeneous indigenous territories (Radhuber and Radcliffe, 2023). Therefore, plurinational claims advanced by indigenous organizations to oppose state extractive and infrastructure projects wouldn't be just about competing agendas for resource management (Radhuber and Radcliffe, 2023). Even though plurinational politics is grounded on concrete territorial struggles, they do not merely refer to ownership, access, and distribution of natural resources. Rather, what is at stake are ways of being, relating, and worldmaking (Sempértegui and Báez, 2024).

The lack of correspondence between the plurinational state model and this complex socio-political space of competing sovereign views explains many tensions and conflicts around the configuration and implementation of plurinationalism. The crucial issue is to what extent plurinationalism as a state form might express plurinational politics and the quest for indigenous sovereignty.

1.2.2 Translating Plurinational Politics

The translation of the plurinational political space into state structures has been mediated through cooptation and bureaucratization. Cooptation means that instead of governing with the plural movements outside the formal party system that brought progressive governments to power, they privileged traditional forms of representation under liberal corsets, maintaining the traditional political system and subordinating or coopting autonomous social organizations (for Bolivia: Gutierrez Aguilar, 2011; Augsburger, 2021; Ranta, 2023). Bureaucratization of plurinationalism in Ecuador and Bolivia meant that indigenous autonomies must be fitted into formal municipal boundaries already defined by the state, regardless of ancestral territories (Tockman and Cameron, 2014; Cruz Rodríguez, 2012). Consequently, administrative requirements and procedures transformed autonomic politics into endless legal processes.

Plurinational politics is also limited by neo-developmental and neocolonial state agendas that reinforce resource extraction dependency. This agenda depoliticizes indigenous discourse and practices, appealing to "decolonization," "*Buen vivir*," and "plurinationalism" as labels to support state claims of national sovereignty and justify extractivist and infrastructural projects (Postero, 2017; Rivera Cusicanqui, 2012; Laing, 2015; Perreault and Valdivia, 2010). In the end, in Bolivia and Ecuador, the development model inspired by Indigenous cosmovisions of *Buen vivir* has come to coexist with classical developmental strategies.

Another limitation of plurinational politics is the very plural nature of grassroots struggles. Whereas many demands reinforce indigenous cosmologies based on different forms of human–nature relationships, some of them might also engage with different types of extractive agendas, as explained by Anthias (2022) in her analysis of local dynamics in the campaign for regional autonomy in the gas-rich Gran Chaco in Bolivia. Plurinational politics, in any case, requires a broad space to negotiate and articulate different grassroots and indigenous views on sovereignty and resource governance at local, national, and international levels.

The international dimension is also critical because Indigenous peoples place their political discourses within international frameworks of indigenous rights, whereas states rely on international forces to advance extractive and infrastructure initiatives. Therefore, global political and economic structures constrain the translation of plurinational politics and, at the same time, are the venues where Indigenous peoples navigate their struggles. This explains why indigenous movements in Latin America promoted *Runasur* as an international platform aimed at creating a new form of regional integration based on plurinationalism (Granja et al., 2022).

Runasur was founded in the Conference of Peoples and Organizations of the Abya Yala "Towards the Construction of a Plurinational America" in December 2020 in Cochabamba, Bolivia, where more than one thousand indigenous leaders from Latin America participated (Manestar, 2023). *Runasur* was created in response to the crisis of political representation of national governments and the need for pressure for the enforcement of human rights, indigenous rights, and rights of nature (Manestar, 2023). Indigenous peoples are the leading actors in this international platform, but it is also open to the participation of different civil society organizations, such as Afro-descendants, social movements, unions, and collectives of artists and intellectuals. By building on the notion of plurinationalism, *Runasur* challenges the idea of the state as a central actor for Latin American regional governance and the traditional model of inter-governmentality based on state representation. In this way, *Runasur* holds an ontology and temporality that differ from the Westphalian foundations of the nation-state and inspire other ways of building regional integration (Granja et al., 2022). Although this initiative has been taken with suspicion and opposition by nation-states for allegedly being secessionist, this is a form of building plurinationalism beyond national systems that reinforces solidarity among Indigenous peoples and social movements.

The theoretical, political, and institutional developments of plurinationalism, at national and international levels, should influence the transformation of the governance of the Amazon. Conceiving indigenous nations as international actors means that there is no more a "one national interest" that legitimizes Amazonian nation-states to decide alone on the future of Amazonian ecosystems. Rather, indigenous sovereignty and plurinational politics among nation-states and Indigenous nations must be translated into proper institutional mechanisms for international decision-making.

1.3 Pluriversal Governance

"Saving the Amazon" has different meanings for the different actors involved. For global conservation NGOs and the international community, this means protecting Amazonian ecosystems as a way to address climate change. For basin states, it mainly means ensuring the availability of Amazonian resources to advance the goals of "sustainable development." For the Indigenous peoples living across the basin, saving the Amazon is saving their natural, spiritual, and social world (Aoki Inoue, 2018).

What is the "world" that Amazonian Indigenous peoples seek to save? When international leaders and scientific communities refer to the climate crisis as an "existential threat," "climate catastrophe," or "climate emergency," they often show concerns about the destiny of the planet and humanity. Indigenous cosmologies problematize the assumptions about the relationships between humanity and the world it inhabits. For instance, Amazonian anthropology (Kohn, 2013; Viveiros de Castro, 2004; Rival, 2016; Descola, 2004) has shown how Indigenous peoples conceive both human and natural beings as persons entangled in social dynamics of respect and survival. Whereas modern multiculturalist ontology assumes a unity of nature and a multiplicity of cultures, indigenous perspectivism presumes a spiritual unity and a corporeal diversity: "one culture, multiple natures/one epistemology, multiple ontologies" (Viveiros de Castro, 2004: 474). Then, the crucial difference is not the different epistemologies or knowledge systems over the forests, but that social actors conceive different worlds based on their different ontological relations with natural beings.

Anthropologists and, in general, social theorists involved in the "ontological turn" define ontology as the study of reality (Kohn, 2015; Viveiros de Castro, 2015). The turn radicalizes postcolonial theory's critique of Eurocentric ways of categorizing the world (Blaser, 2014). "Cultural difference" is not different enough because it relies on the modernist ontological assumption that there is one reality or world and multiple perspectives or cultural representations of it (Blaser, 2014). Cultural diversity is then reduced to a symbol of identity politics (Carrithers, 2010) that treats native thought as a sustained fantasy (Viveiros de Castro, 2015). In this context, appealing to ontology means "taking others and their real difference seriously" (Blaser, 2014: 52).

The ontological turn has been associated with post-humanism authors such as Bruno Latour, Donna Haraway, John Law, or Isabelle Stengers who challenge the modern nature/culture dualism and conceive reality as always in the making through the dynamic relations of heterogeneous assemblages involving the agency of more-than-humans (Kohn, 2015). However, given the dependency on Western epistemologies and ontologies, post-humanism treats the foundational ontological split between nature and culture as universal (Sundberg, 2014; Burow et al., 2018). This leads to the ontological assumption of a singular reality, about which different cultures offer distinct interpretations (Sundberg, 2014). For instance, building on Benedict Anderson's Imagined Communities, Jasanoff and Kim (2009) formulated the concept of "socio-technical imaginaries" as the shared sense that builds the nation's scientific and technological projects. Despite Jasanoff (2015) later acknowledged that there might be different imaginaries in tension coexisting within a society, the concept obscures the fact that imagined cultural differences are often contingent upon concrete differences in what is known to be real rather than imagined (Schelly et al., 2021). In studying Anishinaabe ways of knowing what is real on the earth, Schelly et al. (2021) suggest that the fundamental realities of collective Indigenous knowledges are not imaginaries based on desired futures. In indigenous perspectives, the world is formed of a shared substance/power/essence that ties all things together and provides the potential for human and non-human agency. For this "relational ontology," personhood is not limited to humans, and human societies are only a part of a larger web of relations (Lawres and Sanger, 2022).

Therefore, the ontological turn's engagement with indigeneity introduces the idea of ontological heterogeneity and fluidity (Blaser, 2014). Considering indigenous perspectives, we are not solely dealing with a shifting ontology, a (re)animated world, we are dealing with multiple ontologies, a multiplicity of worlds (Blaser, 2014). This allows the formulation of the notion of political ontology because reality is political: rather than being a stable object to be observed, it varies and is enacted as a process. Then, some ontological enactments are prioritized over others (Yates et al., 2017). The varied processes of "worlding" or enacting realities (Yates et al., 2017) express the "pluriverse," the partially connected unfolding of worlds (Blaser, 2014). Indigenous territories are then conceived as a world of many worlds, and as one small but significant part of this pluriverse, humankind's responsibilities are entangled in the more-than-human relationships that sustain life (Larsen and Johnson, 2016).

1.3.1 Indigenous Ontologies in Environmental Governance

Povinelli (2015) argues that the ontological turn is both symptomatic and diagnostic of the global ecological crisis. Indigenous ontologies would potentially provide wisdom for healing, restoration, and a return to reciprocal and relational systems (Schelly et al., 2021). This premise has been criticized for constructing indigeneity as a speculative way of knowing and being necessary if humanity is to survive the Anthropocene (Chandler and Reid, 2019). For Chandler and Reid (2019), discourses of "becoming indigenous" are not about other ways of being but new ways of constructing the Western self as adaptive and resilient in the face of unknowable adversities. Political ontology has also been criticized for mystifying the material processes that drive the world history of modernity and romanticizing indigenous territories as pluriversal spaces independent of capital (Moore, 2022). These critiques should be taken seriously as recent contributions appeal to pluriversality to challenge how environmental governance naturalizes particular representations, knowledges, and expertise as universal truths, inhibiting alternative forms of existence (Tickner and Querejazu, 2020).

There are two approaches to formulating a pluriversal environmental governance. One formulation relies on "relational ontologies" to overcome dominant governance models (Tickner and Querejazu, 2020). In this view, ideas of relationality, complementarity, and reciprocity between human and natural beings should be widely adopted so that governance norms and institutions are "aligned to the rules of the Earth" (Tickner and Querejazu, 2020: 224). This proposal is problematic because it discursively portrays indigenous values in universal patterns that must be adopted by the whole world (Chandler and Reid, 2019) and disregards how economic and political material relations create constraints of pluriversal projects (Moore, 2022). Moreover, this framework does not consider the plurality of indigenous politics and their different values and relationships with nature. For instance, in the Amazon, indigenous ontologies do not necessarily resemble the relationality, complementarity, and reciprocity ideals. Humans and more-than-human beings are competitors for resources under a "political economy of life," where, from the point of view of social actors, the most scarce resource is their own forces of life (Santos-Granero, 2009). According to this cosmology, the vital force that animates the world is finite and scarce, in constant circulation and unequally distributed. Therefore, the growth of a living being can only be done at the expense of another. This means that all beings constantly struggle to accumulate enough vital strength to guarantee their survival and reproduction. What avoids the anarchic destruction among species is that all are perceived as "persons" and have the right to live, so all aggression would be responded to with a new aggression. This results in an ethic of self-regulation that ensures a natural balance (Santos-Granero and Barclay, 2010).

A more promising approach to pluriversal environmental governance emphasizes the need to make space for ontological differences over the natural world. Torres and Verschoor (2020) identify three forms of governance embedded in different ontologies in the Colombian Amazon: one derived from Western conservation and shared by officials; another that expresses indigenous ontologies; and another focused on economic rewards and pushed by non-local entrepreneurs. In the Peruvian Amazon, there is also a clash of ontologies in the context of "green colonialism," in which conservationists, Indigenous peoples, and local and foreign companies might oppose each other in implementing their different ways of conceiving and managing nature (Merino, 2022). In general, whereas conservationists and Indigenous peoples might agree on the need to fight climate change and establish ambitious targets, ontological differences create disagreements on the means to achieve these goals. For instance, at the COP15 of the Convention on Biological Diversity in 2022, parties approved a new 30 × 30 framework to have 30 percent of terrestrial and marine areas of the world as protected areas by 2030. During negotiations, indigenous organizations alleged their concerns that achieving this target would risk indigenous territorial rights on behalf of conservation. The agreement finally explicitly recognized these rights, but the specific arrangements to protect them, such as models of indigenous protected areas, were left to national governments. Whereas few scientists might support the interests behind corporate actors in continuing to extract "natural resources" as usual, different scientific groups often support either indigenous ways of sustainable exploitation or conservation arrangements advanced by global conservation NGOs that seek to avoid any kind of exploitation. These different views on the management of nature express ontological clashes. For Torres and Verschoor (2020), these differences must be recognized and negotiated rather than avoided.

This last version of pluriversal governance is much more promising as it addresses the discursive critique and the lack of engagement with the political economy. A crucial question remains regarding how the intrinsic value of nature must be incorporated into international governance, considering the trend of the rights of nature in the Amazon and beyond.

1.3.2 Nature Agency in Pluriversal Governance

In the Amazon, along with plurinationalism, the groundbreaking legal recognition of the rights of nature seems crucial to reconsider international governance arrangements. Indeed, when scholars mention new practices of pluriversal governance, they highlight the legal recognition of the rights of nature. The Ecuadorian Constitution of 2008 is the first in the world that formulate these rights as constitutional rights. In Bolivia, under the constitutionalization of the Indigenous principle of *Buen vivir* in 2009, the government developed legislation that protects the rights of the Mother Earth (*Pachamama* in Quechua Indigenous language). In Colombia, the Supreme Court (2016) ruled that the Atrato River in the Amazon is a legal person with fundamental rights to be defended by designated guardians. This is a worldwide trend. Legislative development underpinned by the Treaty of Waitangi in New Zealand (2017) and judicial decisions carried out by courts in India (2017), responding to grassroots and judicial activists, have recognized rivers as legal persons endowed with specific rights. Ecological democracy scholars argue that the legalization of the rights of nature is a significant step toward the granting of political agency to natural beings (Dryzek and Pickering, 2019; De Blic, 2020).

However, the legal recognition of the rights of nature is different from political agency. Governance is not simply rights recognition. Governance means political relations, representation, deliberation, coordination, and articulation to achieve collective goals. In the evolution of the rights of nature, it is possible to identify different strategies for legal recognition and defense, but no provisions for nature's political representation. The original formulation in the seventies often refers to the claims of the American lawyer Christopher Stone (1972) that the environment should have legal standing in a similar way that a corporation or children are represented by others in courts. Whereas legal and political philosophers at this time sought to extend liberal theory toward deep ecologism, recognizing the inherent value of nature as a holder of rights, in institutional terms, this only meant that a guardian (an environmental organization or a government agency) not directly affected by the pollution produced by a company should have the capacity to demand a legal remedy on behalf of nature. Later developments since the 1990s seek to provide personhood to nature through specific legal provisions beyond judicial standing. This resulted in the world's first rights of nature local ordinance in Tamaqua, Pennsylvania (2010) and other sub-national regulations in Maine (2009), New Hampshire (2014), and California (2013) aimed at systematically protecting the environment from the dumping of toxic sewage. New theoretical developments supported these initiatives, such as "Earth Jurisprudence" and "Wild Laws" frameworks that conceive the laws of nature (the principles that govern how the universe functions) as the main source of human laws, and therefore, human legislation should seek to ensure the reproduction of all natural beings to transform our relationship with the natural world from one of destruction to one of mutually beneficial support (Maloney and Siemen, 2015; Berry, 1999; Schillmoller and Pelizzon, 2013; Cullinan, 2002; Burdon, 2012). Despite the ambition of these frameworks, the legal implementation was limited to the discursive recognition of nature rights focused on very specific locations.

More recent developments translate the rights of nature to national legislation and constitutional norms with the involvement of indigenous and environmental organizations. The Ecuadorian Constitution has a section on the rights of nature, which begins stating that Nature or *Pachamama* has the right to the integral respect of its existence and the maintenance and regeneration of its vital cycles, structure, functions, and evolutionary processes (Art. 71). The formulation of these rights would combine radical Western ecology, indigenous thinking, and legal rights discourse (Rühs and Jones, 2016; Akchurin, 2015). Scholars conceive the rights of nature as a hybrid concept (Rühs and Jones, 2016), a mestizo concept (Santos, 2010), and an epistemic pact (Valladares and Boelens, 2017). However, the relationship between Indigenous peoples, the environment, and rights discourses seems to suggest other dynamics. In the Amazon, the Achuar People of Ecuador and Peru conceive many plants and animals as having a soul (*wakan*), similar to the human being, a faculty that classifies them among persons (*aents*) with reflexive conscience and intentionality (Descola, 2004). In general, Indigenous peoples classify a scale of beings in which the differences between men, plants, and animals are of degrees and not of essence. Namely, personhood is an issue of degree and context, rather than a right of the whole natural world. In New Zealand, the Te Awa Tupua Act of 2017 recognized the legal personality of the Whanganui River and stated that ownership of the riverbed is vested in the river itself. For Kramm (2020), the Parliament introduced a new ontology that integrates both the ontology of the Māori (river as an ancestor) and the ontology of the government (river as a legal person) into a comprehensive ontology based on which the two guardians can make decisions about the River's wellbeing. However, while the government restricts deliberation to human beings, the Māori would include all ancestors, including human beings, non-human animals, and nature (Kramm, 2024). The legal definitions of ownership and legal personhood do not coincide with Māori understandings of their relationship with the river (Yates et al., 2023).

The relationships between indigenous groups and natural beings might be of complementarity and reciprocity, respect and power, or others rather than guardianship. In Ecuador, indigenous organizations advocated for the rights of nature not primarily to portray the way they live with nature but as a way of negotiating for expanding their territorial rights and plurinationality. In New Zealand, the goal was to use a legal framework, still considered colonial, to enact something closer to Māori realities (Yates et al., 2023). These complex relationships explain why, when the rights of nature were debated in Ecuador, some indigenous sectors expressed concerns that enacting norms for a domain that had previously been outside the law would grant the state mechanisms for regulating and controlling communities' spaces (Valladares and Boelens, 2017; Akchurin, 2015). Other concerns were that the state would regulate nature's rights only symbolically, transforming it into a hegemonic political paradigm or a buzzword with no real impacts (Valladares and Boelens, 2017; Fitz-Henry, 2012). Some of these concerns were materialized. In Ecuador, subsequent regulations such as the Mining Law (2009), the Organic

Law of Water Resources and Exploitation (2014), and the Organic Code of the Environment (2017) weakened the rights of nature by allowing large-scale mining and extractive activities in fragile ecosystems and protected areas. Only the interest in expanding industrial mining has led the Ecuadorian government to initiate efforts to eliminate unauthorized mining, appealing to the rights of nature. The Ministry of Environment invokes these rights to justify routine administrative actions that are part of its institutional mission (Kauffman and Martin, 2016).

The deepest problem of conceiving the right of nature as a feature of pluriversal governance is that it depoliticizes the whole significance of governing the natural environment. By leaving the concretization of nature rights and interests to administrative and judicial implementation, it remains a mere concept subjected to the discursive appropriation of indigenous thinking and management of indigenous areas (Youatt, 2017). Nature's interests must be located not merely at the legal, but also at the political dimension. This requires establishing democratic procedures to represent these interests in the political arena, considering the different ecological ontologies of state authorities, environmentalists, and Indigenous nations.

1.4 Building a Plurinational and Pluriversal International Governance

Putting in conversation plurinationalism and pluriversality is crucial to examine institutional, epistemological, and ontological tensions in the international sphere and the prospects for building a different kind of international governance. The decolonial framework is inspiring for this endeavor because it provides the analytical lens to deal with both onto-epistemological injustices and the global political economy. For decolonial scholars, such as Anibal Quijano, Enrique Dussel, Walter Mignolo, and Ramon Grosfoguel, the rationalist and universalist ideals of modernity were functionally developed with the colonization of the Americas in the fifteenth century, its colonial racial classifications, and its colonial extractive rationale. This allowed the development of two global processes: a global process of extraction and accumulation of resources from the South to the North, and a global process of naming or imposition of identities (Indians, blacks, and mestizos) as socially and politically inferior to the European white men. Quijano proposed the notion of "coloniality of power" to explain how despite colonialism formally concluded in most of the world, coloniality maintains its force because socio-political and geoeconomic power within countries and among countries resembles these two global processes. Decoloniality, then, means breaking both the legacies of colonial epistemic and ontological violence and colonial extractivist violence of global economic processes. Consequently, to deal with coloniality, international environmental governance must deal with institutional, epistemological, and ontological injustices.

- **Institutional Injustices**
  Principles: State-centrism
  Expressions:
  Extractive states
  Institutional conflicts
  Alternatives: Plurinationalism: Plurinational states & plurinational international governance
- **Epistemological Injustices**
  Principles: Ethnocentrism
  Expressions:
  Political, economic, and ecological imaginaries
  Epistemological conflicts
  Alternatives: Multiculturalism: Epistemic diversity
- **Ontological Injustices**
  Principles: Anthropocentrism
  Expressions:
  Worlding practices
  Ontological conflicts
  Alternatives: Pluriversalism: Pluriversal political spaces

Source: By the author

Institutional injustices codify the extractivist political economy into national and international institutional arrangements. Epistemological injustices consolidate ethnocentrism and Western political, economic, and ecological imaginaries, excluding alternative ways of knowing and managing the natural environment. Ontological injustices legitimate worlding practices that mystify other ways of conceiving the world and humans and more-than-human relationships. These different injustices are deeply interrelated as institutional injustices also express epistemological and ontological injustices and the other way around. Thus, conflicts associated with different representations of the natural environment are not limited to epistemological questions. Conceiving the forest and mountains as resources rather than sacred beings also raises ontological concerns. In the same vein, conflicts related to the exclusion of indigenous sovereignty over the forest are not just about institutional constraints. The denial of Indigenous peoples as sovereign over their territory during colonization and post-colonization was (and is) not just epistemological violence, it is ontological violence (Bawaka Country including S. Wright et al., 2016). Similarly, today's denial of indigenous self-determination in constitutional arrangements expresses institutional injustices and ontological injustices (Kramm, 2024).

These injustices exclude different institutions, thinking, and cosmologies that support the enactment of different paradigms: plurinationalism as a governance model that recognizes indigenous sovereignties; multiculturalism as an epistemic platform that incorporates epistemic diversity; and pluriversality as a political space that contains ontological differences. The attempts to enact these paradigms produce ontological, epistemological, and institutional conflicts. As these institutions, thinking, and cosmologies are embedded in natural environments deemed crucial for global sustainability, questions on the political ecology of international governance require unraveling institutional, epistemological, and ontological tensions. The key aim of this book is to unravel these tensions through the study of the international governance of the Amazon.

The book formulates descriptive and normative claims. Regarding the former, it explains the limitations of explaining the environmental degradation of the basin only in terms of physical/material drivers. Scientists and experts have shown that the main drivers are global climate change, the expansion of extractive industries, the irruption of illegal economies, and mega-infrastructure developments. An analysis of the international governance of the Amazon shows that environmental degradation deeply responds to institutional, epistemological, and ontological injustices. In epistemological terms, the Amazon is conceived either as a place of global extractivism, global conservation, or national development under Western imaginaries. In ontological terms, indigenous worlds and nature agencies are excluded by legitimizing a worldview of Amazonian ecosystems as resources and commodities. In institutional terms, Western ontology and epistemologies support strong sovereignty arrangements that disregard local and global environmental concerns and indigenous ancestral rights. As a result, these injustices create a state-centric, ethnocentric, and anthropocentric framework that facilitates the continued development of the material drivers that affect the region. Concrete expressions of this operation include the exclusion of Indigenous Peoples from the international governance of the basin, the instrumentalization of Indigenous knowledge, the emphasis on the principle of sovereignty, and the predominance of extractive imaginaries over the Amazon.

Regarding the normative claims, the book proposes addressing ontological, epistemological, and institutional injustices by building a plurinational, multi-epistemic, and pluriversal international governance. A plurinational governance would redefine Westphalian conceptions of sovereignty and self-determination to make a substantial space for indigenous sovereignties in international decision-making. This governance goes beyond conventional venues for the international participation of Indigenous peoples through indirect involvement with national commissions; participation in side or parallel events; or the granting of observer status. It entails rethinking international relations and sovereignty arrangements by conceiving Indigenous nations as legitimate international actors with decision-making power in international bodies and processes relevant to their lives. By examining the Amazon through the lens of plurinationalism, ACTO would have to be transformed from being a state-centered international organization to becoming a plurinational organization guided under plural conceptions of sovereignty and self-determination. In addition, a Plurinational Amazon must translate plurinational politics in a way that issues of co-optation, bureaucratization, and extractive dependence found in plurinational governments are not reproduced in international arrangements. For this aim, it would be crucial to incorporate the political representation of Amazonian Indigenous nations in the deliberative processes of the organization.

A pluriversal and multi-epistemic governance would open international deliberative forums to negotiate different ontologies and epistemologies. This entails politically discussing varied environmental measures and targets embedded in both indigenous and Western thinking. More deeply, it would imply discussing the different worldviews on the natural environment. Instead of assuming that state representatives, depoliticized advisory scientist bodies, or indigenous organizations are the only legitimate representatives of the natural world, it would be important to rethink ecological democracy and governance as an instance for negotiating ontological tensions. This pluriversal governance would embrace, rather than avoid, different worldviews emanating from scientist conservationist concerns, indigenous plurinational politics, and state developmental agendas. In this scenario, scientists would have a crucial role along with those people that might coincide with scientists' sense of urgency, but have different views on nature's ontological foundations and propose different means to bring justice to the relationship between ecosystems and communities. By examining the Amazon through the lens of pluriversality, ACTO would have to be transformed from being an anthropocentric and ethnocentric international organization to becoming a pluriversal institutional space. This would mean including independent scientific communities in deliberation processes along with Indigenous nations and nation-states to formulate and negotiate the different ways they portray the representation and protection of the natural environment.

The proposal for a plurinational, multi-epistemic, and pluriversal governance relies on new principles and structures of international governance. Under this framework, instead of governing internationally the Amazon under the principles of "absolute sovereignty" and "common concern of humankind," it reformulates the notions of sovereignty and humanity to make a space for ontological, epistemological, and institutional differences. Ultimately, this proposal challenges polycentricity as an ideal governance model. Polycentricity has fostered regional institutional fragmentation and has legitimized different development priorities of each government, excluding a common sustainable path for the entire region. Moreover, polycentricism has co-existed with top-down arrangements that have instrumentalized Indigenous peoples as mere participants who legitimize environmental and extractive projects. We need to think beyond the current state of affairs. We are not obliged to choose between either a fragmented and polycentric architecture or ideal and utopian global agreements. It is possible to achieve regional agreements over international commons such as the Amazon under new paradigms and frameworks. This governance model can also inspire a transformative path across the world's international commons, in whose governance not solely nation-states, but also conservation scientists and Indigenous peoples should have their voices institutionalized.

1.5 Book Organization

This book is a product of more than ten years of research on indigenous politics, environmental governance, and political ecology in the Amazon rainforest. Through these years, I have engaged with different academic projects using the research methods of document analysis, interviews with national and international officials, NGOs, development bank officials, indigenous organizations and activists, and ethnographic fieldwork in Peru, Brazil, and Ecuador. The book builds on the data collected and the analysis made in previous research projects to present a comprehensive examination of the Amazon rainforest and its international policy architecture as a macro case study. To unpack this case, the book analyzes the interactions between different international actors, policy regimens, and local and international struggles of Indigenous peoples in the basin. Thus, it focuses on ACTO governance to unveil how its international architecture facilitates basin states' extractive agendas while instrumentalizing indigenous participation to legitimize localized environmental initiatives and programs. It also focuses on COICA to explore how its activism is expanding the political space for meaningful inclusion of the indigenous agenda in international processes. The book also delves into the limitations of governing global extractivism in the basin through the analysis of the IIRSA, the most ambitious portfolio of mega-infrastructure projects in the region, aimed at facilitating international trade. It also addresses how global conservation initiatives and the scientific community formulate alternative imaginaries in which the Amazon is a place of global conservation instead of global extractivism. Through this multi-scalar examination, the book provides a nuanced analysis of how Indigenous nations, state developmental agendas, and global conservation provide conflictive worldviews on nature governance.

The book is divided into seven chapters. The introduction has provided the background and empirical and theoretical justifications for the study. It has explained the global relevance of the Amazon and the current drivers of environmental degradation in the basin. It also has discussed three notions that guide the analysis through the chapters: polycentric governance, plurinational governance, and pluriversal governance.

Chapter 2, "The Amazon as an International Commons: Governing Principles for Negotiating Sovereignty and Environmental Imaginaries," analyzes the international environmental governance of the Amazon through the Amazon Cooperation Treaty Organization (ACTO). In particular, it explores how ACTO has incorporated governance principles for governing international commons ("enclosure," "common heritage of humanity," and "common concern of humanity") into its discourses, instruments, and practices. This chapter explains that despite the discursive rejection of international forces, the basin states appeal to "common concern" to embrace international cooperation in localized initiatives, while through "enclosure" they promote transnational extractive and infrastructure projects. Beyond the debate between internationalization and sovereignty, these principles interact under anthropocentric, ethnocentric, and state-centric premises. This produces a fragmented governance that legitimizes the expansion of extractivism under sovereign and developmental imaginaries while excluding the concerns and aspirations of Indigenous peoples and environmentalists.

Chapter 3, "The Amazon as a Place for Global Extractivism: Rethinking Extractivism and Infrastructure in Extractive Frontiers," explores the governance of extractivism in the Amazon by reflecting on IIRSA infrastructure development and how it relates to extractive activities. The analysis of the entanglements between mega-infrastructures and extractive industries also allows a deeper understanding of extractivism. From a scalar dimension, the Amazon becomes an example of global extractivism, a place where infrastructure and extraction coalesce to feed the global economy and the endless transnational circulation of commodities. From material/immaterial dimensions, infrastructure might be a kind of extractivism in itself when its main goal is profit-making from construction, detached from real prospects for connectivity. In turn, its immaterial dimension refers to how extractive logics permeate infrastructure activities, such as the monetarizing of the knowledge and needs of locals to justify the projects' socio-economic viability. Considering the re-dimensioning of extractivism, this chapter provides reflections on how it promotes international economic integration while limiting environmental integration in the Amazon. This raises crucial insights on the proper ways to govern internationally extractive activities.

Chapter 4, "The Amazon as a Place for Global Conservation" unpacks the tensions and conflicts of conceiving the Amazon as a field of global conservation and examines the prospects to scale indigenous politics of conservation and reimagine conservation policies in the local and international spheres. For this aim, this chapter discusses the theories for decolonizing conservation, how they help to explain environmental conflicts in the Amazon, and their strengths and gaps. Then, it provides an overview of the conservation architecture and associated conflicts in the Peruvian Amazon through three cases that show the international and local interactions around conservation politics and policies. Ultimately, this chapter provides insights to revisit critical theories on conservation and the importance of international governance for reinventing conservation practices and policies in the Amazon and beyond.

Chapter 5, "Envisioning a Plurinational Governance for the Amazon," analyzes the role and aspirations of Indigenous peoples in the international governance of the Amazon. Based on the analysis of COICA international politics and ACTO strategies and actions regarding Indigenous peoples, this chapter argues that the international governance of the Amazon has excluded Indigenous peoples by recognizing a limited version of self-determination with no political rights. Many ACTO officials reject the possibility of having the representativeness of Indigenous peoples in the deliberative processes of the organization. However, the continued indigenous activism has opened new opportunities for institutionalizing their participation within ACTO. Despite ACTO's political weakness and the different institutional challenges of COICA, Indigenous peoples struggle to decolonize the international governance of the Amazon and enact what would be a plurinational international governance.

Chapter 6, "Envisioning a Pluriversal Environmental Governance: Scientific and Indigenous Ontologies in the Amazon," examines the prospects for including scientific and indigenous ontologies in the international governance of the Amazon. This chapter assesses the different governance models for enlarging ecological democracy and having nature's interests represented in political spaces. For this aim, it analyzes the most prominent scientific bodies dealing with the climate emergency, the Intergovernmental Panel on Climate Change (IPCC) and the Intergovernmental Science-Policy Platform on Biodiversity and Ecosystem Services (IPBES), compared to the Science Panel for the Amazon (SPA), the first scientist platform dedicated to the largest rainforest in the world. This chapter proposes enlarging ecological democracy under a pluriversal governance in which nation-states, scientists, and Indigenous peoples would share the political stage to negotiate their different worldviews and the authority to represent their own natural worlds. This might trigger ontological clashes, but also the possibility of creating ontological coalitions around indigenous rights, the protection of nature, and the appropriate means to deal with the climate crisis in the basin.

The concluding chapter, "Conclusions: Governing the Amazon and Beyond" provides a summary of the findings and arguments developed in Chapters 2–6. It also provides a reflection on the policy implications of the study for reforming the international governance of the Amazon and other international rainforests, such as the Congo rainforest. Finally, it provides some reflections on how the proposed framework can be applied to global commons, such as the high seas and seabed beyond national jurisdictions and outer space.

CHAPTER 2

The Amazon as an International Commons

Governing Principles for Negotiating Sovereignty and Environmental Imaginaries

2.1 Introduction

International actors and governments have consistently expressed their concerns about the fate of the Amazon. In 2005, former commissioner of the European Union and Director General of the World Trade Organization, Pascal Lamy, proposed that the Amazon and other international rainforests should be considered "global public assets" and, therefore, should be administered by the international community (BBC, 2005). Although Amazonian governments, especially Brazil, strongly opposed these declarations, their failure to substantially reduce deforestation has kept these proposals alive. Despite some improvements at the beginning of the 2000s, in Brazil, satellite imaging shows that during Jair Bolsonaro's administration (2019–2023), the rate of deforestation soared by as much as 92 percent. In Peru, Colombia, and Bolivia, the rate of deforestation has also increased in recent years (Pereira and Viola, 2020; Artaxo, 2019; Cardil et al., 2020).

In 2019, massive forest fires affected vast Amazonian territories, especially in Bolivia and Brazil, allegedly produced by the extension of logging, small agriculture, and cattle. After the fire crisis, French President Emmanuel Macron said that the Amazon forest was a concern for the whole planet and that Brazil should not be allowed to destroy it all (Associated Press, 2019). The Brazilian government rejected this declaration as a form of neocolonialism (López Rivera, 2019). Bolsonaro claimed that developed nations were using an environmental agenda to take over Brazilian natural resources: "Sovereignty of the region and its riches is what is truly at stake … No country in the world has the moral right to talk about the Amazon. You destroyed your own ecosystems" (in Dom Phillips, 2019).

These declarations show the continuity of old debates about the "internationalization of the Amazon" and the conception of the Amazon rainforest as a "global commons." Since the seventies, with the rise of the international agenda for protecting large rainforests, developed nations suggested that the Amazon should be treated as a global commons governed internationally under the principle of "common heritage of humankind." Basin states reacted against these attempts, reaffirming their absolute sovereignty over their respective Amazonian territory (Cazala, 2020; Vogler, 2012). These debates led Amazonian states to approve the Amazonian Cooperation Treaty (ACT) in July 1978 and then create the Amazonian Cooperation Treaty Organization (ACTO) in 1998. With this international architecture for sustainable development, basin states would address international environmental concerns while supporting national developmental agendas based on resource extraction. By this time, the principle of "common concern of humankind" emerged as the most suitable to govern global rainforests in general and the Amazon in particular. This principle allows some indirect influence of international forces through cooperation and assistance but not direct incidence in state environmental and economic policies over the forests (Garcia, 2011; Mgbeoji, 2003; de Sartre and Taravella, 2009; Bastos Lima et al., 2021; Franchini and Viola, 2019).

The failure to stop deforestation and environmental degradation in the subsequent decades obliged regional leaders to compromise to improve the international governance of the Amazon. At the Fourth Presidential Summit under the Treaty of Amazonian Cooperation in August 2023, the governments approved the Declaration of Belém and announced a "new common cooperation agenda in the Amazon" to achieve "sustainable development" and "take urgent actions to avoid the point of no return in the Amazon." The Declaration formulated new principles for this agenda, such as the participation of Indigenous peoples, gender equality, and intercultural and intergenerational approaches; but also reiterated the only principle in force since the conclusion of the Treaty: "The sovereignty of the States, including respect for the national legislation of each country."

This chapter analyzes how the persistent emphasis on national sovereignty influences the international governance of the Amazon and examines how other principles for governing international commons have been incorporated into the actual governance of the basin. Absolute sovereignty (enclosure), common heritage, and common concern are conceived in this study as governance principles for managing global and international commons and not as formal principles of international law. Under this premise, the absolute sovereignty of basin states under the idea of "enclosure" and the principle of "common concern of humankind" would conceive the Amazon as an *international commons* shared among basin states as those principles reaffirm state sovereignty. The principle of "common heritage of humankind" would conceive it as a *global commons* where no nation-state should have strong sovereign claims over Amazonian areas.

After analyzing official documents and regulations produced by the ACTO since its creation and complementing this analysis with fieldwork in its headquarters in Brasilia in 2022 and semi-structured interviews with ACTO officials, this chapter found unexpected interactions among those principles. "Enclosure" and "common concern" have been incorporated in ACTO's governing instruments and practices, excluding the "common heritage" for being a potential vehicle of international forces. Nonetheless, through the principle of the "common concern" international actors are welcomed in the governance of the basin in the form of focalized cooperation. At the same time, through "enclosure" national governments promote transnational extractive and infrastructure projects. In practice, basin states use these principles to validate their sovereignty and environmental imaginaries. They articulate strong sovereignty claims (enclosure) while proclaiming international environmental compromises and partnerships (common concern).

A lesson from the analysis of the Amazon rainforest is that beyond the internationalization vs sovereignty debate, enclosure, common heritage, and common concern have obscured the sovereign claims of Indigenous peoples by relying on anthropocentric, ethnocentric, and state-centric premises. They are state-centric by excluding Indigenous nations from the international governance of the basin. In this operation, they are also ethnocentric by excluding other notions and principles different from Western conceptions of sovereignty and environmentalism. These principles are also anthropocentric by focusing on the welfare of "humankind" instead of the natural world. Indigenous holistic cosmovisions on human-nature relationships and self-determination claims challenge these premises and might assist in reimagining sovereignty and environmentalism and, in this way, restructuring the arrangements for governing international commons.

This chapter is organized as follows: Section 2.2 presents the scholarly debates on the principles for governing the commons and international forests. Section 2.3 introduces the Amazon rainforest as an international commons. Section 2.4 analyzes how the governing principles of enclosure, the common concern of humankind, and the common heritage of humankind have been incorporated in ACTO organization, instruments, and discourses. Section 2.5 discusses the prospects for reformulating those principles in the Amazon and beyond. Section 2.6 formulates the conclusions and implications of this chapter.

2.2 Governing Principles for International Commons

The notion of "global commons" often refers to areas outside national jurisdiction in which international law regulates some special forms of access, such as the high seas and deep seabed, outer space, and the atmosphere (Vogler, 2012; Kurian and Vinodan, 2020). In this regard, other global commons would be the ozone layer (Brown, 2014) and the electromagnetic frequency spectrum (Wijkman, 1982). Global commons have also been conceptualized from an economic perspective as material domains in which common-pool goods exist, such as fisheries in the oceans, characterized by having high subtractability or rivalrousness (its consumption might lead to depletion) and low exclusion (it is difficult to exclude others from using them) (Vogler, 2012; Pokorny et al., 2019). A related but different notion is "global public goods," which are expected to have non-rival properties and low exclusion, therefore suffering from freeriding (Boonen et al., 2019; Schaeffer et al., 2017). Examples of global public goods are global climate protection (Magnan and Ribera, 2016; Wit and Freitas, 2019), epidemics control, and knowledge (Boonen et al., 2019).

One way to deal with global commons is the institutionalization of the principle of "open access" by which the area in question is regarded as of free use, with no exclusionary rights nor institutional rules for collective management. Another way is "enclosure," inspired by Hardin's Tragedy of the Commons. Whereas Hardin focused on the local depletion of common-pool resources for not defining clear property rights, scholars argue that this tragedy occurs on the international level because governments are either unable to design appropriate international authorities or are unwilling to engage with binding international treaties that divide commons at the same time of limiting their sovereign rights (Wijkman, 1982). In this context, "enclosure" means establishing absolute sovereignty arrangements over specific portions of a non-regulated international space. This implies the transformation of a global commons into an international commons shared among some nation-states.

One example of global commons enclosure is the establishment of 200 nautical miles of exclusive economic zones (EEZs) for each nation-state under the United Nations Convention on the Law of the Sea of 1982-UNCLOS (Vogler, 2012). The 200-mile thesis is associated with the demands of developing countries to protect their coastal seas from foreign maritime powers (Young, 2021). Advanced originally by Peru and Chile in the 1950s, it sought a just redistribution of maritime world resources and the empowerment of the smallest states to deny access to their fishing zones to the "distant water fishing nations" (Young, 2021; Boczek, 1984). This trend was reinforced by the New International Economic Order (NIEO) movement against neo-colonialism (Boczek, 1984) and the enactment of declarations and institutions that advanced third-world interests, such as the Resolution on Permanent Sovereignty over Natural Resources (1962), the Declaration on the Establishment of a New International Economic Order (1974), the Charter of Economic Rights and Duties of States (1975), and the Declaration on the Right to Development (1986).

The use of enclosure reinforced the sovereignty of former colonies to deal with international powers under developmental imaginaries (Eslava et al., 2017; Gathii, 2019). This trend, however, excluded Indigenous peoples (Fukurai, 2018). For instance, the NIEO doctrine "Permanent sovereignty over natural resources," formalized in the General Assembly Resolution 626 of December 1952, aimed at protecting developing countries' sovereignty to use their natural resources vis-á-vis powerful foreign states and transnational corporations. Since the original purpose was to strengthen the position of newly independent states, the term "peoples" was understood as referring to post-colonial states, and not constituent peoples. To this day, third-world states employ this doctrine to pursue development projects promoting the national interest, conflating the identities of various groups with that of the state and invalidating ancestral claims to land advanced by Indigenous Peoples (Bayot, 2019). Even when states recognize indigenous territorial rights and enclose forest areas in their favor, this does not entail a substantial recognition of their ancestral rights. As argued by Chandra (2020), the purpose of enclosing the commons in biodiversity zones in the last decades is not to benefit the proximate local interests but to serve the interests of humankind as a whole. The recognition of limited territorial rights of local communities becomes entangled in a global network of rules and decision-making.

Vogler (2012) argues that enclosure cannot always provide a management solution and is blind to distributional consequences or what is known as "tragedies of dispossession" (Balagopal and Chacko, 2020). For instance, contrary to Hardin's logic, world fishing resources have declined due to overexploitation (FAO, 2010), affecting mainly local and indigenous communities that depend on these resources. The deepest problem is that theories and institutions such as EEZ and "permanent sovereignty over natural resources" are justified in nationalistic rhetoric that only serves to promote the self-interest of developmental states with no concern for local and international environmental impacts and inequalities. This questions the potential of these doctrines for true decolonization (Young, 2021).

2.2.1 Common Heritage, Common Concern, and Global Forest

The "common heritage of humankind" has been portrayed as an alternative to enclosure to govern global commons. This principle suggests that the management of the commons would be done on behalf of all peoples; the economic benefits from this management must be shared by the global community, and the area of common global ownership must be a completely demilitarized zone where only can be conducted peaceful activities, such as scientific research (Mgbeoji, 2003; Shelton, 2009a,b). Both common heritage and enclosure were promoted by developing nations under the NIEO campaign during UNCLOS negotiations in the seventies and early eighties (Vogler, 2012). The aim was that the enclosure, through EEZ, be applied to 200 nautical miles and the "common heritage" to the seabed beyond 200 miles (Lodge, 2021). The international community would have full legal ownership of the seabed as "common heritage" through the International Seabed Authority acting as a trustee,[1] with developing states holding preferential rights in the distribution of the area's resources.

Different authors have shown concerns that "common heritage" could be treated more as an intellectual artifact than as a principle with actual implications (Mickelson, 2014). On the one hand, treaties that mention it have the lowest numbers of ratifications (Mgbeoji, 2003; Buck, 1998; Cazala, 2020), except for the Law

[1] Article 137(2) of UNCLOS. See also: Agreement relating to the Implementation of Part XI of the United Nations Convention on the Law of the Sea, adopted in July 1994.

of the Sea Convention and its associated instruments.[2] On the other hand, in those regimens where it has been formalized, it has been unable to stop extractivism. For instance, the International Seabed Authority has granted licenses for the exploration of potential mining sites in the Atlantic, Indian, and Pacific Oceans, fostering a new global gold rush of deep-sea mining. For Hunter et al. (2018), this can be partly explained by the original 1960s "common heritage" framing because it focused on the redistribution of benefits from mineral exploitation with absolute neglect of its social and environmental impacts. In formulating this principle, Maltese diplomat Arvid Pardo presented a fantastical portrayal of almost inexhaustible mineral resources in the seabed to the First Committee of the United Nations General Assembly in 1967. This framing has continued to dominate the deep-sea narrative (Hunter et al., 2018) and has also been incorporated into international arrangements for exploring outer space (see Chapter 7).

More critically, applying this principle in areas subject to clear national jurisdictions, such as the rainforests, is difficult. Although some proposed conceiving the forests as global commons (Vogler, 2012; Pokorny et al., 2019) subjected to "common heritage," sovereignty claims led to the failure to adopt a forest convention at the United Nations Conference on Environment and Development (UNCED), also known as the Earth Summit or Rio Summit in 1992 (Mickelson, 1996). Mohammed Bedjaoui in 1979 had already noted how conceiving the Amazon and the Congo rainforest as "mankind's common heritage"[3] wouldn't be outrageous if there were a fair distribution of rights and duties for all States. For Bedjaoui, this was not the case. Applying common heritage to the forest would mean that the Third World would shoulder the obligations derived from this principle, while the industrialized States would only benefit from it. These fears continued in the following years. In their Declaration of San Francisco de Quito of March 1989, the foreign ministers of the Amazon countries repudiated international interferences with their developmental policies in the region (Nabais, 2000). They criticized the declarations and activities of international environmental organizations as questioning their sovereignty. Regional leaders argued that environmental concerns were only a pretext for the Global North to stop Brazil and other Amazonian states from developing (Kolk, 1998; Bastos Lima et al., 2019).

Despite these tensions, the G7 leaders, with the support of global conservation NGOs, proposed to negotiate a forest convention at the UNCED (Smouts, 2003). At the first UNCED preparatory committee meeting in July 1990, timber-exporting and developing countries, such as Brazil, Malaysia, and Indonesia, resisted any suggestions that forests were a global commons rather than a national resource (Dehm, 2021). Amazonian countries strongly opposed this conceptualization under

[2] For instance, the "Agreement on the Conservation and Sustainable Use of Marine Biological Diversity of Areas beyond National Jurisdiction" on June 19, 2023.

[3] The original formulation referred to "mankind." Current scholarly and normative terminology uses the word "humankind."

sovereignty arguments (Cazala, 2020) and claimed that any attempt to conceive the Amazon as a global commons was a neocolonial tactic of developed nations to have open access to their biological resources (Vogler, 2012). Suspicious of ecological imperialism, they opposed any restrictions on sovereignty and the right to pursue national interests (Brunnée and Nollkaemper, 1996). During the UNCED, Prime Minister Mahathir Mohamad of Malaysia synthesized this position: "Obviously the North wants to have a direct say in the management of forests in the poor South at next to no cost to themselves." He denounced the attempts of rich countries to "regulate the development of the poor countries" (Mickelson, 1996: 240). The conflict led to the decision not to negotiate the convention and only approve the Non-Legally Binding Authoritative Statement of Principles for a Global Consensus on the Management, Conservation, and Sustainable Development of All Types of Forests ("Forest Principles"). These principles are generally regarded as a broad and non-substantial set of guidelines.

After Rio, some proposals tried to reactivate the discussions for negotiating a forest convention. Mickelson (1996) proposed integrating the concerns of developing nations through the principles of sovereignty over natural resources and the right to development. Brunnée (1996) proposed the emerging principle of "common concern" as the basis for a new proposal. This principle was first formulated by General Assembly Resolution 43/53 of 1988 ("climate change is a common concern of mankind") and the 1990 General Assembly Declaration on International Economic Cooperation, which acknowledged the threat to the environment as "the common concern of all" (Dehm, 2021: 125).

The principle of common concern has gained prominence in the international architecture of the environment. The United Nations Framework Convention on Climate Change (UNFCCC), the Convention on Biological Diversity, and the Paris Agreements included it in their preamble to emphasize the global responsibility of states to assist in addressing climate change and biological diversity. The concept has three dimensions: First, the global dimension involves the cooperation of all states when responding to environmental threats because the subject of the concern is of significance to the international community. Second, the temporal dimension results from the long-term effects of major environmental problems, like climate change, that affect the rights and obligations of present and future generations. Third, the social dimension requires the engagement of all sectors of society, including governmental organizations, businesses, NGOs, civil society, and individuals (Horn, 2015). Under this framework, all countries have differentiated obligations to address the common concerns: developed countries have an ethical duty to cooperate to conserve biodiversity in areas beyond the limits of their jurisdiction; "less capacitated countries" should promote this cooperation and take advantage of it to make international agreements effective (Bellinkx et al., 2022).

Unlike the common heritage, "the common concern" indicates that all states have interests in ecological protection rather than an internationalization of ownership of resources (Horn, 2015; Brown, 2014). The common concern principle, then, does not prevent developing states from exploiting their natural resources but only requests that these resources be exploited considering the international interest in environmental sustainability (Shelton, 2009; Dine, 2019). The application of the concept, thus, is considered useful for resources or areas where national sovereignty claims remain strong (Weiss, 2012). For these reasons, in current discussions on forest governance, "common concern" is considered better suited than the "common heritage." By not focusing on the ownership dimension of forest resources but merely on its function or use dimension as carbon storage, protecting this function would be a shared responsibility (Brunnée and Nollkaemper, 1996).

In the post-Rio context, the interest in achieving a forest convention diminished. NGOs feared that the timber industry would dominate the process and lead to low standards. They had a more pragmatic view: instead of engaging in a long and costly process, it would be better to solve pressing problems and implement existing agreements (Smouts, 2003). This was actually the triumph of "common concern" as this principle does not necessarily require global solutions, it might be advanced through national strategies, plans, or programs (Weiss, 2012). Thus, developing countries were committed to maintaining their forest cover and preserving the biological diversity contained in their forests. In exchange, industrialized countries would contribute with financial support and technology. All states, funding agencies, the private sector, and NGOs, would cooperate to promote the sustainable use of the forest while developing trade in forest products (Smouts, 2003). Amazonian governments reaffirmed that the sustainable development of the Amazon is of common concern to humankind, but the final responsibility and authority over the management of this area lies with each Amazonian government (Garcia, 2011; Nabais, 2000).

In this context, forest protection advocates prioritized voluntary mechanisms and those that reinforce national sovereignty, such as the private governance of forest certification (Long, 2013) and the control of illegal logging (H van Asselt and McDermott, 2016). Along with these efforts, a new wave of non-binding declarations and plans emerged, such as the UN's 2014 New York Declaration on Forests and the UN Strategic Plan for Forests 2017–2030 (Paim, 2021). In this fragmented governance, the most salient mechanism has been the program "Reducing Emissions from Deforestation and Forest Degradation" – REDD+.

2.2.2 REDD+ and the Fragmented Internationalization of Rainforests

The "common concern" principle is fully exemplified in the design and implementation of REDD+. It emerged from the climate change regime as the most feasible way to preserve tropical forests by focusing on the economic gains from forest protection (Long, 2013; Eikermann, 2015). The integration between the climate and forest regimens started after the 1997 Kyoto Protocol with the Clean Development Mechanism (CDM), which included afforestation and reforestation but not incentives to protect already-established forests (Dalla and Korber, 2024). It was just at COP13 in 2007, with the Bali Action Plan, that the Parties decided to promote actions to reduce deforestation and forest degradation emissions with REDD+ (Giacomini, 2022). REDD+ rationale is simple: the costs of preventing emissions by reducing deforestation are projected to be significantly less than the cost of reducing emissions in many sectors within developed countries, and thus, anti-deforestation is seen as the most cost-effective mitigation option in the short term (Long, 2013). It was agreed that developing countries should be supported by the international community with financial and technological resources to bring existing forests into carbon markets. Thus, the UNFCCC institutionalized REDD+ under a national approach in which each party submits the outcomes of deforestation rates below a baseline and receives "payments by results" from international sources (Dalla and Korber, 2024; Cifuentes, 2021). The voluntary nature of REDD+ for developing countries and its incentive scheme sought to overcome the sovereignty and finance concerns that had meant a deadlock in past forestry negotiations. Countries such as Brazil, once a strong opponent of a global forest convention, started embracing REDD+ (Long, 2013).

Today, REDD+ is conceived as the main international climate change mitigation mechanism (Cifuentes, 2021); a policy tool for forest conservation incentive (Lozano et al., 2024; Dalla and Korber, 2024); the main approach to addressing deforestation and forest degradation (Schroeder and González, 2019); and the dominant policy paradigm in the global forestry sector (Aryal et al., 2024). Although initially seen as the world's largest experiment in payment for ecosystem services (PES) schemes, it evolved to support a broader set of policies (Recio, 2022), starting from reducing emissions from deforestation to measures against degradation and, finally, enhancement of carbon stocks through afforestation, reforestation and sustainable forest management, as included by the Cancun Safeguard Principles adopted at COP 16 in 2010 (Bayrak and Marafa, 2016). At COP 19 in 2013, parties adopted the Warsaw Framework, creating national focal points to verify "result-based actions" and for the transfer of "result-based payments" (Godden and Tehan, 2016). The Paris Agreement (2015) and the UN Sustainable Development Goals (2015–2030) further promoted result-based payments and net-zero emissions targets (Aryal et al., 2024). The Parties decided not to create a centralized international mechanism and rather emphasized the national and decentralized character of REDD+ (Recio, 2022).

REDD+ entails a transnational transaction between producers (Global South countries, communities) and buyers (State, private actors) of forest ecosystem services, which takes shape through multilateral, bilateral, or private agreements (Lozano et al., 2024). Private agreements rely on market-based mechanisms that involve the trading of carbon offsets. Multilateral and bilateral agreements rely on fund-based mechanisms that support developing countries in implementing REDD+ programs and receive "result-based payments" (Garcia et al., 2021). The expectation was that the public funding support would be gradually replaced by carbon markets (Recio, 2022; Sunderlin, 2015). However, for many years, there was no global regulatory framework under the UNFCCC for establishing this market (Sunderlin, 2015), and just recently, at COP 29 in Baku, in 2024, parties agreed to establish international carbon market standards. Current "compliance carbon markets" rely on national legislation and regional agreements such as the European Union's Emissions Trading Scheme. "Voluntary carbon markets" rely on decentralized demand for carbon offsets and credits under guidelines such as the Climate, Community and Biodiversity Standard (CCB) and the Verified Carbon Standard (VCS) (Bayrak and Marafa, 2016). Given low carbon prices, public funding from developed countries has been the main source of support for REDD (Norman and Nakhooda, 2014). This process of "aidification" has been facilitated by the existing mechanisms that the aid sector already had in place. In 2015, it was calculated that bilateral programs managed 51 percent of the finance pledged since 2006, and multilateral funds accounted for around 33 percent (Recio, 2022).

The main multilateral REDD+ program is the United Nations Program on Reducing Emissions from Deforestation and Forest Degradation (UN-REDD), established in September 2008 at the COP13, which provides support to developing countries to implement REDD+ in three phases: capacity building and the development of national policies and measures; their implementation; and verification of results-based actions. The UN also administers the Green Climate Fund (GCF), the main source of payments, and the World Bank launched the Forest Carbon Partnership Facility (FCPF) in 2007 and the Forest Investment Program (FIP) in 2009 to assist developing countries with Readiness Mechanisms (Bayrak and Marafa, 2016). These institutions establish bureaucratic processes to manage REDD+ and deal with national governments. Bilateral donors, such as Norway, Germany, Japan, and the state of California, also contribute to REDD+ financing and have been prominent in shaping influential standards (Dalla and Korber, 2024; Recio, 2022; Zelli, 2019). In addition, institutions like the Global Environment Facility and regional banks administer their own funding mechanisms, such as the Amazon Fund or the Congo Basin Forest Fund (Zelli et al., 2019). NGOs also perform agenda-setting, implementation, and evaluation functions, generating private environmental and social safeguard schemes (Zelli et al., 2019).

These processes are currently mediated through a "rights-based approach" that recognizes the value of sustainable indigenous management over one-fifth of the tropical forests (Popkin, 2015; Aryal et al., 2024; Bayrak and Marafa, 2016) and the need to not overrule local norms, values, and initiatives in implementing REDD+ (Aryal et al., 2024; Schroeder and Gonzalez, 2019; Cifuentes, 2021). Poznan safeguards on indigenous knowledge, FPIC, and participation in COP 14 and principles of transparency, inclusiveness, and accountability incorporated in the Cancun Agreement in COP 16 express this trend (Giacomini, 2022; West, 2015; Schroeder and González, 2019). A further proposal has been Indigenous REDD+, developed by indigenous organizations in Peru and promoted by COICA to ensure that indigenous rights are guaranteed based on principles of territorial and human rights and self-determination under the UNDRIP (Rengifo, 2010; AIDESEP, 2011; Espinoza and Feather, 2012; Cifuentes, 2021). As in the case of a "climate justice approach" to REDD+ (Osborne et al., 2024), the aim is to incorporate indigenous communities as qualified partners in environmental co-management (Schroeder and González, 2019). Although this approach seems incompatible with conventional ones, authors argue that parallel implementation is possible for coexisting programs at different administrative scales (White, 2014).

In this context, REDD+ ended up at the intersection of the governance systems on climate change, biodiversity, forestry, and development, driven by a variety of actors that come together, collaborate, or compete (Dalla and Korber, 2024; Zelli et al., 2019). The result is a complex, fragmented, and multilevel governance, marked by the proliferation of intergovernmental and transnational institutions for standard-setting, financing, implementation, and evaluation (Gupta et al., 2016; Müller, 2020; Lozano et al., 2024). Given that these actors exert authority at multiple scales in the absence of a multilateral treaty and top-down governmental structures, REDD+ has been seen as a polycentric paradigm of governance that both promotes experimentation and is in itself an experiment of payments for ecosystem services (Bushley, 2014; Long, 2013; Sunderlin, 2015; van Asselt and McDermott, 2016). This polycentric framework would also be beneficial because it allows for the co-existence of alternative governance frameworks with plural power balances, offering a voice to those who often struggle to be heard (H van Asselt and McDermott, 2016). Critiques over REDD+, however, have been consistent over the years.

2.2.3 REDD+ Limitations to Govern International Forests

Between 2006 and 2014, more than US$8.7 billion was pledged for REDD+ from public and private sources and directed to over 80 countries, 40 percent of the funds went to Indonesia and Brazil. By mid-2017, US$218 million of the US$2.9 billion pledged to pay for actual REDD+ emission reductions had been disbursed (Dehm, 2021). Between 2018 and 2020, 377 REDD+ projects started implementation in 56 countries, covering 53 million ha of the 2.08 billion ha of their total forest cover (Atmadja et al., 2022). Despite investing billions of dollars in two decades of discussions and programs, REDD+ has not been applied at the expected scale and has not been effective in climate change mitigation (IPCC report, 2019; Aryal et al., 2024; Dehm, 2021; Osborne et al., 2024).

Many critiques focus on the leakage, permanence, and additionality challenges of implementation. Leakage refers to how implementing REDD+ in a specific location might simply displace environmental degradation in another place. This is problematic given the impossibility of verifying that carbon "saved" through sequestration is equivalent to carbon emissions released elsewhere, especially on a North-South global scale (Dehm, 2021). Permanence refers to the risk that carbon is just temporarily stored in the forests and the prospect of restarting emissions in the future because of economic pressures or natural hazards. Additionality refers to the risk that reduced carbon emissions would have occurred anyway, even without REDD+ payments (Bayrak and Marafa, 2016; Aryal et al., 2024).

More deeply, "offsets" have been blamed for being a "dangerous distraction" that legitimates the ongoing fossil extraction and avoids structural transformations (Dehm, 2021). Indeed, between 1850 and 2015, the contribution of deforestation to the total net emission increased only by 11 percent (Houghton and Nassikas, 2017). This suggests that ignoring fossil fuel emissions and commercial farming, while blaming small forestry practices for global emissions, is counter-productive and allows the super-polluters to continue polluting in the name of carbon offsets (Aryal et al., 2024; Giacomini, 2022). A study (Grant et al., 2021) found that switching from coal/oil to natural gas would cut one-third of emissions, whereas the adoption of carbon-capture technologies might reduce it by half (Monjane et al., 2022). Rather, developed countries, corporations, and financial institutions promote "net-zero" emissions measures and voluntary carbon markets in a strategy that has been blamed for greenwashing (Gürçam, 2022; Streck, 2021; Whitington, 2016) and for consolidating temporary and patchy voluntary markets that delay building a solid REDD+ framework (Aryal et al., 2024). For example, a study into Verra, who managed the world's leading voluntary carbon markets program, has found that over 90 percent of rainforest offset credits are likely to be "phantom credits" adopted by big corporations including Disney, Gucci, and Shell (Greenfield, 2023; Aryal et al., 2024).

Structural concerns relate to the critique of REDD+ neoliberal logic: forests are protected to get financial benefits from carbon credits (Dalla and Korber, 2024; Bayrak and Marafa, 2016). This means converting forests into legible and tradable carbon units by extracting them from their embeddedness in social and ecological life, obscuring social, ecological, and cultural values and uses, clashing with Indigenous conceptions of nature (Cifuentes, 2021; Bayrak and Marafa, 2016). Although the forests are not necessarily commodified and incorporated into international carbon markets, the offset discourse and institutional fundamentals of carbon markets make this possible (Aryal et al., 2024; Dehm, 2021; Giacomini, 2022). For Fletcher et al. (2016), the problem is that "conservation markets" are unable to replace "extractive markets." The latter generates profits by externalizing environmental and social costs, whereas the former cannot provide the same level of revenue despite valuation efforts. Consequently, conservation markets become increasingly less market-like and must incorporate subsidies and regulations to achieve conservation. In this view, the aim of reconciling the people, planet, and profit in market-based conservation is a contradiction. Solving this requires moving away from market mechanisms toward a more fundamental redistribution of resource control.

There is also a problem with REDD polycentricity since rules and standards developed in different institutions, such as illegal logging regulations, indigenous rights, and international trade, may be in contradiction (H van Asselt and McDermott, 2016). Different institutions might also have different approaches, such as FCPF "risk-based" policies versus UN-REDD "rights-based" ones (McDermott et al., 2012). Besides, the proliferation of standards, funding, programs, and discussion forums means a challenge for local communities, with limited resources to navigate the various processes (H van Asselt and McDermott, 2016). Indeed, REDD+ is blamed for being an expert-oriented global project in which academic elites and NGOs dominate forest management practices (Aryal et al., 2024; McDermott et al., 2012). Lord and Sareen's (2025) study on Tanzania explains how REDD+ technification could deepen fragmentation by privileging the few elite actors qualified to fulfill monitoring requirements with a disproportionate share of developmental funding, impeding locally driven decision-making. National Forestry Inventories (NFI) development under the Cancun and Warsaw frameworks further promotes a techno-managerial orientation and benefits the local forestry industries rather than other stakeholders (McDermott et al., 2012). Dominant monitoring approaches overlook socioeconomic, cultural, gender, and biological aspects of forest management (Nielsen, 2014; Zelli, 2019). More internationally, Dehm (2021) criticizes the "capacity paradigm" of the North–South difference in terms of a "lack," where the focus is not on questions of historical and ongoing responsibility but on building capacity in the Global South.

Other critiques address the problem of "recentralization" given that under the UNREDD and FCPF frameworks, the State is the main actor in REDD+ projects. Technocratic requirements to establish national forest management plans, reliable baseline data, MRV mechanisms, and others, and the increase of funding might increase forest rents, incentives for corruption, and recentralize control (Bayrak and Marafa, 2016; Lord and Sareen, 2025; Phelps et al., 2010; West, 2015), leading to state-led "green" land grabs (Schroeder and González, 2019). Many concerns emerge on how countries with weak safeguards might remove the locus of control and motivation for preservation away from the local scale, generating greater forest loss and undermining the autonomy, rights, and resources of local communities (Phelps et al., 2010; McDermott et al., 2012; Osborne, 2015; Bayrak and Marafa, 2016). Other authors found that decentralization does not always meet its objectives, especially in terms of strengthening local resource management (Ribot et al., 2006). Along with decentralization initiatives, governments often impose restrictions to maximize their own goals, facilitating the subversion of democratic processes by more powerful actors (Lane, 2003). Research on 23 subnational initiatives in six countries (Brazil, Peru, Cameroon, Tanzania, Indonesia, and Vietnam) found that at the sub-national level, horizontal cross-sectoral challenges persist related to conflicts over interests and power (Ravikumar et al., 2015; Sunderlin, 2015). In countries such as Nepal, there is tension between formal decentralization initiatives and informal efforts to maintain control over forest management, with many cases of exclusion, elite capture, corruption, and collusion between community leaders and external actors (Bushley, 2014).

In general, the results of REDD+ funding delivery are not predictable; they could result in recentralization or fragmentation with similar inefficient, ineffective, and inequitable forest protection (Lord and Sareen, 2025). The exclusion of local and indigenous knowledge and agency exemplifies these processes. REDD+ technocratic discourses and practices are seen as a strategy for the education and subjectification of local communities as carriers of global carbon responsibility (Müller, 2020). As a result, the literature points to several cases of limited understanding of local dynamics, leading to not aligning project goals with local needs and values (Schroeder and González, 2019). Rather, some REDD+ prescriptions are against them, producing local conflicts (Aryal et al., 2024). For instance, conceiving forests as "carbon sinks" only highlights their economic value when, for indigenous communities, the forests represent their homes, livelihoods, water, shelter, culture, beliefs, and religion (Giacomini, 2022; Bayrak and Marafa, 2016; Aryal et al., 2024). This explains why REDD+ has faced opposition among Indigenous, peasant, and civil society groups globally (see Cifuentes, 2021). Indigenous organizations have framed REDD+ projects as new forms of colonialism or "CO2lonialism," undermining their right to access to land and resource control on behalf of the green economy under a top-down approach to conservation (Giacomini, 2022; Lozano et al., 2024). When these concerns address private initiatives, project developers are labeled as "carbon cowboys" for designing profit-oriented REDD+ activities without respecting social safeguards (West, 2015). A study of the Asia Indigenous Peoples Pact (AIPP) mentions that "carbon cowboys" are entering indigenous forests to profit from carbon market speculation. A study by Espinoza and Feather found an explosion of carbon piracy in pilot REDD+ initiatives in Peru. Taking advantage of weak social safeguards, "carbon pirates" convinced the communities to sign away their land and carbon rights in favor of commercial interests. REDD+ unintentionally provided them an increasing control over forests and the intellectual property of these communities (Bayrak and Marafa, 2016).

The high amount of evidence suggests that the problem of REDD+ is not simply implementation. There is a need to reevaluate the market and polycentric fundamentals and assumptions of this mechanism and how it is justified and consolidated by the principle of "common concern of humankind."

2.2.4 Beyond "Common Concern" over the Forests?

By reinforcing international cooperation and sovereign power, market initiatives and cooperation projects such as REDD+ institutionalize the common concern principle. In this way, those mechanisms reinforce the fragmented and market-oriented international governance of rainforests. In this context, it seems crucial to assess the benefits and risks of this principle and its polycentric mode of governance.

Only a few scholars have advanced these tasks. Engaging with Third World Approaches to International Law (TWAIL) premises, Dehm (2021) formulates a critical assessment of the common concern principle. She explains how, since the 2000s, tensions over ownership and control over tropical forests were sidestepped by avoiding the conflictual question of the dominium over these areas and instead focusing on the functions that forests serve. In this view, although the national sovereignty over forests was formally declared, the understanding of forests' carbon sequestration functions as a matter of global common concern led to actualizing global authority over forested areas. This means that Global South countries can be differently compelled to act according to a "common concern," including through mechanisms of conditionality and finance. Those responsible for the greatest proportion of current and historical GHG emissions, in contrast, are least subject to an international jurisdiction pursuant to a "common concern." For Dehm, this global authority consolidates pre-existing relations of power by locating the problem of deforestation within nation-states, obscuring global drivers of deforestation, such as the global financing that enables the production of timber, agricultural goods, and palm oil that contribute to deforestation; the global supply chains through which these commodities circulate; and the global consumption of these products.

Chandra (2020) also criticizes "common concern" from a TWAIL perspective. She notes how under this principle, the international community seeks to protect the forest from the "tragedy of overuse." International law then provides the meta-frames of governance, national states provide the regulatory framework, and local communities must work with and alongside these global and government actors. This means that the sovereign eminent domain of the state and the internationalization of nature protection are not contradictory, but complementary. The common concern principle serves to frame the rules that enclose the forest. It legitimizes both, state sovereignty granting land rights for local communities and international actions on these areas by global entities that use environmental discourses (international organizations, corporations, NGOs). For Chandra, once the commons have been endowed with a value that transcends their utility to the local communities, the collective rights of these communities no longer allude to their interests but to the larger collective of humankind. This obscures the social history of the place and the social relations that produced the commons. These communities become subjected to a larger network of rules and decision-making.

These reflections emphasize the North-South divide in the different ways of exerting state authority over the forest (Dehm) and how international and state forces instrumentalize local communities' authority over the forest (Chandra). Dehm's position resonates with the general TWAIL's critique of global environmental law as being dominated by the priorities and concerns of rich countries, whereas the concerns of poor countries are frequently marginalized (Atapattu and Gonzalez, 2015). In this framework, even the tensions recognized within the South remain state-centric as those mainly refer to the different environmental priorities of leading Southern states, such as China and India, in contrast to more ecologically vulnerable small island states. Chandra's critique is attentive to internal forms of hierarchies and oppression within Third World nation-states (an early questioning on TWAIL) but with little attention on the political agency of indigenous communities and how indigenous thinking and politics might renew discussions on governing the forests. These two aspects, the political agency of Indigenous peoples and indigenous ecological knowledge, are crucial to reshaping the principles for governing international commons.

2.3 The Amazon as an International Commons: Official and Indigenous Perspectives

Amazon's geospatial boundaries have been historically defined by three criteria. One is hydrographical and is based on the extent of the basin and the rivers' systems. Another is ecological and relies on definitions of rainforest ecoregions. Another criterion is political-administrative and responds to how each Amazonian country legally defines its Amazonian region (Tigre, 2017). In the last years, and with the rise of satellite technologies, Amazonian boundaries are being increasingly understood by the extent of rainforest cover by country, recorded by satellite data (Butler, 2020). In this sense, the Amazon's distribution is the following: Brazil (59%), Peru (12%), Colombia (8%), Bolivia (7%), Venezuela (6%), Guyana (3%), Suriname (2%), Ecuador (2%), and French Guyana (1%). The Amazon is also divided into four sections (Northeast, Southeast, Central, and Western Amazonia), and between the upper and lower areas (Brazil has most of the lower Amazon, but conservation and endemic biodiversity mainly concern the upper Amazon, located in Ecuador and Peru).

Given the current sovereignty boundaries in the basin, rather than being a global commons, the Amazon might be conceptualized as an international commons. This means that the Amazon is shared among basin countries under sovereignty rules established in post-colonial nation-building processes. These complex processes began in the eighteenth century after former Spanish and Portuguese colonies gained independence in the region. These processes implied military tensions, wars, and peace treaties among basin states during the nineteenth and twentieth centuries. The Rio Protocol, signed by the states of Peru and Ecuador in January 1998, was the last international instrument to settle a boundary dispute in the Amazon (Figure 2.1).

The conceptualization of the Amazon as an international commons might also be found in the pre-colonial context because hundreds of Indigenous nations had their own territorial claims over the rainforest. Archaeologists and historians explain that by the sixteenth century, around 10 million people were living in either small semi-permanent settlements or large permanent villages in the region. The consolidation of cultural niches in the basin supported the development of vast societies that did not over-exploit the resources (Neves et al., 2021). Indigenous peoples with larger populations, such as the Omagua and Machiparos from the upper Amazon had friendly political relationships and agreed to fight against other Indigenous peoples from the lower Amazon (Morales, 2000). In

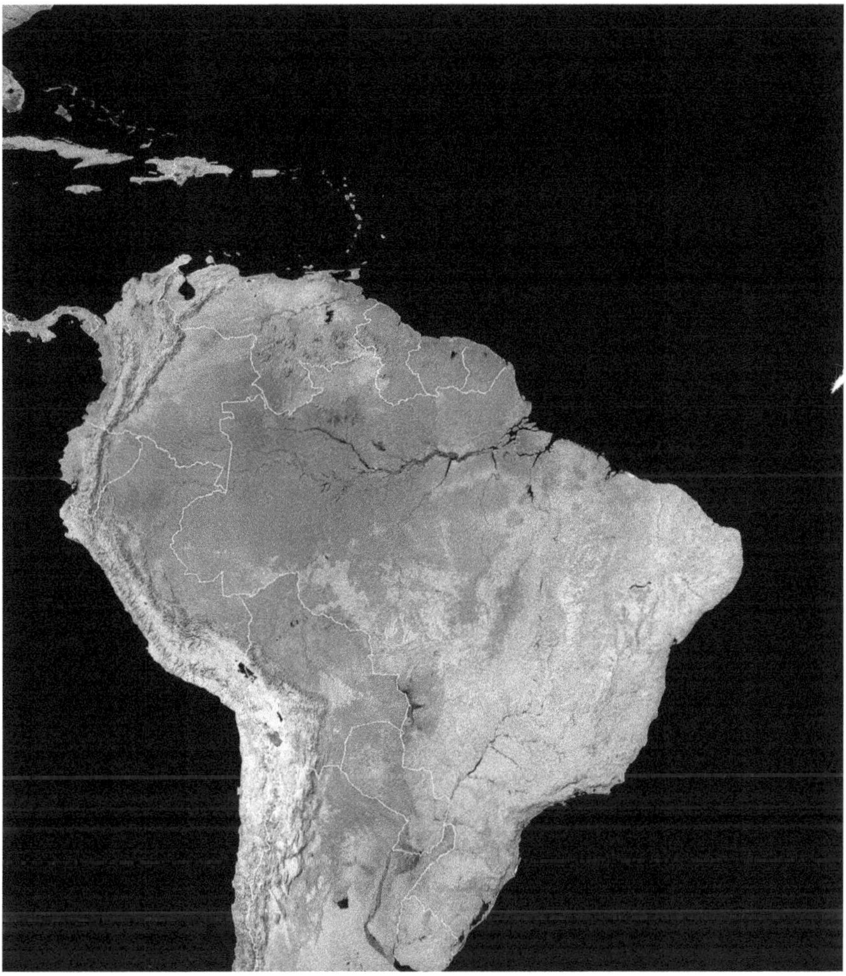

Figure 2.1 Amazon Rainforest map by NASA Earth Observatory Group, 2025

general, Amazonian Indigenous peoples shared and enclosed Amazonian areas under their own arrangements, which were then reconfigured by colonial powers and post-colonial nation-states.

During colonization, indigenous communities were exterminated by foreign diseases, enslavement, and plunder for the "gold rush." In the early republic era, the "rubber rush" implied the slavery and displacement of Indigenous peoples, especially in Brazil and Peru. Under the developmental agenda of the last century and the responses of basin states against "the internationalization of the Amazon," governments strongly reaffirmed state sovereignty and promoted large-scale neo-colonization of the region (de Sartre and Taravella, 2009; Bastos Lima et al., 2019; Mgbeoji, 2003). The Amazon was again conceived as the last frontier to develop mega-infrastructures, oil, mining, and agribusiness, while illegal economies (logging, drugs) started to develop in the shadows of the state. Today, nearly 2.2 million indigenous individuals live in the Amazon (SPA, 2021), and they are still subjected to displacement and land degradation (Picq, 2017; Fontaine, 2006).

Indigenous peoples have consistently formulated their views on how to govern the Amazon rainforest. Nemonte Nenquino, Waorani indigenous leader in the Ecuadorian Amazon, explains indigenous perspectives in these terms: "As Indigenous peoples, we are fighting to protect what we love – our way of life, our rivers, the animals, our forests, life on earth" (Goldman Environmental Prize, 2021). In this view, the Amazon is not only a rainforest whose natural functions serve human interests. The protection of the Amazon is ethically grounded on the need to protect life on Earth. For this endeavor, Indigenous peoples have a critical role. Olivia Bisa, President of the Autonomous Chapra Government in the Peruvian Amazon, claims: "Thanks to indigenous peoples, the Amazon has historically been protected. The Peruvian State itself talks about the importance of the Amazon, as it covers 80% of the country's biodiversity. This is not by magic, it is because there are Indigenous peoples who are living there, who conserve it, who take care of it" (Interview, 15.05.2024).

Indigenous cosmovisions and their practical governance over the forest, however, have been obscured by nation-states. As stated by Bisa: "We, as Indigenous peoples, preexist the Peruvian State. The state was formed with its laws, policies, and government systems, but we were never participants in decision-making in those moments and spaces, even though this altered our territory, our lifestyles, our cosmology" (Interview, 15.05.2024). For this reason, Indigenous peoples are reenacting their sovereignty over the forest. As stated by the Shipibo-Conibo leader Julio Cusurichi, "The goal is for Indigenous people to be the protagonists. We have to administer the Amazon regions that are our ancestral territories and not just leave it to the government" (Goldman Environmental Prize, 2021).

These claims resonate in international spheres, where the Coordinating Body of Indigenous Organisations of the Amazon Basin (COICA), representing more than 500 Indigenous Peoples across the Amazon, has achieved some prominence. At the World Economic Forum in 2024, Fany Kuiru, the first woman appointed General Coordinator of COICA, emphasized the need to ensure that Indigenous peoples are given a place at the table. During a session in Davos, she stressed the need for the world to ensure "full and effective participation in decision-making regarding policies affecting the Amazon" (World Economic Forum, 2024).

Indigenous cosmovisions on human-nature relationships and their quest for having a voice in the international governance of the Amazon oblige us to reexamine how ACTO has engaged with the governing principles for managing the basin. This analysis will assist in exploring how those principles might be reconceptualized, attending to indigenous claims and concerns.

2.4 The International Policy Architecture of the Amazon: ACTO

The creation of ACTO in 1998 implied the enactment of a complex and bureaucratic international organization with different governing bodies, units, and processes. ACTO's governing bodies are the Permanent Secretariat, the Meeting of Foreign Affairs Ministers of Member States (The Meeting), the Council of Amazonian Cooperation (The Council), and the Commission of Coordination of the Amazonian Cooperation Council (CCOOR). The General Secretary represents the organization and is elected by unanimity in the Meeting for 3 years (might be reelected once). The Meeting is ACTO's supreme unit, celebrates ordinary summits every two years, and establishes the general directives for the organization. The Council is a deliberative body integrated by diplomatic representatives of each member state. It holds annual meetings and supervises the fulfillment of both treaty goals and decisions taken by the Meeting. The CCOOR is responsible for monitoring the activities of the Permanent Secretariat. High-level authorities from member countries integrate CCOOR and celebrate trimestral meetings.

The Meeting, the Council, and CCOOR are political-strategical bodies and periodic forums of decision-making. They are in charge of designations, enactment of declarations, approval of conventions and partnerships, among others. These bodies are also very hierarchical since decisions in one unit often escalate for approval to the upper unit. National implementation of treaty stipulations and governing bodies' decisions are the responsibility of Permanent National Commissions. These Commissions are organized by the Foreign Ministries of each member country and incorporate representatives of different governmental offices.

At the operative level, ACTO's Permanent Secretariat has two Directors (Executive Director and Administrative Director) and 7 coordinators of thematic areas: environment, indigenous affairs, health, tourism, infrastructure, science and technology, and transport and infrastructure. They are delegates from each Treaty member and work inside the organization as permanent officials for the period of each new administration. These are technical-administrative offices in charge of executing ACTO's everyday activities.

In general, ACTO is considered a weak international organization limited to diplomatic coordination as a cooperation forum. As such, it promotes focalized development projects and the knowledge exchange about regional issues. Despite being conceived as a multilateral platform, it has no meaningful influence on state agendas and common policies because of its lack of supranational power, dispute resolution bodies, and enforcement mechanisms (Pereira and Viola, 2020; Pio, 2020; Zárate and Motta, 2020). The next sections discuss how enclosure, the common heritage of humankind, and the common concern of humankind have been incorporated into ACTO discourses and processes and how these principles influence the democratic governance of the organization (Figure 2.2).

Figure 2.2 Meeting Room of the council at ACTO, Brasilia, 2022. Photo by the author

2.4.1 Enclosure

Under the doctrine of national security, Bolivia, Brazil, Colombia, Ecuador, Guyana, Suriname, Peru, and Venezuela signed the Amazonian Cooperation Treaty in July 1978. The main objective of the Treaty was to "defend the sovereignty of Amazonian countries" (Interview with ACTO Director 14.03.2022) and "avoid that other international forces might interfere in the Amazon" (Interview with former ACTO Director, Brasilia 07.03.2022). At the First Chancellors Meeting under the Treaty (Belém, Brazil, October 23 and 24, 1980), the Ministries proclaimed: "The use and exploitation of all the natural resources of the Amazon is the sovereign and exclusive right of each of the States located therein … Initiatives that tend to raise doubts about the sovereignty of States … regarding the use and preservation of their forest resources are unacceptable."

The parties decided to create a Permanent Secretariat under the Treaty in 1995 and the Amazonian Cooperation Treaty Organization (ACTO) in 1998, with headquarters in Brasilia. Considering the Treaty framework, ACTO was born as an international and intergovernmental organization of cooperation heavily dependent on national legislation rather than being a supranational organization for integration. Between 1978 and 2023, only 3 meetings of presidents and 13 meetings of ministers of foreign affairs were held under the Treaty.

Former General Secretary (2004–2007) Rosalía Arteaga led a phase of institutional development (Pio, 2020; Tigre, 2017). Under her mandate, the VIII Meeting of Ministers of Foreign Affairs (Manaus, Brazil, September 14, 2004) approved ACTO Strategic Plan 2004–2012. The main goal of the Plan was the institutional consolidation of ACTO and stated: "the determination of ACTO Member States to reaffirm the full exercise of their sovereignty over the resources of the Amazon, to promote the economic and social development of the region and the protection of its cultural and environmental heritage, for the benefit of their respective populations."

With the appointment of Manuel Picasso as General Secretary in 2009, the organization inaugurated a new phase of strengthening with the enactment of the Manaos Declaration in November 2009 (Pio, 2020; Tigre, 2017). The Manaos Meeting was attended by the President of France, Nicolas Sarkozy, representing for the first (and last) time the non-member French Guyana (Tigre, 2017). The declaration set forth the content of a new agenda that redefined ACTO as an international organization for sustainable development, encompassing both environmental and socio-economic goals (Tigre, 2017).

With the Lima Declaration approved at the X Meeting of Ministers of Foreign Affairs in 2010, the parties approved the Strategic Agenda of Amazonian Cooperation (AECA, 2010–2018). The updated AECA (2020–2030) strategic objectives are: "Facilitate exchange and cooperation between Member Countries promoting sustainable development ... in the region to improve the quality of life of its inhabitants .... Ensure that the interests and sovereignty of the Member Countries are respected and promoted." At the Lima Declaration, the parties also ratified "The sovereign right of each country over its natural resources."

The emphasis on state sovereignty is repeated in most documents produced by the different units of the organization and might explain deep disagreements among country members. Former ACTO General Secretary, Francisco Ruíz, said that at the beginning of the 2000s, the main tensions referred to the position of Venezuela on some international financing. Venezuela opposed the financing of US-based organizations for allegedly risking the state's sovereignty (Interview, 18.03.22). A former Coordinator of Environment said that for many years, ACTO discussions implied two dominant groups: Venezuela, Bolivia, and Ecuador, leading one block, and Brazil, Peru, and Colombia, leading the other. There was no way of reaching a consensus because there were eight countries, and the table was often divided four against four. The political discrepancies impacted ACTO's administration. Given that, in practice, Venezuela was excluded from ACTO governance since its ambassador was not recognized by Brazil, the organization was unable to designate a new General Secretary in 2021 (the mandate of María Moreira was de facto extended). For some diplomats, the Venezuelan issue implied three years of paralysis. This situation has also implied the lack of designation of coordinators for thematic areas, and by 2022, the organization only had three designated officials: The General Secretary and the two directors; the rest of the personnel worked temporarily as consultants for specific cooperation projects.

Discourses of sovereignty have not been so critical in other international organizations and forums with more influence on regional governance (Pereira and Viola, 2020). For instance, the international organization Andean Community of Nations (CAN), made up of four Amazonian countries (Peru, Bolivia, Ecuador, and Colombia) has two legislative units that enact binding decisions on issues of international commerce and intellectual property: The Andean Council and the Commission of the Andean Community, with delegates from each country member. The CAN also has the Andean Tribunal of Justice, one of the most active international courts, that facilitates dispute resolution and compliance with Andean obligations (Helfer et al., 2009). Another example is the Initiative for the Integration of the Regional Infrastructure of South America (IIRSA). IIRSA included ACTO members and developed an ambitious portfolio of infrastructure projects (Rubiños and Betancout-Santiago, 2021). To implement the IIRSA, Amazonian countries ceded in practice their sovereignty to multilateral banks and transnational corporations to develop more than 150 mega infrastructure projects across the region (Agostinis and Palestini, 2021). ACTO actively supported this endeavor. In the Iquitos Declaration approved at the IX Meeting of Ministers of Foreign Affairs (Iquitos, Peru, November 25, 2005), the parties "Agree to intensify national and regional efforts to advance studies on the development of navigation routes, waterways and other means of transportation in the Amazon system, contributing to the advances made within the framework of ... IIRSA ...." For ACTO Strategic Plan 2004–2012, IIRSA is of "the greatest relevance for the Amazon in the development of physical integration, communications and energy, which will bring closer intra-Amazonian markets ... with international markets."

CAN and IIRSA (through infrastructure) promote commercial integration, both impacting the Amazon, but with no emphasis on environmental and social goals. ACTO has focused on low-scale social and environmental projects, but it has not been a space for formulating or promoting international environmental policies. For Roberto Espinoza, former COICA assessor (Interview, 26.04.2022), the extractive political economy of Amazonian countries explains this situation and the difficulties for a dialogue between ACTO and Indigenous peoples represented by COICA. COICA is an autonomous organization, whereas ACTO depends on the conditions imposed by the states. These states often prioritize extractive policies that disregard the rights and agency of Indigenous peoples.

As ACTO does not properly govern the Amazon rainforest, Amazonian states engage with other international initiatives that overlap with ACTO's competencies. For example, the Leticia Pact, signed in 2019 by Amazonian countries (except Venezuela), formulated general commitments to share information, curb deforestation and wildfires, restore degraded areas, monitor climate change and biodiversity loss, and empower women and Indigenous people (SPA, 2021). The Pact worked outside ACTO arrangements. Although CCOOR members said that the Leticia Pact was not a competitor but a complement to ACTO, it overlapped with ACTO's goals and actions, and ACTO was not the orchestrator of the Pact; specific governments outside of ACTO coordination promoted it. The Pact, however, repeated ACTO's fundamental limitations. It did not establish concrete binding compromises or enforcement mechanisms.

The recent Declaration of Belém of 2023 seems to address the problem of regional fragmentation. In its preamble, it states that Amazonian governments recognize ACTO as "the sole intergovernmental coordination body for the eight Amazon countries concerning jointly implementing projects, and actions that produce equitable and beneficial results to Amazon countries." Could the new impulse of ACTO proclaimed by this Declaration foster environmental policy integration? Former ACTO officials consider it important to undertake reforms to empower ACTO and increase its regional authority, but they are skeptical about the possibility that all members agree on changing ACTO's foundational limitation focused on cooperation instead of policy integration, given the emphasis of state representatives on national sovereignty. During the Belem negotiations, Colombia proposed to create an International Tribunal for Environmental Justice in the Amazon, but the Declaration ended up reinforcing the cooperative character of ACTO and did not establish any measures to enact binding decisions and enforcement mechanisms. Moreover, the Declaration creates the Presidential Meeting as another unit, which would make the organization more bureaucratic in making decisions.

2.4.2 Common Heritage and Common Concern in the Amazon

No ACTO instrument nor official declaration has mentioned the "common heritage" principle. Some sources include notions such as the "heritage" of the Amazonian forest and "future generations," but only refer to the resources belonging to current or future Amazonian generations, not world generations. The principle of "common concern" rather seems relevant in official documents and discourses. For instance, former ACTO General Secretary Rosalia Arteaga (Interview, 18.03.2022) said "I oppose … the internationalization [of the Amazon] because the sovereignty of our countries would be at risk," but at the same time she highlights how in her mandate ACTO had a great openness to international cooperation: "We knock the door of many countries and had positive responses … We also signed agreements with multilateral institutions, such as CAF, World Bank, the InterAmerican Development Bank, and others."

Early ACTO instruments already highlighted the importance of international cooperation. The Declaration of the II Meeting of Chancellors under the Treaty (Cali, Colombia, December 7–8, 1983) proclaimed that states would examine "the possibility of having financial, technical and personnel support from international organizations and institutions …." The Manaus Declaration of the first President

Meeting in May 1988, stated "... we welcome the cooperation of countries from other regions of the world and international organizations that can contribute to the implementation of national and regional projects and programs that we freely decide to adopt ... in accordance with the priorities of our governments ...." The Declaration of the Second Meeting of Presidents (Manaus, February 11–12, 1992), stated that national efforts "will not be sufficient without international cooperation to support the efforts made by our States ...." In this Declaration the parties also recognized "The greater responsibility of developed countries in the progressive deterioration of the environment ... reason why ecological controls and conditionalities cannot be imposed on developing countries ...." They demanded a new approach of international cooperation based on "the expansion of financial resources and trade flows" and "access to technologies," and acknowledge that cooperation is critical "for the conservation and rational use of the natural heritage."

At the V Meeting of Foreign Ministers (Lima, November 4–5, 1995), state representatives emphasized "... the importance of non-reimbursable technical and financial cooperation provided at the national and regional level by various friendly countries and international organizations ...." The members made "an urgent call" to "significantly expand" cooperation to the "efforts made by the Parties in favor of sustainable development of their respective Amazonian territories." ACTO has continued developing cooperation projects with the support of multilateral agencies, developed countries, and global NGOs.

For instance, the project *Monitoring of Forest Cover in the Amazon Region* (2011–2018) was a regional cooperation project on deforestation monitoring aimed at arming member countries with the necessary data to curb deforestation (Tigre, 2017; Pereira and Viola, 2020). This project had the support, among others, of the International Tropical Timber Organization (ITTO), the Directorate-General for International Cooperation of the Netherlands (DGIC), and the German Development Cooperation (GIZ). The project *Integrated and Sustainable Management of Transboundary Water Resources of the Amazon River Basin* (2012–2016) documented the needs and interests of Amazonian populations to propose strategic mechanisms to protect water resources. The project was supported by the Global Environmental Facility (GEF), a multilateral environmental fund located in Washington that includes 186 member countries and international agencies. The project *BIOMAZ* is a technical cooperation project currently in execution, funded by the German Federal Ministry for Economic Cooperation and Development (BMZ). This initiative supports ACTO and its Member Countries in developing a regional strategic framework for the sustainable use and conservation of the Amazon forest's biological diversity. For this aim, the project promotes the provision of information on the status and trends of biodiversity and ecosystem services, as well as dialogue and exchange of experiences among experts and officials from Member Countries.

One of the most diffused projects of ACTO is the Regional Project for the Management, Monitoring, and Control of Species of Wild Fauna and Flora

Threatened by Trade (Biomazonia Project). This project aims to contribute to the conservation of Amazonian biodiversity and is financed by the German Development Bank – KfW (ACTO, 2021). The specific goals of the project are to increase the efficiency and effectiveness of management and monitoring of wild fauna and flora species threatened by trade in the ACTO Member Countries. The first phase of the project (2016–2022) concluded with the launch of the Regional Amazonian Observatory, a mechanism to collect and exchange detailed information about biodiversity among Amazonian countries.

Only two cooperation initiatives have specifically addressed Indigenous peoples. The Strategic Framework to Develop a Regional Agenda for the Protection of Indigenous Peoples in Voluntary Isolation and Initial Contact (PIACI) was a program executed between 2011 and 2016 to propose policies and actions aimed at protecting the PIACI of the Amazon. The project's activities were executed in two phases: "Strategic Framework" and "Indigenous Peoples in Border Regions." The program was implemented with the support of the Inter-American Development Bank (IADB). The other initiative is the project Contingency Plans for Health Protection of Highly Vulnerable Indigenous Peoples and in Initial Contact, currently in execution with the support of the Pan American Health Organization (PAHO). This project seeks to consolidate cooperation actions in bordering territories of the Amazon to mitigate the COVID-19 impacts and the threats of endemic tropical diseases. The project expects to contribute to policy formulation, promotion, and institutionalization for the provision of health services that "effectively meet the demands of these populations." The activities of the project "will be aligned … to national policies, processes, and technical developments, as well as to the institutional framework and operation of the countries' health services and indigenous issues." This project also announces dialogue spaces with Indigenous peoples, but these "will be framed under those defined by each of the national governments participating in the project" (ACTO, 2024).

This project-oriented governance has been reinforced in the new Strategic Agenda of Amazonian Cooperation 2020–2030 and the Declaration of Belém of 2023. The Declaration engages with the principle of common concern by urging "developed countries to meet their obligations to provide and mobilize predictable and adequate support to developing countries, including development financing, climate financing and biodiversity conservation." It also highlights that international cooperation is fundamental to implementing national policies and programs for the sustainable development of the Amazon. By 2023, ACTO reported 16 cooperation projects in implementation, almost all of them with the support of North-South international cooperation from the GEF, the IADB, the UN, the European Union (Euroclima), Spanish Cooperation (AECID), and the German Cooperation (GIZ). ACTO also announced new projects and partnerships for 2024 with USAID, the World Bank, the Green Climate Fund (GCF), the Italian Cooperation, among others (ACTO, 2023).

The proliferation of regional cooperation under ACTO and the own cooperation agenda of each country member under the UNFCCC Nationally Determined Contributions has produced overlapping goals and policy fragmentation. A former ACTO Director said (Interview, 23.03.22) that the priorities of international actors and organizations, such as the World Bank not always fit within what the ACTO prioritizes because of a lack of coordination: "They finance some projects and we are working on other projects with overlapping areas." ACTO's financial limitations reinforce this situation. The budget of the organization depends on differentiated contributions from each government,[4] but former officials confirmed that not all pay on time or complete. For a former ACTO Coordinator of Environment, the key problem is that ACTO is not a priority for the member parties (Interview, 03.03.2022). ACTO officials have no option but to work with funding from international cooperation. For a CCOOR diplomatic representative (Interview, 29.04.2022), the lack of countries' technical capacities would also reinforce the reliance on international cooperation. In his view, the organization must reinforce technical cooperation at local and national levels, just as ACTO meant to work from the beginning.

This cooperation approach shows the limitations of the democratic governance of the organization. A crucial feature of ACTO governance is that the participation of Indigenous peoples is restricted to cooperation projects and programs focused on specific Amazonian areas. In general, the cooperation projects consider Indigenous peoples as "stakeholders" who are invited to workshops or as "key informants" who provide information to formulate and implement the projects. In the only two projects in which Indigenous peoples are directly involved, they are considered as beneficiaries of health services and not as political agents in policy-making processes. An ACTO official (Interview, 12.04.2022) confirmed that ACTO only interacts with Indigenous peoples in the implementation of cooperation projects, and another said (Interview, 03.03.2022) that there is no intention of involving them in higher decision-making.

This approach has been institutionalized in ACTO policies and instruments. Indigenous issues are merely addressed in strategic plans as a matter of "exchange of experiences of country-members" (AECA, 2010–2018). In all minutes from the meetings of the different ACTO units, Indigenous peoples are subjects of protection, not political actors. This results in a paternalistic approach that only proclaims "the protection of indigenous cultures and natural resources" (Resolution of the XII Meeting of Foreign Ministers) as if Indigenous peoples were ancient relics and no collectives with political agency.

[4] The VI Meeting of Foreign Affair Ministers in 2000 approved the scale of contributions of each member party in percentages from the total budget (at that time, US$1.139.600): Bolivia, 6.5 percent; Brazil, 35 percent; Colombia, 16 percent; Ecuador, 6.5 percent; Guyana, 2 percent; Perú, 16 percent; Suriname, 2 percent; Venezuela, 16 percent.

In 2022, ACTO announced a more participative approach with the creation of the Amazonian Regional Platform of Indigenous Peoples and Climate Change, as a space to make known Indigenous peoples' practices of forest conservation. In 2023, the Declaration of Belém created the Amazonian Mechanism of Indigenous Peoples with the aim "to strengthen and promote dialogue between governments and indigenous peoples in the Amazon region for management and coordination concerning topics relating to Indigenous Peoples and that contribute to achieving ACTO's objectives" (Article 6). However, these initiatives still must be implemented, and they locate indigenous participation at the lowest levels of ACTO structures. This means that the "platform" and "mechanism" are conceived as programs or initiatives annexed to some of the ACTO units. Their key goal would be to show ACTO's commitment to indigenous participation rather than incorporate Indigenous peoples in the decision-making processes of the organization.

2.5 Reinventing International Principles to Govern the Amazon

The sovereignty vs internationalization debate about Amazonian resources is a false dilemma. The principles of "enclosure" and "common concern" have been explicitly and implicitly incorporated into ACTO instruments and practices. Whereas basin states strongly proclaim their sovereignty over their specific Amazonian territories against international forces, they give up their sovereignty to foster transnational investments, mega-infrastructures, and commercial integration. They also invite international cooperation to contribute to the fight against climate change. International forces are welcomed and empowered insofar as they align with states' extractivist interests and the apparent fulfillment of their international environmental commitments.

This framework has proved to be limited for the sustainable governance of the Amazon. By reinforcing the principle of enclosure, basin states reject environmental integration as establishing binding environmental standards and enforcement mechanisms might risk extractive interests. The "common concern" legitimizes the current state of affairs of the proliferation of cooperation projects that help portray Amazonian states as committed to international environmental goals. This results in a fragmented governance with little possibility of providing regional solutions and with no participation of Indigenous peoples. The first step to challenge this framework is to examine the state-centric, anthropocentric, and ethnocentric assumptions of these principles, as they disregard other ways of conceiving and governing international commons.

State-centrism refers to the reinforcement of a Westphalian conception of sovereignty and the pursuit of developmental goals under this conception. Thus, ACTO members have defended their sovereignty over the Amazon against external forces while marginalizing the claims of Indigenous nations to be international actors with self-determination. The recent creation of the Amazonian Mechanism of Indigenous Peoples within ACTO might be promising, but it does not tackle the colonial nature of international relations based on Westphalian sovereignty. If Indigenous peoples are not recognized as peoples or nations, therefore, with international political agency in deliberative processes, their participation in regional spaces will be very limited (see Chapter 5). In this context, a crucial governance problem in the Amazon is not that the international authority of basin states over the forest is diminished by international powers (Dehm, 2021). The key issue is that the authority of Indigenous peoples over their Amazonian territory is obscured or denied.

The principles for governing the commons are also anthropocentric because "humankind" is the only beneficiary of the commons' management. This avoids more holistic conceptions of "life on the planet" (Horn, 2015) to the benefit of the non-human natural environment, such as the forest and rivers, as subjects of rights. Indeed, Amazonian Indigenous peoples conceive human and natural beings as persons entangled in social dynamics of respect and survival (Kohn, 2013; Viveiros de Castro, 2004; Descola, 2004). Moreover, the abstract notion of "humankind" obscures the historical hierarchies attached to the formulation of the idea of humanity, in which Indigenous peoples were conceived as less human and in urgent need of assimilation. In this context, indigenous territorial claims and cosmologies are instrumentalized as expressions of "common concerns" (Chandra, 2020), disregarding their own concerns on the way how to govern the rainforest beyond anthropocentric assumptions.

Finally, these principles are embedded in ethnocentrism because all the discussions about sovereignty, internationalization of resources, and so forth are framed under Western epistemological and ontological systems. This is the case even when these principles are advanced by Amazonian country leaders as third-world champions, as they heavily rely on state-centric and anthropocentric assumptions. This is also a problem for the common heritage principle and the attempts to incorporate it into the Amazon governance. This principle relies on the protection of Amazonian resources by world nation-states, conceiving the notions of sovereignty and resources under Westphalian frames that seem to imagine the Amazon as an empty space, devoid of people. However, the Amazon has been occupied by Indigenous peoples for over 12,000 years. During this long history, Indigenous societies developed technologies that allowed cultural and agro-biological development (Neves et al., 2021). In the Amazon, "natural heritage is cultural heritage" (Neves et al., 2021: 29).

It is crucial to reformulate the principles for governing international commons in general and their application to regional areas, such as the Amazon. We must enlarge the meaning of sovereignty to include indigenous sovereignty as a governing principle for managing international commons. Indigenous struggles for self-determination question the state-centric basis of enclosure, common concern, and common heritage, as those principles conceive nation-states as the only actors with international political agency. We might also reformulate the notion of humankind in "common concern" and "common heritage" principles and challenge their anthropocentric nature based on the centrality of human interests. The aim is to include the interests of different human collectives, not only represented by nation-states, and the interests of the natural environment in international decision-making. Indigenous knowledge and ontologies of human–nature relationships support this innovation, as they suggest that protecting the forest is not only a question of humankind but also a question of protecting life on the planet.

By reformulating these principles and allowing the broadening of inter-national interests for governing the Amazon, Indigenous nations would be enabled to participate in regional decision-making, and they could push for enacting regional binding standards to achieve ecological and social goals. This is the case because they live and suffer from environmental degradation of the Amazon, regardless of the national state borders where they live.

The examination of sovereignty arrangements, imaginaries, and discourses in the Amazon suggests that the ultimate aim shouldn't be decolonization in the sense of portraying third-world states as developmental champions against powerful Western states; it is about decoloniality in the sense that the third world needs to fight the ethnocentric, anthropocentric, and state-centric legacies and realities of colonialism in international and national stages. Ultimately, this means disputing current sovereignty and environmental imaginaries that exclude indigenous self-determination in the international arena and their struggles to protect Amazonian ecosystems.

2.6 Conclusion

This chapter has problematized the principles for governing global and international commons and has examined how these principles have been incorporated into the discourses, instruments, and practices of the governance of the Amazon.

The principles of "enclosure," "common heritage," and "common concern" have been formulated or advanced by third-world countries in the international struggles for governing global and international commons in a way that resources deemed essential for humankind are fairly distributed and protected. Regarding international forests, these countries have both reaffirmed strongly their sovereignty and rejected conceiving these areas as a common heritage. In this discussion, the principle of common concern emerged as the most suitable principle to reconcile international concerns and national sovereignty.

However, these efforts have been framed under sovereignty, developmental, and ecological imaginaries grounded on Western state-centrism, ethnocentrism, and anthropocentrism. This excludes indigenous conceptualizations of sovereignty and human-nature relationships. The abstract notion of humankind and the pursuit of benefits for human collectives represented by all nation-states reject indigenous claims for self-determination and more holistic perspectives of life on the planet. Ultimately, this framework legitimizes coloniality in the international arena and within nation-states' power structures in the South and the North.

This chapter has evaluated the international governance of Amazon through ACTO and has found unexpected interactions among the principles for governing international commons. Whereas the sovereignty vs internationalization debate has suggested the proclamation of enclosure and the rejection of international forces in the governance of the basin, ACTO's instruments and practices suggest the contrary. Member states strongly proclaim their sovereignty over their specific territories against international forces, but they give up their sovereignty to foster extractivism in the form of transnational investments, mega-infrastructures, and commercial integration. They also request international cooperation to contribute to reaching their international environmental commitments.

The result is a fragmented and precarious governance. By reinforcing enclosure, basin states reject environmental integration as establishing binding environmental standards and enforcement mechanisms might risk extractive interests. The "common concern" legitimizes the current state of affairs of the proliferation of small-scale cooperation projects that help portray Amazonian states as committed to international environmental goals. The recent Declaration of Belém promises the strengthening of the international governance of the Amazon and the inclusion of Indigenous peoples. However, it reinforces the cooperative nature of the organization, incorporates Indigenous peoples as participants in a specific mechanism (not as an international actor with self-determination), and has not created new institutions to advance toward regional policies and international enforcement.

This chapter suggests that this framework should be reformulated, and for this aim, it is important to reformulate the principles for governing international commons. Beyond state-centrism, it is important to enlarge the meaning of sovereignty to include indigenous sovereignty as a governing principle for managing international commons. We might also reformulate the notion of humankind in "common concern" and "common heritage" principles to include indigenous holistic cosmovisions that conceive the natural and human worlds as deeply entangled. In practice, this reformulation should lead to including Indigenous nations as meaningful participants in the Amazonian governance with the political agency to push for international policies beyond general declarations. Ultimately, this would mean changing the dominant geopolitical imaginary in the region. From conceiving the Amazon as governed under classical state sovereignty and small-scale, project-oriented environmental cooperation, to imagining the basin governed by plural sovereignty and environmental arrangements inspired by indigenous cosmovisions and struggles.

CHAPTER 3

The Amazon as a Place of Global Extractivism

Rethinking Extractivism and Infrastructure in Extractive Frontiers

3.1 Introduction

At the outset of the 2000s, a wave of optimism swept through the Amazonian region regarding the potential to achieve sustainable development. Governments in the Amazon appeared committed to curbing deforestation and safeguarding forest ecosystems under international environmental agreements and cooperation programs. Policies were introduced to mitigate forest loss through the establishment of protected areas, land use planning, environmental monitoring, and remediation strategies. These measures led, at least temporarily, to a decline in deforestation rates below historical averages (Walker et al., 2019).

However, these environmental gains were short-lived, as policy reversals and institutional weakening followed. In Ecuador, for instance, progressive environmental measures – such as the initiative to ban oil extraction in Yasuní National Park – were overturned due to a lack of international financial support and the state's urgent need to stimulate economic growth. Similarly, in Brazil, the administrations of Presidents Dilma Rousseff and Michel Temer reduced the extent of protected areas to accommodate large-scale infrastructure projects, including dams and mining ventures (Walker and Simmons, 2018; Diele-Viegas et al., 2020). Under President Jair Bolsonaro (2019–2022), environmental institutions suffered further setbacks through significant budget cuts (Diele-Viegas et al., 2020). Satellite data reveal that deforestation rates during Bolsonaro's tenure surged by as much as 92 percent (Pereira and Viola, 2020). Comparable trends were observed in Peru, Colombia, and Bolivia during the 2010s (Pereira and Viola, 2020). After a brief period of improvement in 2012, deforestation rates across Amazonian countries began to climb steadily once again (Pereira and Viola, 2020).

At the heart of this enduring environmental degradation lies a prevailing imaginary of the Amazon as a zone primarily for intensive resource extraction. Despite increasing global concern for environmental conservation and the rights of Indigenous peoples whose livelihoods depend on the rainforest and its waterways, economic interests continue to dominate regional policy agendas. Between 2013 and 2015, approximately USD 1.07 billion was invested in regional environmental protection efforts – primarily by bilateral and multilateral institutions. However, these figures pale in comparison to the significantly larger investments in infrastructure and energy projects that drive deforestation and facilitate extractive industries. For example, between 2015 and 2020, thirty-three major European financial institutions collectively invested over USD 20 billion in companies directly implicated in deforestation activities in Brazil (SPA, 2021).

Proposed solutions to this crisis often reflect the prevailing dominance of economic rationalities and market-based mechanisms. Following the global media attention on the 2019 wildfires that devastated vast areas of the Amazon, 251 investors issued a public statement urging companies to adopt zero-deforestation policies (Aljazeera, 2020). However, initiatives such as green certification have proven insufficient in guaranteeing deforestation-free supply chains (Walker et al., 2019). The case of the soy moratorium – a voluntary agreement among Greenpeace, the Brazilian government, and agribusiness actors to avoid purchasing soy cultivated on recently deforested land – illustrates these shortcomings. To circumvent the moratorium, some actors first cleared land for cattle grazing and later converted these pastures into soy plantations, thereby technically complying with the agreement. Today, cattle ranching accounts for approximately 80 percent of deforestation in the Amazon (Yale Global Forest Atlas, in Matthew, 2021; Chan and Araujo, 2020).

Flexible environmental regulations similarly facilitate large-scale infrastructure projects designed to expand the production and export of commodities. One illustrative case is the Ferrogrão railway project, intended to create a new transportation corridor for soybeans between the Brazilian states of Mato Grosso and Pará. A study conducted by the Federal University of Minas Gerais found that the proposed railway would traverse several Indigenous territories in the Xingu River Basin and lead to the deforestation of approximately 230,000 hectares (568,000 acres), thereby threatening the Xingu Indigenous Park. Although the project was temporarily halted due to sustained Indigenous resistance and a 2021 ruling by the Brazilian Supreme Court, it remains a priority for the current government (Oliveira, 2023).

Eduardo Galeano's seminal work The Open Veins of Latin America (1971) posited that Latin American history has been fundamentally shaped by violent processes of resource extraction. Contemporary scholarship on extractivism, in a way, builds upon this legacy when examining the dependence of Global South economies on the intensive extraction of raw materials for global markets. In the Amazon, extractivism is commonly associated with the exploitation of minerals, oil, timber, and agricultural commodities. Infrastructure development is often regarded as an enabling condition for these extractive activities (Nobre, 2016; Lees et al., 2016;

Bebbington et al., 2018; Runde et al., 2020). However, infrastructure should not merely be viewed as a passive facilitator of extractivism, but rather as an integral component of extractive practices themselves.

This chapter explores the complex relationship between extractivism and mega-infrastructure projects in the Amazon. It engages with recent academic debates that emphasize the multi-scalar and intangible dimensions of extractivism. These include discussions on the reconfiguration of value chains and territorial frontiers with local, regional, and global consequences (McNeish and Shapiro, 2021; Chagnon et al., 2022), as well as the notion of extractivism extending to the appropriation of data and subjectivities (Ye et al., 2019; Gago and Mezzadra, 2017). The aim is to critically examine how infrastructure development in the Amazon is embedded within extractive processes, thereby contributing to a more comprehensive understanding of extractivism and its modes of governance.

Historically, mega-infrastructure projects were framed as instruments of national development, social progress, and state-building. Today, however, these projects are increasingly oriented toward enhancing global connectivity to facilitate international trade. This chapter argues that this shift in discursive framing has deepened the integration of infrastructure within extractive paradigms. In the Amazon, mega-infrastructure and extraction have become inseparable, jointly fueling the global economy through the continuous transnational flow of commodities. This integration produces profound social, economic, and ecological consequences with implications that extend beyond national borders, situating the Amazon as a paradigmatic case of global extractivism. In this context, infrastructure may be conceived as a form of extractivism in its own right – where investments are primarily motivated by profit rather than genuine connectivity or development outcomes. Under this logic, the Amazonian territory itself becomes the principal object of extraction. Moreover, infrastructure projects increasingly rely on the extraction of intangible resources – such as community knowledge and socio-economic needs – to justify their feasibility and legitimacy.

Given these dynamics, the Amazon's role as a site of global extractivism necessitates robust international governance mechanisms that prioritize ecological sustainability and social justice. Yet, such governance arrangements have been notably absent in the region. Instead, prevailing international governance frameworks have facilitated the advancement of mega-infrastructure projects with scant regard for environmental or human rights concerns. A case in point is the Initiative for the Integration of Regional Infrastructure in South America (IIRSA), a sweeping portfolio of mega-projects aimed at enhancing trade connectivity, which has been met with strong opposition from environmentalists due to its detrimental impact on biodiversity (Wegner and Pereira, 2018; Fontaine, 2006). To operationalize IIRSA, Amazonian states effectively ceded aspects of their sovereignty to multilateral development banks and transnational corporations, thereby enabling the implementation of over 150 large-scale infrastructure projects across the region (Agostinis and Palestini, 2021).

By examining the interrelationship between extractivism and IIRSA-related infrastructure, this chapter contends that the structural entanglement of extractive logics and infrastructural development explains why Amazonian countries have achieved partial regional integration without establishing binding environmental standards. Such standards are often perceived as obstacles to the advancement of extractive circuits. Consequently, effective governance of extractivism in the Amazon must entail not only the regulation of extractive activities but also the international governance of infrastructure systems that sustain them.

3.2 Exploring the Meaning of Extractivism

Contemporary scholarship increasingly regards extractivism as an "organizational concept" that frames global debates on political economy, political ecology, and sustainability. While the term has gained prominence in recent years, particularly in global discourses on development and the environment, its roots in Amazonian studies are well established. Since the 1980s, Brazilian academic literature has used extractivism to describe a specific form of localized economic activity centered on the harvesting of natural resources. This mode of production was conceived as fundamentally distinct from – and often in opposition to – large-scale agricultural development, which entailed massive deforestation and the establishment of monoculture plantations (Homma, 1992, 1995; Costa, 2019; De Almeida, 2004; Porro, 2005).

Despite its more limited economic scale and comparatively minimal environmental footprint, forest-product extractivism – particularly rubber extraction – played a pivotal role in both local livelihoods and national economies for several decades. Its peak occurred during the early twentieth-century "rubber boom," which has since been thoroughly documented as a period of significant human and ecological cost. In Brazil and Peru, the boom was marked by forced displacement, enslavement, and in some cases, outright genocide of Indigenous populations, as extractive enterprises sought to exploit forest territories and coerce Indigenous labor into rubber collection.

Following the decline of rubber prices in the international market, a new developmental paradigm emerged in the 1970s, characterized by state-led colonization and the expansion of the agricultural frontier. Backed by military regimes, these initiatives aimed to convert Amazonian landscapes into monetized, agriculturally productive zones, radically altering the region's socio-economic configuration. In Brazil, this shift deeply affected traditional Amazonian communities – composed of Indigenous peoples, descendants of escaped slaves (*quilombolas*), itinerant farmers, and impoverished migrant settlers from the Northeast – who now faced displacement and unsustainable development models (Dürr, 2020; Costa, 2019). Similarly, in Peru, legal reforms incentivized Andean peasants to migrate to the Amazon and engage in agriculture and cattle ranching. Infrastructure development, particularly road construction, was promoted as a means to stimulate commerce and catalyze economic growth.

Despite the expansion of agricultural activities, extractivism continues to play a significant role in Amazonian economies. Scholars have categorized extractive practices into two principal types: predatory and non-predatory. Predatory extractivism occurs when the rate of resource extraction exceeds the natural regeneration capacity of the ecosystem, leading to the depletion or extinction of those resources. Examples include commercial logging, overharvesting of palm hearts and rosewood, and unregulated hunting and fishing. In contrast, non-predatory extractivism involves sustainable practices that preserve the source plant or animal, ensuring the long-term availability of the resource. The collection of latex from rubber trees or the harvesting of Brazil nuts exemplifies this model, as these activities can be conducted in ways that do not often harm the parent organism and maintain ecological balance (Homma, 1992, 1995).

Brazil has institutionalized non-predatory extractivism through the establishment of extractive reserves (*reservas extrativistas*) – protected areas under communal ownership that permit traditional populations to harvest forest products under strict environmental guidelines. Introduced in 1990, these reserves aim to support the livelihoods of marginalized rubber tappers and other forest-dependent communities while mitigating deforestation (Clüsener-Godt and Sachs, 1995). Although some scholars regard these reserves as a model for sustainable land use (Homma, 1992), others view them as utopian or limited in their practical application (De Almeida, 2004). In particular, critics have noted that many extractive peasants are transitioning into cultivation-based agriculture and even cattle ranching – activities that often run counter to the ecological goals of the reserves (Porro, 2005).

Overall, scholarly assessments of extractivism in the Amazon emphasize the need to interrogate its economic viability, social equity, ecological impact, and agricultural sustainability. The evolving nature of extractivist practices – and the pressures exerted by market forces, state policies, and infrastructural development – suggest that extractivism is not a static concept, but rather a dynamic and contested terrain within the broader framework of Amazonian development.

3.2.1 New Versions of Extractivism

Since the early 2000s, political ecologists have redefined extractivism to emphasize the predatory nature of resource extraction driven by global markets and new technologies. In this renewed perspective, extractivism entails large-scale environmental degradation and resource depletion (Gordon and Webber, 2008; Bebbington and Humphreys, 2011). Influenced by David Harvey's (2003) concept of "accumulation by dispossession," these analyses foreground how extractive frontiers are less about the exploitation of labor and more about the appropriation of land and resources from Indigenous and marginalized populations.

Decolonial scholars have deepened this critique by linking extractivism to the enduring structures of coloniality. According to this view, extractivism not only perpetuates global inequalities – where the Global South supplies raw materials to enrich the Global North – but also constructs and reinforces racialized subjectivities deemed expendable or disposable (Quijano, 2000).

Building on these insights, Latin American scholars influenced by neo-Marxist and decolonial traditions (e.g., Gudynas, 2017; Svampa, 2015) have employed extractivism as a critical category to describe an economic model characterized by high-volume extraction for export, supported by institutional and legal frameworks that enable such operations. These processes generate profound socio-environmental consequences and provoke widespread resistance (Gudynas, 2017; Riofrancos, 2017). Although the literature has primarily focused on the mining and oil sectors, it also recognizes the rise of agro-extractivism – an extractive model rooted in monocultures, genetically modified organisms (GMOs), and agrochemical inputs driven by global food markets (Merino, 2020).

During Latin America's "Pink Tide" (roughly 2000–2010), extractivism scholarship distinguished between classic extractivism and neo-extractivism. The former, typical of neoliberal regimes (e.g., Mexico, Colombia, Peru), involved the privatization of natural resources, minimal regulation, and limited redistribution of revenues. By contrast, neo-extractivist governments such as Bolivia and Ecuador implemented "post-neoliberal" policies, expanding state control over extractive sectors and channeling rents into social programs. However, these approaches continued to generate conflict, environmental degradation, and displacement, particularly affecting the most marginalized communities (Siegel, 2017; Holst, 2016; Merino, 2016; Bebbington and Humphreys, 2011). This continuity reflects what Arsel et al. (2016) call the extractive imperative: a political and economic logic that prioritizes extraction regardless of ideological orientation or market conditions.

Despite its critical traction, extractivism as a concept has faced several critiques. Empirical critiques often target the assumed uniformity of local resistance, arguing instead that Indigenous and rural communities exhibit diverse responses to extractive projects, ranging from opposition to strategic engagement and negotiation (Valdivia et al., 2018; Lyall, 2021). Policy critiques highlight the lack of viable large-scale alternatives proposed by extractivism scholarship, noting that while innovations like the "rights of nature" have gained legal recognition, they often suffer from weak implementation and limited scalability.

More recent critiques have challenged the conceptual boundaries of extractivism itself. Rather than restricting the term to the material extraction of natural resources, scholars have expanded its scope to include financial and digital forms of extraction. From this perspective, extractivism also encompasses the spaces where extraction is planned, legitimized, and operationalized, often far removed from the physical sites of resource removal (Martin, 2017). Digital and financial infrastructures are inherently extractive in that they control the logistics of global trade, influence commodity prices, and shape investment flows.

This expanded conception further highlights how value is extracted from human labor, knowledge, and life itself (Ye et al., 2019; Gago and Mezzadra, 2017). Both rural and urban populations are subjected to the same extractive logics.

For instance, data extractivism describes how individuals become both the source and target of data collection practices that generate profit for digital platforms. These platforms, rather than factories, serve as the new operational centers of extractivism (Ye et al., 2019). Nevertheless, even digital systems depend on material infrastructures, including the mining of lithium and rare earth elements, fossil-fuel-based energy, and the construction of global logistics networks, all of which reproduce classical extractive patterns (Chagnon et al., 2022).

Dunlap and Jakobsen (2020) refer to this convergence of material and immaterial extractive networks as total extractivism, underscoring the pervasive reach of extractive processes across physical and virtual realms. Relatedly, McNeish and Shapiro (2021) introduce the notion of hyper-extraction to describe the ever-expanding frontiers of resource exploitation – from polar regions and the deep sea to the moon and asteroids, as well as increasingly targeted urban spaces. The broader concept of global extractivism encapsulates these dynamics, emphasizing the planetary scope and implications of extractive practices (Chagnon et al., 2022).

Global extractivism considers not only the spatial expansion of extractive operations but also their temporal and metabolic effects. At the macro level, it contributes to soil degradation, water depletion, and biodiversity loss. At the micro level, it alters the metabolisms of individual organisms through pollutants, toxins, and microplastics. This view moves beyond the traditional core–periphery dichotomy, recognizing that extractivism shapes diverse societies and roles across both the Global North and South, linking global supply chains, consumption habits, energy regimes, and extractive frontiers in a web of interdependent but unequal relations.

3.2.2 The Amazon as a New Extractive Frontier

The notion of the extractive frontier has traditionally been understood in material terms, referring to the geographic expansion of mining, energy, or agricultural exploitation into territories previously considered peripheral or unproductive by capital (Svampa, 2015). These frontiers are not a recent phenomenon; rather, they can be traced back to the origins of capitalism and European imperialism (Moore, 2017). Today, the concept acquires renewed urgency in the context of the Anthropocene, as the planet approaches ecological limits and the contradictions of capitalist overaccumulation become increasingly apparent. In the Amazon, this dynamic is particularly salient: the so-called spatial fix (Harvey, 2001) has extended to nearly the entire basin, resulting in overlapping and interconnected extractive interventions.

However, contemporary conceptualizations of extractivism invite a broader understanding of the frontier itself. While classical accumulation operated through the exploitation of labor and the dispossession of land (Harvey, 2003), contemporary forms of accumulation now extend into immaterial terrains, encompassing the commodification of data, knowledge, and even subjectivities.

In this book, Amazonian territories are analyzed as extractive frontiers in both their material and immaterial dimensions. On the one hand, areas previously inaccessible or unprofitable due to logistical or financial constraints are increasingly being targeted for extractive development through large-scale infrastructure investments. These include roads, dams, ports, and digital connectivity projects, which open up vast regions to mineral, hydrocarbon, and agro-industrial exploitation. On the other hand, these material interventions are deeply embedded in immaterial processes. Extractive projects require not only the mobilization of capital and machinery but also the extraction of data, local knowledge, and even aspirations, all of which are instrumental in legitimizing and enabling these operations.

In this context, the concepts of global extractivism, hyper-extraction, total extractivism, financial/digital extractivism, and data extractivism are not mutually exclusive but rather refer to different but interrelated dimensions of a shared phenomenon. Material and immaterial extractivism denote distinct practices and targets of appropriation – ranging from minerals and forests to information and biocultural heritage. Likewise, scalar dimensions reflect the entanglement of local, national, and transnational dynamics that shape the development and consequences of extractive endeavors.

Infrastructure projects in the Amazon exemplify these multi-scalar and multi-dimensional processes. They are not merely conduits for the circulation of goods and capital but also mechanisms that integrate Amazonian territories into broader regimes of knowledge production, investment speculation, and socio-environmental transformation. In this sense, the Amazon is not only a resource-rich space being opened to new cycles of exploitation but also a complex arena where material and immaterial frontiers are simultaneously forged and contested.

3.3 The Amazon as a Site of Global Extractivism

The Amazon has long been projected as an isolated, inhospitable wilderness or as an untouched natural sanctuary. However, historical and contemporary accounts show that it has always been deeply interconnected with global economic, political, and technological systems (Picq, 2017; Palacio, 2012). During the colonial era, the Amazon became a conduit for the transatlantic traffic of precious metals like Inca silver and gold, triggering geopolitical competition over territorial claims – a "scramble for the Amazon" among European powers (Hecht, 2013). In the post-colonial period, international interests were rearticulated around infrastructure development for national integration, border defense, and the exploitation of natural resources (Fontaine, 2006). As early as the nineteenth century, resource-based projects like the extraction of cinchona and rubber laid the groundwork for riverine and terrestrial transportation systems, urban settlements, and population displacements (SPA, 2021).

In the post-World War II era, state-driven initiatives intensified, promoting agrarian reform, urbanization, and expanded energy and mineral extraction. By the late 1970s, neoliberal reforms facilitated the privatization of public and communal lands, displacing vast rural populations and transforming them into precarious urban dwellers (SPA, 2021). This wave of liberalization ushered in a new phase of resource-export development centered on commodities such as beef, iron, gold, timber, cocoa, and soy for global markets.

Today, Amazonian countries play a pivotal role in the global supply of primary commodities: Brazil exports iron ore, soybeans, and beef; Peru, Ecuador, and Colombia are key oil producers; Bolivia and Peru supply natural gas; and Venezuela, Brazil, and Peru are major gold exporters. Hydroelectric power is a significant energy source across the basin (SPA, 2021). As of April 2025, the Amazon contains 794 oil and gas blocks, many of which overlap with 441 Indigenous territories and 61 protected areas (Milhorance et al., 2025). By 2020, mining concessions covered 18 percent of the Amazon and intersected with over 450,000 km^2 of Indigenous lands (Quijano et al., 2020). Furthermore, by 2022, 434 hydroelectric dams had been completed or were under construction across the Amazon Basin (Caldas et al., 2022).

While extractivism in the Amazon has often been studied through specific sectors such as mining, oil, and agribusiness – or through emblematic national and subnational case studies – it also includes less tangible forms. Immaterial extractivism involves the commodification of ancestral knowledge, transformed into products within international bioprospecting and intellectual property regimes (Vásquez and Cojtí, 2020). Meanwhile, illicit extractivism – including illegal logging, mining, and narcotics cultivation – thrives in regions marked by limited state presence and deepened inequalities (Pereira and Viola, 2020).

All forms of extractivism in the Amazon are closely tied to large-scale infrastructure projects. Hydropower plants, waterways, highways, railways, and ports are not simply supportive; they are enabling technologies for the circulation of commodities at global scale (Bebbington et al., 2018; Runde et al., 2020; Lees et al., 2016; Peralta, 2021). For instance, Brazil's Ferrogrão railway project aims to transport 40 million tons of soy annually along the Tapajós River corridor to meet rising demand in China and Europe by 2050 (Chan and Araujo, 2020).

Infrastructure is frequently framed by governments and corporations as a vehicle for modernity, development, and connectivity. Promises of job creation, improved public services, and market integration are persuasive narratives used to garner local support. However, communities exhibit a wide spectrum of responses: while some view infrastructure as a path to development, others resist these projects, concerned about displacement, ecological degradation, and socio-cultural disruption (McCormick, 2010; Abers et al., 2017). Infrastructure, therefore, is not neutral, it is a site of contested political imaginaries and socio-environmental claims (Carse and Kneas, 2019).

From a global perspective, this pattern has been conceptualized as an "infrastructure scramble" (Kanai and Schindler, 2019), in which infrastructure emerges as a central political and technological apparatus of global capitalism. It is a political technology that not only reconfigures physical space but also shapes perceptions of what development means and what futures are possible (Lesutis, 2021). Infrastructure reframes underdevelopment by spatially reorganizing territories through corridors, networks, and nodes that link remote extractive zones with global markets (Enns and Bersaglio, 2020).

In the Amazon, extractivism is inseparable from infrastructure. Extraction demands the development of logistical and transport systems, while infrastructure projects themselves often justify their costs through the promise of expanded commodity flows. These interdependencies reinforce a cycle of extraction and expansion that frequently ignores or overrides the environmental, social, and cultural aspirations of local populations. As such, infrastructure and extraction constitute two sides of the same coin in the logic of global extractivism.

The next section explores this relationship further by examining the region's most ambitious infrastructure development strategy to date.

3.4 The Intersection between Extractivism and Infrastructures: The Case of IIRSA

The historical trajectory of infrastructure development in the Amazon reveals the deep entanglement between state-led development goals, extractive expansion, and regional integration. In the 1970s, initiatives such as the Trans-Amazonian Highway in Brazil sought to consolidate national sovereignty and stimulate economic development through territorial integration (Walker et al., 2019). Despite contributing to significant deforestation (Diele-Viegas and Rocha, 2020), the primary obstacle to such large-scale projects was not environmental concern but rather a chronic lack of financial resources. A major turning point occurred under President Fernando Henrique Cardoso's administration in Brazil, when the Initiative for the Integration of Regional Infrastructure in South America (IIRSA) was launched in 2000 during the First Summit of South American Heads of State. Framed as a comprehensive program of mega-infrastructure projects, IIRSA aimed to bridge infrastructure deficits across the twelve South American nations by organizing investment along development corridors (Walker et al., 2019; Bebbington et al., 2018; Walker and Simmons, 2018).

IIRSA is widely regarded as the most ambitious intergovernmental infrastructure initiative in South America to date, achieving a rare regional consensus (former CAF Director, Interview, 02.03.2022). It also represents a distinctive form of regionalism, wherein states delegated significant authority to multilateral development banks, such as the Inter-American Development Bank (IDB) and the Development Bank of Latin America (CAF). These banks were not merely financiers; they played a critical role in designing, coordinating, and implementing infrastructure agendas by convening both state and non-state actors (Agostinis and Palestini, 2021). The Brasilia Declaration, which formalized IIRSA, effectively functioned as a binding contract wherein states delegated technical and planning authority to these financial institutions.

IIRSA's governance was structured around two principal bodies: an Executive Steering Committee, composed of national officials responsible for transportation, energy, and telecommunications; and a Technical Coordination Committee, staffed by representatives from IDB, CAF, and FONPLATA. This arrangement enabled the orchestration of cross-border infrastructure planning on an unprecedented scale.

By 2004, IIRSA had delineated ten integration and development hubs to link the Atlantic and Pacific coasts through a portfolio of 335 infrastructure projects. Of these, 169 projects (over half the total) were located in Amazonian countries, including forty-seven binational and two multinational projects. Most of these were transport-related (89.35%), followed by energy (9.47%) and telecommunications (1.18%) (Betancourt-Santiago and Rubiños-Cea, 2021).

The Amazon Hub proposed a vast multimodal transport system linking Pacific ports (Buenaventura in Colombia, Esmeraldas in Ecuador, and Paita in Peru) to Brazilian ports such as Manaus, Belém, and Macapá. The project aimed to integrate a market of 61.5 million people across an area of 5.7 million km^2 (IIRSA 2010a,b). According to an IDB assessment, exports from this hub increased by 79.4 percent between 2000 and 2008, dominated by commodities such as crude oil, iron, soy, copper, and petroleum derivatives. These accounted for 34 percent of the region's total export value, though 95.5 percent was transported by maritime means – only 1.4 percent moved via road, highlighting a mismatch between IIRSA's investment focus and actual logistics flows (IIRSA, 2010a,b).

Despite this, IIRSA played a critical role in re-scaling extractive operations by enabling commercial connectivity across remote areas (Betancourt-Santiago and Rubiños-Cea, 2021). Infrastructure corridors served not only to facilitate commodity movement but also to attract new investments and consolidate state and corporate presence in resource-rich but historically marginalized territories.

In 2008, IIRSA was absorbed into the newly created Union of South American Nations (UNASUR), specifically under its Infrastructure and Planning Council (COSIPLAN), which sought to institutionalize and expand the regional infrastructure agenda (Bebbington et al., 2018). However, by 2018, shifts in the political landscape and the subsequent dissolution of UNASUR curtailed multilateral collaboration. In the aftermath, countries reverted to bilateral agreements, executing projects on a more ad hoc basis (Agostinis and Palestini, 2021).

Nevertheless, IIRSA/COSIPLAN continues to shape the Amazon's infrastructural and extractive landscape. As of 2022, 32.5 percent of Amazon hub projects had been completed, 27.8 percent were under execution, and the remainder were in the planning phase (Betancourt-Santiago and Rubiños-Cea, 2021). COSIPLAN's 2017 Project Portfolio identified seventy Amazon Hub projects grouped into eight categories, all scheduled for completion by 2026 (Peralta, 2021) (Figure 3.1).

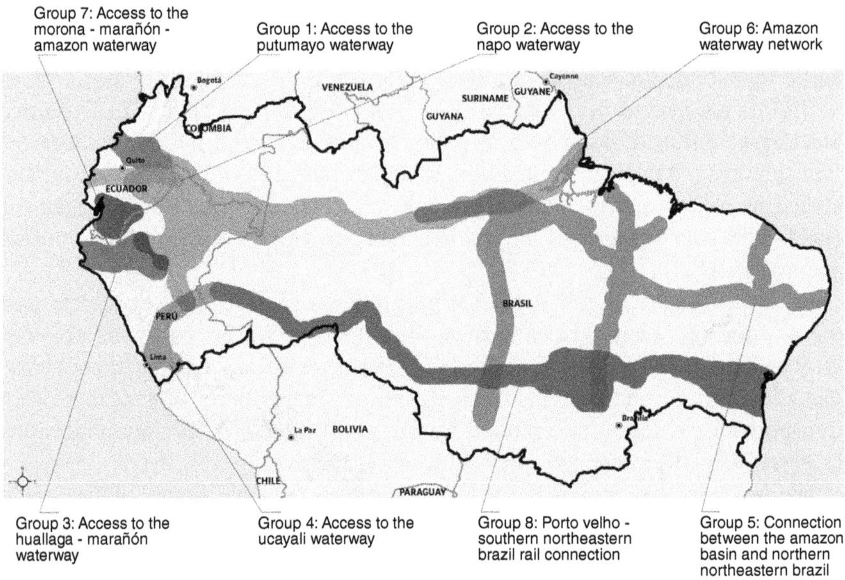

Figure 3.1 Project groups of the Amazon Hub.
Source: COSIPLAN (2017)

The strategic vision behind these investments has shifted. While early infrastructure projects were framed within national development and integration paradigms, the current logic focuses on transforming the Amazon into a multimodal transportation platform geared toward global markets (Wegner and Pereira, 2018). As Bebbington et al. (2018) argue, the goal is no longer merely state-building but rather the facilitation of international commodity circulation through infrastructure systems that support and expand extractive operations.

3.5 IIRSA and the Continued Allure of Mega-Infrastructures

Despite the substantial social and environmental consequences associated with mega-infrastructure projects – such as widespread deforestation triggered by new roads and railways cutting through frontier forests – IIRSA's governance framework systematically overlooked the development of regional environmental standards. Officials involved in IIRSA often justified infrastructure development as a tool for sustainable development, claiming that enhanced connectivity would strengthen state presence in remote territories and thereby curb illegal deforestation and mitigate ecological harm. Some argued that environmental considerations had been integrated into project planning (Interviews with former CAF officials, 17.02.2022; 02.03.2022). However, interviews with former IIRSA, CAF, and IDB officials confirmed that the criteria for defining development hubs were based exclusively on connectivity imperatives, with no formal environmental framework guiding these decisions (Interviews, 17.02.2022; 26.04.2022; 18.05.2022).

The only notable environmental policy proposal was the Environmental and Social Evaluation under a Strategic Approach (EASE-IIRSA), a methodology approved by CAF in 2010. It was intended to evaluate cumulative social and environmental risks across interconnected projects within a corridor. Yet, the initiative yielded minimal outcomes. Beyond its proposal for implementation, no country applied the methodology in a comprehensive or systematic manner (Interview with EASE official, 23.02.2022).

Environmental organizations have consistently criticized IIRSA and COSIPLAN projects for prioritizing connectivity and extractive interests over ecological sustainability. For instance, International Rivers expressed concern about the Madeira–Mamore–Beni–Madre de Dios hydroelectric dam and hydroway, arguing that these projects facilitated the expansion of soybean cultivation into rainforest regions (Myers, 2018). Road projects under IIRSA have also raised alarms about enabling extractive incursions into protected areas inhabited by uncontacted Indigenous peoples (Harvey and Knox, 2015). In Peru, the South and North Interoceanic highways – completed in 2010 and 2011 respectively – were approved without preliminary geological, engineering, or environmental impact assessments, despite traversing Indigenous territories and ecologically sensitive zones (Durand, 2019).

Activists have also highlighted how infrastructure can facilitate illegal forms of extractivism, including wildlife trafficking, unauthorized logging, and illegal mining. Little (2013) found that the lack of environmental planning for the South Interoceanic Highway in Peru contributed to the expansion of illegal gold extraction and trafficking across the Peru Bolivia Brazil corridor. Although these activities predated the highway, critics argue that it significantly accelerated their scale and scope, transforming the road into a conduit for unregulated exploitation (Wegner and Pereira, 2018; Durand, 2019). As one former NGO official put it: "the highway served illegal activities to plunder the Amazon" (Interview, 01.06.2022).

Not all critiques have focused on environmental concerns alone. Some have questioned the economic logic of mega-infrastructure projects. The Interoceanic South Highway, for instance, was widely criticized for its financial inefficiency. Critics contend that it was driven less by trade needs than by excess capacity in Brazil's construction sector, with limited regard for commercial viability. Despite costing approximately USD 2 billion, the highway generated just USD 3 million annually in foreign trade (Fowks, 2017). It ultimately became the most expensive highway in the region's history (Durand, 2019). Former officials noted that IIRSA's underlying philosophy was less about fostering regional trade than about channeling massive public investments into construction without rigorous oversight or evaluation (Interviews, 18.05.2022; 01.06.2022).

Geopolitically, the infrastructure-extractivism nexus in the Amazon is increasingly embedded within broader global dynamics. Rather than strengthening regional integration, many IIRSA-linked projects have sought to position the Amazon as a global commodity corridor, particularly in light of shifting trade flows from the Atlantic to the Pacific under China's economic ascendancy (Durand, 2019). China's Belt and Road Initiative (BRI), launched in 2013, has reinforced this trend, aiming to expand China's influence through strategic investments in infrastructure across Latin America.

Though some critics argue that Chinese infrastructure investment may reflect surplus construction capacity more than genuine development needs (Interview with former IDB official, 18.05.2022), the BRI has advanced a powerful ideological narrative centered on infrastructure-led development – what Gonzalez-Vicente (2019) describes as the promise of "making development great again." This infrastructure-driven vision reinforces extractive logics, particularly in response to China's increasing demand for commodities such as soy, beef, and minerals, which is projected to grow over the coming decades (Herrera, 2019; Jauregui, 2020; Bebbington et al., 2018).

Brazil already hosts two BRI-linked projects in the Amazon: the high-voltage transmission system linked to the Belo Monte Dam, and the expansion of the São Luís port. A third potential project is the Ferrogrão railway (Chan and Araujo, 2020). By 2019, China had become a more significant source of sovereign infrastructure financing for Latin America than the World Bank or IDB (Gallagher and Myers, 2019). Major recipients include Ecuador, Bolivia, and Peru, countries where Chinese firms and policy banks have invested in energy and transport projects that directly affect the Amazon.

Nevertheless, many of these Chinese-funded initiatives have encountered social resistance and raised serious environmental concerns. For example, the Sao Manoel dam in Brazil, granted to China Three Gorges Corporation and State Grid Corporation of China, was approved without adequate consideration of Indigenous rights (Fearnside, 2018; COICA, 2018). In Peru, the IIRSA Amazónica Hydroway, developed by Sinohydro, has been criticized for insufficient evaluation of the health and social impacts on riverine Indigenous communities (Merino, 2022). Similarly, oil and mining projects backed by Chinese capital – such as the Mirador mining project in Ecuador and El Nogal oil block in Colombia – have been marked by forced displacement, lack of prior consultation, and contested environmental assessments (Figueroa, 2018; COICA, 2018).

While China has issued several guidelines for overseas social and environmental responsibility – such as the Guide on Social Responsibility for Chinese International Contractors (2012), and the Guidelines for Environmental Protection in Foreign Investment and Cooperation (2013) – these remain non-binding. Compounding this challenge, South American states lack the institutional capacity, legal harmonization, and technical oversight mechanisms needed to monitor and regulate foreign infrastructure investments (Wegner and Pereira, 2018). As a result, Amazonian countries continue to promote the region as a space for global extractivism, rather than advancing a coherent framework for international environmental governance.

3.6 Infrastructure as Extractivism

Mega-infrastructure projects constitute manifestations of extractivism in two key dimensions. From a scalar perspective, infrastructure is integral to the extractive cycle, as exemplified by regional initiatives such as the Initiative for the Integration of the Regional Infrastructure of South America (IIRSA), which prioritizes physical integration and connectivity to facilitate the global circulation of Amazonian commodities. Building on scholarship that expands the scalar understanding of extractivism (McNeish and Shapiro, 2021; Chagnon et al., 2022), one can argue that infrastructure entails planning, construction, extraction, and the mobilization of commodities through logistical corridors. While governments continue to present such mega-projects as harbingers of progress and development, they increasingly reflect the imperatives of global connectivity aimed at sustaining international commodity flows.

From a material and immaterial dimension, infrastructure constitutes a form of extraction in itself. In the case of the Interoceanic South Highway, the official economic rationale was framed as improving trade across Amazonian countries and with the broader world. However, the underlying justification was often the surplus capacity of construction firms, whose primary interest lay in profiting from the act of building. Some observers contend that infrastructure plans – particularly those involving large-scale Chinese investment – respond to this same logic of surplus capacity (Interview with former IDB official, 18.05.2022). In this context, infrastructure is not merely a conduit for extractivism; it is itself a mode of commodifying and appropriating Amazonian space for speculative and profit-driven purposes.

Moreover, infrastructure operates as a material expression of extractivism and simultaneously enacts extractivist logics in immaterial ways. Prior to construction, infrastructure must be technically and politically legitimated. Technically, this involves feasibility studies assessing terrain, foundation materials, routing, and the estimation of costs and benefits. In the case of roads, designs incorporate projections regarding life span, traffic volume, vehicle weight, and cumulative surface stress (Harvey, 2018). In these projections, local communities are rendered into statistical indicators used to estimate potential benefits and trade volumes. Thus, affected populations are instrumentalized as variables to rationalize infrastructure development.

Critics of the Interoceanic Highway have noted that its economic rationale was inadequately articulated and questioned the extent to which the region would benefit from the project (Harvey, 2018). A limited number of studies supported the highway by citing interviews with local residents, who identified possible transported commodities and indirect benefits such as tourism (Bonifaz Fernández and Urrunaga Pasco-Font, 2012). For then-Minister of Transport and Communications, Enrique Cornejo, the project was self-justifying: "Experience shows that when the government announces the construction of a road, traffic increases, economic agents start taking decisions, land value increases, commerce develops, passengers and commodities transport start a new dynamic… Never as in this case is applicable the

'Say Law', which we rephrase: 'Any offer of infrastructure creates automatically its own demand" (Cornejo, 2012). Such arguments illustrate how infrastructure developers mobilize local knowledge, expectations, and data to promote extractive agendas.

This dynamic exemplifies a form of immaterial extractivism. Echoing the logic of data extractivism (Gago and Mezzadra, 2017; Ye et al., 2019), local populations are both the source of extractable information and the nominal beneficiaries of infrastructure ostensibly aimed at development. In practice, these communities are often materially dispossessed: such projects may entail displacement, environmental degradation, or the undermining of local livelihoods. Roads designed for high-speed international trade are seldom aligned with the needs of locally oriented development (Harvey, 2018). Along the Interoceanic Highway, many communities perceived the infrastructure as detrimental, fostering resettlement, land speculation, displacement from rivers, and fueling the gold rush and illegal logging (Harvey and Knox, 2015).

According to some scholars, this reflects the intrinsic unpredictability of infrastructure development: it does not always function as envisioned by state planners (Harvey, 2018). This is true if we focus on the technical and formal justification for infrastructure but not on its subjacent extractive logic. Infrastructure supports extractive interests in multiple ways: it generates profits for construction firms and benefits political actors who leverage developmentalist narratives. When infrastructure fails to support formal trade networks – often due to speculative motivations – it is appropriated by illegal actors, including illegal miners and loggers.

Thus, infrastructure and extractivism are inextricably linked. At the scalar level, the global economy depends on this synergy to extract and circulate commodities via transnational corridors. Within the paradigm of hyper-extractivism (McNeish and Shapiro, 2021), infrastructure enhances the value chain by connecting remote resources to global markets. This necessitates the expansion of extractive frontiers into ecologically sensitive areas and territories inhabited by Indigenous peoples in voluntary isolation.

From a material/immaterial perspective, infrastructure is extractive when it facilitates the speculative appropriation of territory or when it harnesses local knowledge and needs for political and economic legitimization. This dual embeddedness helps explain why Amazonian countries have achieved some degree of infrastructural integration, yet remain unable to agree on regional environmental standards – since such regulations would hinder or delay extractive circuits.

This extractive vision underpins national and transnational institutional frameworks that prioritize territorial commodification over ecological integrity. The institutional and epistemic injustices embedded in this framework marginalize not only alternative imaginaries and governance models but also Indigenous ontologies and their relational cosmologies. Forests, rivers, and landscapes are not mere resources or sites for infrastructure – they are integral to socio-political and cosmological orders.

In response, grassroots actors across the region have mobilized against extractive ontologies through occupations of mining sites, oil blocks, and road blockades.

These political interventions resist extractive incursions while advancing alternative forms of governance (Davis, 2021). Authorities must attend to the transformative potential of these practices. Such engagement could catalyze regional discussions on infrastructure moratoria for high-impact projects (Interview with former IDB official, 18.05.2022; Interview with former NGO official, 01.06.2022), the comprehensive implementation of Indigenous peoples' right to free, prior, and informed consent, and a reorientation of regional development priorities toward sustainability.

As a former CAF official emphasized, the protection of forests and carbon reservoirs must take precedence over connectivity. Infrastructure should serve ecological resilience and community well-being: "We must invert the logic – start with identifying environmental services and then design infrastructure to support them" (Interview, 26.04.2022). In sum, addressing the degradation of the Amazon requires a paradigmatic shift – from envisioning the region as a site of global extractivism to one of international and plurinational environmental governance.

3.7 Conclusions

This chapter has contributed to current debates on the conceptual boundaries of extractivism by examining the critical role of infrastructure in enabling and embodying extractive operations. Drawing on empirical evidence from mega-infrastructure projects in the Amazon, it has demonstrated how such initiatives reflect extractivist discourses, practices, and logics that privilege global connectivity and profit-making over environmental sustainability and the integrity of Amazonian territories. Ultimately, the chapter has reflected on how these interventions have transformed the Amazon into a locus of global extractivism, while highlighting the challenges involved in reimagining it as a space of international environmental governance.

Recent scholarship has underscored the significance of mega-infrastructures in facilitating extractive activities and enabling the transnational circulation of commodities. In the Amazon, this process has been driven in large part by the IIRSA initiative and its extensive portfolio of projects – including ports, highways, railways, hydrovias, and bridges – designed to integrate regional markets with global trade networks. These developments call for a deeper theoretical interrogation of the mutual entanglement between extractivism and infrastructure. This chapter has shown that such entanglement operates across two interrelated dimensions.

From a scalar perspective, infrastructure plays a central role in extractive operations. While historically infrastructure has been associated with nation-building, modernization, and local development, its contemporary function is increasingly tied to transnational connectivity and competitiveness in global markets. Infrastructure serves as a necessary condition for activating commodity flows across new extractive frontiers, areas previously deemed inaccessible due to technological or logistical constraints. In this regard, extractivism must be understood not merely as a discrete economic activity, but as a broader cycle encompassing planning, exploration, construction, extraction, production, transportation, and the appropriation and redistribution of resource rents.

However, infrastructure is not only a means of enabling extraction, it can also be considered a form of extractivism in itself. From a material/immaterial perspective, particular infrastructure projects function as direct mechanisms of appropriation. This occurs when the primary objective is not the transportation of commodities but rather the speculative profits generated through construction. In such cases, infrastructure becomes a modality of commodifying and extracting value from Amazonian space. This logic was evident in the case of the IIRSA Interoceanic Highway, where the project, framed in terms of connectivity and competitiveness, appeared instead to respond to the surplus capacity of construction firms and the speculative interests of state and corporate actors seeking to capitalize on territorial appropriation.

The extractive rationale also manifests in the political and economic justifications mobilized to advance mega-infrastructure projects. This immaterial dimension parallels the logic of data extractivism, wherein the knowledge, expectations, and needs of local communities are instrumentalized to legitimize infrastructure initiatives. Communities are positioned simultaneously as sources of data and as the presumed beneficiaries of development. However, across various IIRSA projects, participatory mechanisms, environmental safeguards, and social standards were either insufficiently implemented or altogether absent. In many instances, affected communities resisted the projects, perceiving them as harmful to their ecosystems and livelihoods, and as facilitators of lawless activities such as illegal mining and logging.

In this context, the Amazon emerges as a paradigmatic site of global extractivism, a region in which the scalar and material/immaterial dimensions of extraction intersect and reinforce one another. Yet this global extractivist imaginary is increasingly contested. Local communities and Indigenous peoples challenge the territorialization of extractive interests through road blockades, protests, and the occupation of mining and oil facilities. These actions must be understood not merely as resistance, but as political practices that articulate alternative imaginaries and claims to territorial governance.

Recognizing these practices opens up the possibility of reimagining the Amazon not as a strategic frontier for global extractivism, but as a region at the heart of international environmental governance. Such a shift requires addressing institutional, epistemic, and ontological injustices embedded in current infrastructure and development paradigms, and affirming the political agency and ontological perspectives of local and Indigenous communities. Only by doing so can we move toward a more just and sustainable vision for the Amazon, one that prioritizes ecological integrity, cultural diversity, and the collective right to self-determined development.

CHAPTER 4
The Amazon as a Place for Global Conservation

4.1 Introduction

Protected areas and Indigenous territories occupy important portions of the Amazon. They both cover 45.5 percent of the basin, around 3.55 million km^2, of which 28.1 percent are indigenous territories and 11.9 percent are protected areas with the strictest legal protection (RAISG, 2015). Scholars conceive this trend as "one of the most significant waves of conservation designations in history," explained by the "enthusiastic political support," especially in Brazil and Peru, since the nineties (Gullison and Hardner, 2018).

The becoming of the Amazon as a field of global conservation also responds to the fact that, in the last three decades, conservation and Indigenous territorial rights have been packed together under the global climate agenda. Since the 2003 World Parks Congress in Durban, South Africa, there seems to be a global consensus among conservationists to promote the combination of social and ecological goals, the development of social standards in conservation, and the inclusion of local governance. This consensus relies on a global discourse of Indigenous peoples as forest stewards based on scientific studies and satellite data showing how indigenous territories contribute to enhancing the biodiversity adjoining their territories (Mistry and Berardi, 2016; Garnett et al., 2018). Satellite images show, for instance, the stark contrast between the deforestation caused by commercial soy plantations and the natural forests of the adjacent Xingu Indigenous territory, in the southeastern Amazon in Brazil (Gullison and Hardner, 2018). As a result, the model of fortress conservation that justified the displacement and marginalization of entire peoples from protected areas is no longer acceptable in conservation forums, either national or international. The "new conservation," internationally diffused since the 1992 UN Rio Declaration, advanced the models of Community-based conservation (CBC) and Rights-based approaches (RBA). The former emphasizes the importance of co-management with locals in conservation initiatives. The latter emphasizes recognizing land and participatory rights to Indigenous peoples and local communities under international laws and standards. The conservation community today advances these approaches and repudiates the practices of green colonialism.

This trend, however, obscures many tensions between Indigenous peoples' territorial rights and the expansion of protected areas. While funders and practitioners have adopted the rhetoric of equitable and inclusive conservation, these principles have had less impact on site-level governance, creating a gap between policy and practice (Witter and Satterfield, 2019). Multilateral policy debates such as those that approved the Global Biodiversity Framework of the Convention on Biological Diversity (CBD) have focused on what proportion of the planet to conserve rather than how it should be conserved (Bhola et al., 2021). Green colonialism has been formally erased from the global conservation agenda, but "green grabbing" and "blue grabbing" are still common practices (Dawson et al., 2021). For instance, Becker (2022) and Sullivan (2022) unveiled how conservancies in Namibia (the poster child of CBC in Africa) are based on racialized land distribution systems and conservation laws that consolidate the power and wealth of a minority, whereas restricting communal grazing in areas closed for wildlife, recreational hunting, and tourism. In practice, CBC demands that deprived Indigenous communities cede control over their land in exchange for employment and public services (Ybarra, 2017). The RBA is also limited because the relations between indigenous rights and conservation are mostly regulated in international declarations, policies, and standards that are not legally binding and rely on voluntary compliance. In sum, RBA and CBC remain window dressing to mask the disempowerment of local and Indigenous communities by the global conservation agenda (Sène, 2023).

Given the shortcomings of the "new conservation," critical scholars name it as a conventional, mainstream, neoliberal, Western, and extractive form of conservation. It is Western because it has not substantially changed the colonial "conservation via dispossession" that displaces Indigenous Peoples and accumulates Indigenous lands under settler control (Stein et al., 2023). It is neoliberal because it aligns conservation with the creation of profit in its efforts to find ways to simultaneously "save" the environment and establish long-term modes of capital accumulation (Sullivan, 2022; Büscher and Fletcher, 2015; Stein et al., 2023). It is extractive because conservation practices are entangled with extractivism: as conservation happens "here," it is presumed that extraction can continue to happen "there" (Stein et al., 2023). It is mainstream and conventional because these practices are common across the globe and produce similar conflicts.

These discussions deeply resonate with conservation arrangements in the Amazon. The basin is the scenario of several conflicts in which protected areas, indigenous territories, and different legal and illegal extractive interests overlap. This is not only a territorial, material overlapping; there are also overlapping cosmologies and ways of territorial governance. These different dimensions have local and extra-local scopes. Regarding the external sphere, critical approaches to conservation question the lack of consideration of the international political and economic forces that dominate conservation beyond the space of concrete initiatives. Regarding the local scale, critical scholars unveil how concrete practices instrumentalize Indigenous subjects through mechanisms of inclusion and exclusion. Local and extra-local critiques acknowledge that the problem of conservation goes beyond specific conservation sites and advocate for meaningful local self-determination and authority. However, these critiques have left a gap in the way these local and international spheres can be integrated in theoretical and policy terms. In other words, they have not answered how local social-ecological knowledge and politics can be integrated into higher levels of decision-making, beyond the community, and into governance at national and international levels (Dawson et al., 2021).

To contribute to this endeavor, this chapter unpacks the tensions and conflicts of conceiving the Amazon as a field of global conservation and examines the prospects to scale indigenous politics of conservation and reimagine conservation national and international policies. For this aim, this chapter first discusses the critical theories for decolonizing conservation, how they help to explain environmental conflicts in the Amazon, and their strengths and gaps. Then, it provides an overview of the conservation architecture and associated conflicts in the Peruvian Amazon. Once the general context is explained, the chapter focuses on three case studies that show the international and local interactions around conservation politics and policies. The final section provides insights to revisit critical theories on conservation and the importance of international governance in reinventing conservation.

4.2 A Policy Framework for Decolonizing Conservation?

Green colonialism still resonates in Amazonian countries. Seventy-six protected areas in the State of Minas Gerais in Brazil share similar patterns of conflicts with indigenous and local Amazonian communities, related to, among others, issues of land tenure regularization, agriculture, livestock, and restrictive legislation (Silveira-Junior et al., 2021). In Colombia, 29 of 54 national parks overlap partially or completely with 53 indigenous *resguardos* (Premauer and Berkes, 2015), and, in general, 62.7 percent of the Parks registered conflicts with local and indigenous communities (Monsalve and Vargas, 2018). One of the main drivers of conflicts would be the legacies of the Fortress Conservation model in the management of the parks (De Pourcq et al., 2017).

Given the persistence of colonial legacies and racialized power relations in conservation practices, there are increasing calls for decolonizing conservation worldwide, meaning the opposition to the expansion of non-indigenous protected areas and the demand for international recognition of indigenous resource sovereignty and self-determination as a form of addressing global biodiversity loss (Dawson et al., 2023; Sène, 2023; Dawson et al., 2021; Tauli-Corpuz et al., 2020).

Decolonizing conservation advocates for a transition toward more locally rooted, plural, socially just, and convivial forms of conservation that move away from typical conservation approaches (Corbera et al., 2024). This transition does not imply a simple correction of the status quo by making conservation science and practice more "participatory." It aims at disrupting the processes of knowledge production that underpin the policy and practice of mainstream conservation (Corbera et al., 2024). Decolonization, then, must involve a material shift in decision-making power in which consultation, collaboration, and co-management interrupt, rather than uphold, colonial power dynamics (Schneider, 2023).

Corbera et al. (2024) propose six principles for decolonizing conservation that highlight the revalorization and empowerment of local and indigenous communities and indigenous-led initiatives. One of those principles, "limits," has an external scope by emphasizing biophysical and environmental limits for human development, which implies curtailing the material and energy consumption of the rich. Relatedly, Büscher and Fletcher (2019, 2020) propose "convivial conservation" by promoting co-existence, biodiversity, and justice, and challenging broader drivers of environmental degradation rooted in the primacy of economic growth. These authors propose moving from protected to promoted areas, which means shifting from saving nature to celebrating human and nonhuman nature interdependencies. They also propose shifting from touristic voyeurism to engaged visitation, proposing that seeing "wild" nature should not be a short-term elite privilege but a long-term democratic engagement based on socio-ecological justice. Convivial conservation also implies moving away from privatized expert technocracy to common democratic engagement, and from monetized value to a nonmonetized "embedded value" through humans and nonhumans living together (Krauss, 2021).

Decolonizing and convivial conservation enrich each other as they both emphasize the interdependence of humans with their environments and involve challenging the excesses of industrial production and resource extraction. The concrete actions proposed by convivial conservation are aligned with decolonizing goals: compensating marginalized communities for past conservation injustices; a conservation basic income for community members in or around protected areas; promoting a different economic model prioritizing extraction limits and degrowth; a global "convivial conservation coalition" promoting just conservation. However, these approaches do not deepen conservation's internal and external dynamics. On the one side, they neglect unequal power dynamics and internal conflicts among local and indigenous communities; on the other side, they do not explain how to deal with a "global economic model" that prioritizes extraction and growth.

4.2.1 Conservation and Capitalism: External Critique

Decolonizing Conservation's concerns on global capitalism and economic growth relate to different reflections that I call "external critiques" of conservation. These critiques highlight how conservation and global capitalism are entrenched

(Sène, 2023), as conservation is embedded in the function and reproduction of capitalism, which is itself a vehicle of diverse forms of colonization worldwide (Corbera et al., 2024). Protected areas, eco-tourism, and the commodification of ecosystem services and biodiversity are tied to a depoliticized agenda of economic growth and development, foreclosing the nature of the social and economic forces causing biodiversity loss (Corbera et al., 2024). In this context, as many extractive activities occur in or close to conservation areas, some conservation organizations seek to work with extractive companies to build their programs on the legacies of colonial conservation practices. Conservation thus becomes a "green alibi" to displace communities and access mineral resources, as reported in the case of diamonds for the Basarwa in Botswana (Boonzaier, 2011; Mosweunyane, 2017). While conservation initiatives may help to counterbalance some of the "bads" resulting from extraction, the resulting extraction-conservation system extends its impacts onto communities and the world at large (Le Billon, 2021).

These dynamics are common in South America. In Brazil, the state of Minas Gerais created five protected areas of restricted use (68,281 ha in total) and two of sustainable use (94,500 ha) between 1998 and 2000, as a form of environmental compensation for the development of the Jaíba Project, the largest irrigated perimeter in Latin America, situated at the margins of the São Francisco river. The area of three of these state parks (Verde Grande, Lagoa do Cajueiro, and Mata Seca) overlapped the territories of vazanteiros communities of de Pau Preto, Quilombo da Lapinha, and Pau de Légua. As state parks do not allow for the human presence or the use of natural resources, these communities were forced to leave their territories without compensation or resettlement, and those who resisted eviction suffered severe restrictions to their livelihoods and well-being (Anaya et al., 2018). These communities have been struggling against these parks through the years. In 2010, they joined other vazanteiros communities to create the "Movement of the People Cornered by Parks" (Movimento dos Encurralados pelos Parques). They organized collective actions for territorial repossession, delimitation of their ancestral territories, and proposals to change the nature of the Parks, from restricted to sustainable use (Anaya et al., 2018).

In Peru, a military government imposed the model of fortress conservation in one of the first protected areas, the Manu National Park, created in 1973. The government banned all human activities in the park, evicted the Machiguenga people, and forced them to settle in an area that years later became the Camisea gas complex. In 2002, the Inter-American Development Bank approved a credit in favor of the Peruvian state to develop this gas complex with the condition to reinforce the environmental system. The commitment implied the creation of four protected areas surrounding the complex: the Ashaninka Communal Reserve in Junin; the Otishi National Park (Junin and Cusco); the Machiguenga Communal Reserve in Cusco; and the Megantoni National Sanctuary in Cusco. Indigenous peoples in alliance with conservation NGOs conceived and promoted those areas as a form of territorial protection given the expansion of illegal mining and illegal logging nearby, however, in these protected areas Indigenous peoples have limited authority and some areas overlap with projects of extending the territorial dimension of the gas complex (Watson and Davidsen, 2022).

In these cases, conservation cannot be understood without considering the economic and international forces surrounding and conditioning conservation arrangements. Without solving these tensions, global attempts to conserve "half of the Earth" or "30x30" agendas would only reveal how powerful individuals, organizations, and countries of the Global North influence the affairs of less powerful countries and communities of the Global South (Collins et al., 2021; Sène, 2023). More dramatically, conservation might end up being a global project that authorizes "green wars," meaning the limitation of life chances of Indigenous peoples in protected areas through their legal dispossession, denial of basic state services, military repression, and tacit sanctioning of private violence against "conflictive" communities (Ybarra, 2017).

Carmenta et al. (2024) propose "Connected Conservation" as a new approach to address the global character of conservation. This approach criticizes the emphasis of contemporary conservation on in-site initiatives, foreclosing distant geographies that drive environmental degradation. In this framework, Connected Conservation requires two broader groups of actions: (1) telecoupled conservation actions that reduce and filter the dominant systemic flows of one-world development, climate change, and trade from centers of wealth and (2) collaborative conservation actions that enhance and amplify the positive yet marginalized forms of local governance, diverse knowledge systems and plural values of nature from bioculturally diverse regions.

Whereas this proposal is valuable, it is still unclear how telecoupled actions would be deployed in practice beyond the usual affairs of international climate summits and activism. The meaning of "collaborative conservation" is also ambiguous, as it seems to refer to groups that "collaborate" to some predefined aims and not to self-determination. In sum, there is a need to rethink how feasible connect global and local critical conservation agendas.

4.2.2 Indigenous Conservation: Internal Critique

Decolonizing conservation also provides what I call "internal critiques" to context-based conservation through critical approaches such as "indigenous conservation" and "nation-building approach to conservation." These approaches, informed by ancestral knowledges and practices, seek to build or reinforce Indigenous Nations and center Indigenous Peoples as the primary decision-makers about what, where, and how conservation should occur on their territories. These practices oppose tokenistic and symbolic representation and recognition of Indigenous peoples in conservation initiatives, for not shifting underlying power relations and failing to change the processes through which the most powerful groups maintain control (Stein et al., 2023).

The paradigmatic conservation model of decolonizing conservation is Indigenous Peoples Conserved and Protected Areas – IPCAs, in which Indigenous Peoples are the authority of a management system aimed at both environmental sustainability and cultural integrity (Krauss, 2021; Borrini-Feyerabend, 2013; Schuster et al., 2019). As IPCAs are managed under Indigenous legal and knowledge systems, they are designed to facilitate not only ecological conservation, but also sustainable livelihoods, cultural and language revitalization, and self-determination (Youdelis, 2021). After being developed in British Columbia, Canada, this model gained international attention at the 5th IUCN World Parks Congress in 2003, which recognized the contribution to conservation goals of protected areas under indigenous administration (Vincent et al., 2004). The parties of the Convention on Biological Diversity adopted the broader term "Indigenous and Community Conserved Areas" (ICCAs) that also include local communities different from Indigenous peoples.

Although Canada is supporting IPCAs through certain initiatives, the country's extractivist dependency along with jurisdictional inconsistencies, undermines this model (Youdelis, 2021). The traditional territories and proposed or declared IPCAs overlap with various tenures (mineral, forestry, oil and gas, hydroelectric, etc.) that threaten their ecological and cultural viability (Youdelis, 2021). IPCAs live thus in a "legal grey zone," as no federal or provincial statute explicitly recognizes the right of Indigenous Nations to declare or govern their own conserved areas (Bulowski, 2022; Zurba et al., 2019). Zurba et al. (2019) also warn that treating IPCAs primarily as vehicles to meet conservation targets under the Convention on Biological Diversity risks undermining the importance of IPCAs for Indigenous peoples. For example, some ministries in British Columbia stated they lacked a cabinet mandate to establish or increase IPCAs since the province had exceeded the 17 percent terrestrial conservation target (Youdelis, 2021). Courtois suggests IPCAs may be understood as "an interim land back action," noting that government support for IPCAs comes in the form of programs rather than nation-to-nation partnerships (Stein et al., 2023).

Amazonian countries consider Indigenous territories as fundamental for achieving conservation goals, but there is no formal recognition of IPCAs, and co-management is, in general, not effective. In Brazil, the Institute of Environment and Renewable Natural Resources (IBAMA) designed the National System of Conservation Units, which is organized into two broad categories: the sustainable use group and the full protection group, which can be managed by different levels of government (Law 9985, 2000). The "Chico Mendes Institute for Biodiversity Conservation," created in 2007, is responsible for managing, protecting, monitoring, and supervising the 335 federal conservation units (Decree No. 5.758), and among its functions, it must "develop policies with traditional communities that live within or nearby conservation units" (Decree No. 5.758). The National Plan for Protected Areas (Decree No. 5.758, 2006) stated that Indigenous lands only might be included in the planning and implementation of conservation actions and integrated biodiversity management, and the National Protected Areas Policy considers that the lands of indigenous and traditional populations are strategic for conservation policies (Da Costa et al., 2022). This is clear considering that indigenous lands represent 13.8 percent of the national territory (National Indian Foundation FUNAI) and are home to about 700 thousand Indigenous people, over half of them live in the Brazilian Amazon (Silva-Junior et al., 2023). Silva-Junior et al. (2023) found that, by ensuring indigenous land rights, these territories could decrease deforestation by up to 66 percent.

However, the overlapping of conservation units and Indigenous lands is a common problem. The Federal Constitution of 1988 states that the "lands traditionally occupied by Indians" must be identified, delimited, demarcated, and approved by the Union (Article 231). By 2022, the areas claimed reached almost two million acres and there were 285 demarcation processes paralyzed (Modardo, 2022). This would respond to a contradictory process of agrarian development historically based on land concentration: By April 2020, 1.78 percent of Brazilian farmers own almost 50 percent of the country's land (Modardo, 2022). Another explanation is that the demarcation procedure is bureaucratic, complex, and time-consuming, and there is no comprehensive rural land registry, resulting in rights' overlapping (Chiavari and Lopes, 2020). Moreover, although Indigenous peoples have exclusive access to the soil, rivers, and lakes in their lands (Article 231, §2º of CF/1988), those lands still are assets of the Union (Article 20, XI of CF/1988). The National Congress might authorize infrastructure and mining in indigenous lands with the only safeguard that those affected communities "must be heard" (Article 231, §3º of CF/1988). The Supreme Court decision in the case of Belo Monte Hydroelectric Plant concluded that the hearing of indigenous communities is not a condition of the authorization process (Rocha et al., 2015; Chiavari and Lopes, 2020). As a result, mining activities are being requested on 28 million hectares of indigenous lands (Chiavari and Lopes, 2020). Regarding the overlapping of Indigenous lands and conservation units, authorities assume that there is compatibility and that the area can have a double designation (Chiavari and Lopes, 2020).

The case of the Catimbau National Park exemplifies the problems of limited hearing of local communities and the broad compatibility of protected areas and indigenous land. The park was created in 2002 as one of the largest protected areas in the Caatinga, Pernambuco State. Despite its legal status as a strictly protected area, the park is home to over 300 Kapinawá households and is neighbored by the Kapinawá Indigenous Territory, where 2,000 inhabitants occupy an area of over 12,000 ha. Most households raise goats and practice subsistence agriculture and handicrafts. The park was established through a workshop in 2002, at which policymakers and scientists agreed that a strictly protected area was the most suitable. This was the only formal interaction with the villagers. Those who attended that meeting recalled that the local mayor and IBAMA staff sought to persuade inhabitants by emphasizing that the Park would bring employment and income, neglecting any explanation about boundaries and regulations. In the coming years, people perceived they gained little or none of the benefits promised and rather suffered resettlement and many restrictions in the use of the Park resources (Dawson et al., 2023).

In the case of Colombia, the National System of Protected Areas (Decree 1076, 2015) classifies the areas according to their management (national and regional), governance (public or private), and permitted activities. Those conservation spaces that did not fall within this categorization are "complementary conservation strategies," the equivalent of the IUCN "Other Effective Area-Based Conservation Measures" (OMEC), which might include indigenous territories. Indigenous and Afro-descendant peoples have rights to collective titling of their ancestral territories as "Indigenous *resguardos*" or as "Collective Territories" under the 1991 Constitution. Colombian legislation (Decree 2164/1995) defines resguardos as special legal and socio-political institutions formed by one or more indigenous communities holding a collective property title to possess and govern their territory. Communal land and resguardos cannot be sold (art. 63) and are granted to perpetuity as territorial entities (art. 286). They have autonomy to be governed by their authorities and manage their own resources (art. 287) through Councils created and operated according to their own traditions (Art. 330). These rights have been reinforced and expanded by the Constitutional Court in landmark decisions (Constitutional Court of Colombia. Decision T-693/2011; Decision SU-123/2018).

Indigenous territorial rights seem to be strong in Colombia, considering that only 4.4 percent of the population is indigenous (census 2018) and that by April 2019, 767 Indigenous resguardos were occupying 32,653 has, 53.3 percent of the Colombian Amazon (Gullison and Hardner, 2018). However, the government's decision to expand indigenous lands through resguardos over almost 30 percent of the country's territory was a pragmatic policy to delegate governance over remote regions, given the state's failures to expand the agricultural frontier and combat guerrilla groups (Rueda-Saiz, 2017). This strategy of control also fostered the assimilation of Indigenous peoples and lands into a model of economic development based on resource extraction. Natural resources, including subsoil resources, are controlled by the State (Arts. 102 and 332). As a result, the multicultural constitutional regimen has not challenged the prioritization of extractive activities. There are many pending petitions for recognizing or enlarging resguardos, and indigenous organizations accuse authorities of privileging the formalization of oil blocks and other economic activities (Gullison and Hardner, 2018). Many Indigenous communities have conflicts with mining companies exploiting Strategic Mining Areas approved by the Executive Branch. Indigenous Peoples Arhuaco, Kogui, Wiwa, and Kankuamo from Sierra Nevada of Santa Marta have been protesting since December 2017 against 132 mining titles granted over their ancestral territory, despite the Constitutional Court (decision T-766/2015) ruled that it is compulsory to make prior consultation with Indigenous communities when mining activities are intended to be developed in their territories. Similar conflicts emerged in the oil industry, such as the long judicial dispute between EcoPetrol and the U'wa people (Hill, 2015).

The contentious relationship between indigenous territories and protected areas has a long history in Colombia. Decree 662 of 1977 established that it is not incompatible to declare a protected area on indigenous territories (regulated then as "indigenous reserves"). It specifies that, through a Special Regime, the permanence of the Indigenous people and the economic use of natural resources are respected under the condition of using technologies compatible with the objectives of the system of protected areas. The state must only coordinate actions of common interest with Indigenous peoples about the management and use of the overlapping areas (Cortes, 2018). Despite this, Indigenous peoples consider that adapting to non-consensual conservation objectives in overlapping areas does not respect their right to self-determination (Cortes, 2018). The resulting conflicts became one of the main reasons for Parques Nacionales, the state agency in charge of protected areas' policies, to formulate the "Parks with People" policy in 1998 in which collaborative governance between parks authority and Indigenous peoples is based on Indigenous rights recognition, local governing authority, and cross-cultural practices. The policy has suffered through changes in government priorities that have weakened environmental and indigenous rights' standards to give priority to the mining sector (Premauer and Berkes, 2015). In 2002, Parques Nacionales adopted the "Policy for Social Participation in Conservation." This policy prescribes the need for dialogue with indigenous, Afro-descendant, and peasant communities, as well as their participation in the management of the parks. However, Colombian legislation (Law 2 of 1959; Decree 2811 of 1974; Decree 622 of 1977) has not been adapted to the principles of this policy, causing legal gaps. In practice, the old regulation prevails, so community participation is limited (De Pourcq et al., 2017).

Indigenous conservation has gained relevance in international discourses and norms, but not in concrete national policy actions and practices. Although the new 30 × 30 CBD framework broadly recognizes the rights of Indigenous and local peoples vis-a-vis conservation initiatives, implementation on how and to what extent to recognize those rights depends on national governments; many of these governments have a history of discrimination and exclusion of indigenous and local communities and privilege extractivism over self-determination.

4.3 The Peruvian Amazon as an Example of the Mismatches of Global Conservation

The second largest share of the Amazon belongs to Peru, and the Peruvian Amazon concentrates 85 percent of the 246 protected areas of this country (Orihuela, 2019). Between one-third to half of this region has been designated by the authorities as protected areas and indigenous territories in a similar proportion (Orihuela, 2019; Watson and Davidsen, 2022; Aidesep and FPP, 2014, IBC, 2016). Undoubtedly, international forces have contributed to this trend. By 2016, Peru received around US$613 million in climate funding. The main part (73 %) consists of bilateral funding (mainly from Norway, the United States, Germany, and Japan), whereas the main multilateral contributors are the World Bank's Forest Investment Program (FIP), the Inter-American Development Bank (IADB), and the Global Environment

Facility (GEF) (Che Piu et al., 2016). A good portion of this funding is used to create and manage protected areas.

Internal forces also explain the expansion of protected areas. Historical accounts explain how Peru evolved from being a laggard in conservation policy during the 1960s to becoming a leader by the late 1970s, thanks to the work of "policy entrepreneurs" within the state, and that continued in the next governments (Orihuela, 2019). In 2008 the government created a specialized agency, the National Service of Protected Areas (SERNANP), and throughout the years, the Peruvian State subscribed to several climate compromises, such as the Paris Agreement, and enacted conservation policies, such as the National Program for Forest Conservation and Mitigation of Climate Change (2010) and the Climate Change Law (2018). Today, Peruvian legislation regulates three types of protected areas: national, managed by SERNANP; regional, managed by regional governments; and private, under private management. By 2022, there were 75 national, 25 regional, and 139 private protected areas. National protected areas have different subtypes. National parks have the strictest protection, excluding commercial resource exploitation, whereas in the other protected areas, authorities allow some degree of exploitation.

External and internal drivers for expanding protected areas have not incorporated the concerns and rights of Indigenous peoples. The protected area that resembles IPCAs is the "communal reserve." The first model of "Communal Reserves" was created with the Forest Law of 1975 as a way to protect the territories and livelihoods of native communities (Palacios and Sarmiento, 2021); however, it did not recognize indigenous governance mechanisms over these areas and was poorly implemented in practice (only one was created under this legislation, the Yanesha communal reserve in Pasco, 1988). The new forest regulation in the nineties allowed the creation of seven communal reserves, representing then 10 percent of the national system of protected areas (1.8 million hectares) (Orihuela, 2014). Under the current legislation (Forest Law, 2011), indigenous communities do manage communal reserves, but not as landowners; they are administrators under a contract with SERNANP. Administration contracts allow Indigenous communities to implement specific management activities, but only if they narrowly align with the plans and strategies defined by state authorities. Indigenous co-management partners are expected to follow these governance guidelines that may be at odds with Indigenous perspectives (Sarmiento and Rolando, 2024). In total, Peruvian governments have implemented communal reserves only in 10 of the 246 protected areas (SERNANP, 2020).

Scholars and practitioners often consider the Amarakaeri Communal Reserve (400,000 ha) created in 2002 in Madre de Dios as a good example of co-management, as it has received international awards and acknowledgment, including its addition to the IUCN Green List in 2018 and the UN Equator Prize 2019. This reserve was promoted by the Native Federation of the Madre de Dios River and Affluents (FENAMAD) as a defense mechanism to protect Harakbut, Matsiguenka, and Yine communities and territories as mining concessions were expanded in the area (Palacios and Sarmiento, 2021). Community representatives constitute the "Executor of the Management Contract" and have signed a co-management contract with the state. Under the reserve governance, communities can practice hunting, fishing, and harvesting, whereas commercial activities such as logging and gold extraction are not allowed. In the beginning, some villagers had great expectations of the reserve, given the prospects of creating a communal ecotourism company, whereas others perceived the reserve as a limitation that benefited those defending conservation interests (Boillat et al., 2010). The communal company, however, never materialized, and the government signed an oil and natural gas exploration contract with Hunt Oil for Lot 76, which overlapped most of the reserve. This situation exacerbated the critiques and led to protests about the coexistence between a mega extractivist project and conservation (Palacios and Sarmiento, 2021).

Another co-governance mechanism is "management committees," applied to most protected areas (except for those under private management). Management committees are platforms of NGOs, local communities and organizations, business representatives, and municipal, regional, or national authorities. They have a more consultative status rather than a normative one. They are vehicles for dialogue, consensus-building, and knowledge exchange for assisting plans made by state authorities (Sarmiento and Rolando, 2024). In both administration contracts and management committees, the state maintains full authority throughout the process: from terms of reference to supervision of compliance, and approval of compatible activities (Watson and Davidsen, 2022). An indirect co-governance mechanism is prior consultations on the creation and zoning of protected areas. By 2024, different governments developed 14 processes of prior consultation with Indigenous peoples, although these are applied to new areas, and many communities demand consultations for areas already created. Moreover, some processes have been very contentious, and communities are not totally satisfied with consultation agreements (as discussed in Section 4.4).

4.3.1 Conservation and Territorial Rights

In general, the growth of protected areas and indigenous lands in Peru has been accompanied by intensified extraction that has led to messy and overlapping land rights allocations and ecological degradation (Watson and Davidsen, 2022). Moreover, when communities inhabit forest areas, national legislation does not recognize them as having property rights, but only "assignment of a right to use," with limited territorial control. Indigenous peoples are socially organized and legally recognized as "peasant" (in the highlands) and "native" (in the Amazon) communities. One of the key demands of Indigenous peoples relates to territorial rights. As 38 percent of all communities (around 4,000) still lack titles (IBC, 2016), indigenous territorial claims within protected areas have increased in recent years.

These claims have international and local implications. At the COP negotiations, the consensus was that titling was an "enabling condition" for protecting forests, and as such, it needed the support of international cooperation. In Peru, high-level government officials, such as the Minister of Environment (2019), announced a commitment to titling: "Titling of all native communities is our goal... it has taken years to understand the importance of this right." Titling has been accepted as a means for achieving both conservation and social justice for Indigenous peoples, the reason why it has been incorporated in important international cooperation projects, such as the Joint Declaration of Intent involving Peru, Norway, and Germany, implemented by the United Nations Development Program (JDI-UNDP); the "Cadaster, Titling and Registry of Rural Lands in Peru" (PTRT3) project, supported by the IADB; and the Saweto Dedicated Grant Mechanism, funded by the World Bank's Forest Investment Program – FIP (DGM-Saweto). The JDI-UNDP project, with an investment of US$300 million, seeks to reduce 50 percent of land-use change through the creation of protected areas, provide incentives for the conservation of two million hectares of forests, and "formaliz[e] the tenure of 5 million hectares of native communities' land." PTRT3 involves an investment of US$80 million, and although it focuses on conservation, it is implemented by the Ministry of Agriculture (in Peruvian legislation, this ministry enacts titling regulations, and regional governments execute those regulations). The DGM-Saweto, with an investment of US$5 million, seeks recognition for 310 indigenous communities, the titling of 130 as communal land (800,000 hectares), and support for communal forest management projects for 18 regional indigenous organizations. It is being directly implemented by indigenous organizations with the support of WWF.

Although these projects highlight the importance of indigenous rights, their main priority is fighting climate change through forest conservation and titling. Most international conservationists working in the Amazon share this idea, including the Gordon and Betty Moore Foundation (USA), Andes Amazon Fund (USA), and Rainforest Foundation (Norway). Other organizations with a social justice focus, such as the Ford Foundation and Rights & Resources International (USA), have also included their goals under the climate and forest conservation umbrella. An international NGO official says, "Although we have a social justice agenda, we use environmental discourses to advance the rights agenda" (Interview, 10.10.2019). For indigenous organizations, the conservation argument is mainly seen as a tool for obtaining territorial recognition and some indigenous organizations reject conservation when they see that this becomes a threat to self-determination (Boillat et al., 2010). Overall, these different projects illustrate how diverse actors have appropriated and used the indigenous environmental steward discourse in different ways for furthering competing policy agendas.

4.3.2 Conservation and REDD+

The entanglements between protected areas and titling projects also reach REDD+ international programs (Chapter 1) and become arenas of contention where Indigenous peoples seek to have a role in forest governance. Since its creation, the

Ministry of Environment has committed to preserving forested hectares through a mix of policy instruments, including REDD+. In this respect, Peru has taken part in multilateral REDD+ funding initiatives, including the Forest Carbon Partnership Facility (FCPF) since 2008, the Forest Investment Program (FIP) since 2010, UN-REDD+ since 2012, and bilateral agreements with Germany (2010) and Norway (2016). By 2019, financial flows associated with REDD+ were around US$0.52 billion, including both executed funds and committed funds for 2030 (Lozano et al., 2024).

The injection of resources provided the means to implement the REDD+ readiness phase, including rulemaking, knowledge production, and policy design. The legal framework for REDD+ was materialized in the 2011 Forest Law, the 2015 Forest Regulations, the 2014 Ecosystem Services Law, and the 2015 REDD+ strategy. The REDD+ strategy emphasized three policies: disincentive policies, such as law enforcement; enabling conditions policies, such as individual and collective tenure rights; and incentives policies, such as the cash-payment program for Indigenous communities (MINAM, 2015). The readiness phase also incorporated social and environmental regulations proposed by each donor, which included indigenous participation and tenure rights.

In this context, for Lozano et al. (2024), the process of tailoring REDD+ to a national context has been an opportunity to address historically neglected institutional challenges concerning Indigenous rights. The strategy used by Indigenous organizations has been developing "scale-jumping processes" by which they bypassed national governments to directly connect with the REDD+ donor and activist communities, including NGOs, scientists, and broader Indigenous networks such as COICA and the Indigenous Caucus. With this strategy, they pushed to create REDD+ spaces at the national level as dialogue platforms to negotiate different interests and worldviews between state authorities and Indigenous peoples (Lozano et al., 2024). However, these spaces have limitations: whereas incorporating tenure rights under (limited) national laws, these platforms excluded governance mechanisms and financial institutions managed by Indigenous organizations.

This suggests that conservation and forest arrangements are seen as opportunities to bring disruptive agendas and, at the same time, present strong limitations given the very nature of a market-oriented mechanism inserted in extractive international structures. In Brazil, Indigenous peoples also hold ambiguous relationships with REDD+. The Suruí People were the first Indigenous group to adopt a REDD+ project worldwide and agreed to engage in carbon markets to safeguard their territory against mining and logging (Cifuentes, 2021). One of the 19 REDD+ projects in the Brazilian Amazon registered under Verra (formerly the Verified Carbon Standard – VCS) was the Suruí Forest Carbon Project (SFCP) in Rondonia, initiated in June 2009 (Garcia et al., 2021). The SFCP also developed the Suruí Fund, a financial mechanism to secure equitable REDD+ allocation (West, 2015). However, in 2018, Suruí leaders formulated several criticisms to the project for excluding indigenous management, affecting their autonomy, and establishing monetary conditions that divided the people, requesting the extinction of the project (da Silva et al., 2024).

Apart from market mechanisms, Brazil has been the major recipient of REDD funds worldwide (31 % of the total), as well as the largest recipient of bilateral funding (Aryal et al., 2024; Recio, 2022). Since 2008, the Norwegian government has contributed more than US$1.2 billion to Brazil, accommodating its sovereignty concerns by granting the country a certain degree of autonomy in managing REDD projects through the Amazon Fund, the primary global example of a national REDD scheme independent of carbon markets (Recio, 2022). Thus, the first "payments for results" project approved by the Green Climate Fund (GCF) started in Brazil in 2020 as part of the National Program for Payments for Environmental Services – Floresta+ (2020–2026). The financing reaches 96.4 million dollars, which represents nearly one-fifth of the 500 million dollars committed by the GCF to programs worldwide. For Dalla and Korber (2024), the architecture of Floresta+ has the potential to reinforce neoliberal rationality, insofar as it creates the technical and discursive conditions for conservation to become a paid "activity." Producers will be able to receive payments for four years for conserving these areas. The neoliberal logic is also expressed in the structuring of rules and procedures based on managerialism, control, and monitoring. The project focuses on small communities, but those are not the main source of emissions. The current efforts are not directed at the main GHG emitters and drivers of deforestation, such as mining, organized crime, and agribusiness (Dalla and Korber, 2024). Moreover, despite these efforts, Brazil lost 62.8 Mha of tree cover from 2001 to 2021, mostly due to high beef and soybean demand in Europe and China (Aryal et al., 2024).

In Peru and Brazil, REDD+ projects are entangled with conservation arrangements and do not seem to have fulfilled their promises because of external and internal drivers.

4.4 Local and Global Dynamics in Conservation: Three Cases

This section discusses three cases where conservation, indigenous rights, and different extractive interests overlap over critical areas in the Peruvian Amazon. The dynamics illustrate the external and internal drivers of a colonial mode of conservation that has not been overcome yet.

4.4.1 Cordillera Escalera Regional Conservation Area

The international cooperation agenda on fighting climate change and coca crops' eradication portrays the Department of San Martín as a "green region." A former oil company official said, "...in San Martín, authorities can be environmentalists because they receive much money from USAID..." (Interview, 09.01.2019). For officials from the Regional Government (GORESAM), international green funds, prizes, and carbon bonds have been an important concern (Interview, 12.11.2019). For national pro-indigenous NGOs, however, it is contradictory to be considered a poster child of green funds and cooperation and, at the same time, grant rights for infrastructure, land-use change, and agribusiness in forest areas (Interviews, 11.11.2019; 04.04.2019).

In 1996, the then-national office in charge of protected areas, with the support of German Cooperation (GIZ), classified Cordillera Escalera in the Department of San Martin, provinces of Lamas and San Martin, as a priority zone for conservation. The Regional Government (GORESAM) pushed for years for the creation of this area. The GORESAM proposed creating a Regional Conservation Area (ACR), with support from a local environmental NGO and funding from the Finnish government. The proposal was finally approved by the national government in December 2005. The ACR includes five river basins that feed the Huallaga and Marañón rivers and covers an area of 149,870 hectares.

The creation of the RCA conflicted with Occidental Petroleum, which obtained concession rights in 2004 over Block 103, spanning an important portion of the area. In October 2006, a local environmental NGO filed a request for a constitutional injunction (*demanda de amparo*) to suspend oil activities on the grounds that they threatened water sources located within the area. The Constitutional Tribunal sided with the plaintiff and suspended exploration until the RCA management plan, an instrument approved by SERNANP, explicitly approved the activities (Constitutional Court of Peru. Exp. 3343-2007-PA/TC). For former oil company executives, the main opposition came from environmental NGOs, not from indigenous communities (Interviews, Lima, 9 and 15 January 2019). Indeed, indigenous organizations also opposed the RCA but on different grounds. They considered the area an imposition that, in practice, criminalizes their ancestral activities (Interviews, San Martin, 8 November 2019) (Figure 4.1).

The "Coordinator of San Martin Indigenous Peoples" (CODEPISAM), the regional office of the national "Interethnic Association for the Development of the Peruvian Rainforest" (AIDESEP), has been struggling against the ACR. One of its eight local federations, the Ethnic Council of Kichwa People of the Amazon (CEPKA), in particular, has promoted titling projects in the area, demanding the recognition of their ancestral rights. Six native communities located within the area and others nearby have used the area's resources ancestrally. However, the only titled community within the RCA is "Nuevo Lamas," a Kichwa community titled in 2016 thanks to persistent demands to regional authorities. The GORESAM titled only 1.8 percent of Nuevo Lamas territory located outside the RCA as property. For the rest of its territory, inside the RCA, the community received "assignment of rights to use." Indigenous leaders complain that communities must request permission from GORESAM to fish, hunt, and gather, becoming "intruders in their own land" (Interview, San Martin, 7 December 2018).

Indigenous communities engaged with the three international titling projects in the area to defend their territorial rights (JDI-UNDP, PTRT3, DGM-Saweto). These projects conceive Indigenous peoples as environmental protectors and titling as a means to fighting climate change. However, they obtained few results as these

Figure 4.1 Regional Conservation Area "Cordillera Escalera," San Martín, 2021. Photo by the author

projects also pursue the titling of land under the category of "assignment of rights to use." Pro-indigenous local NGOs complain that international organizations and NGOs focus on meeting targets rather than ensuring territorial rights and that there is scant progress on titling (Interview, 11.11.2019). This is due to the tendency to avoid addressing "conflictive cases" or overlapping with protected areas (Interview, 05.12.2019), and most communities have overlapping claims, conflicting with settlers, regional zoning, and the ACR. Regional officials and NGOs that promoted conservation argued that titling is delayed not because of a lack of funding, but because of excessive demands on the part of indigenous organizations and pro-indigenous NGOs (Interview, 20.09.2019), who would advise communities to claim rights to which they were not entitled.

In August 2017, Nuevo Lamas and CEPKA – with the support of the Institute of Legal Defense, a human rights NGO- filed a constitutional complaint against GORESAM for not titling the entire territory as property, against the Ministry of Agriculture for not adapting the legislation of indigenous rights to international standards, and against the Ministry of Environment and SERNANP for not having held a consultation on the RCA creation. GORESAM officials are the most reluctant about the claims. The office in charge of the RCA rejected titling and offered the communities "conservation agreements" to make them "forest protectors" (Interview,

San Martin, 20 September 2019). In a public statement (2019), CODEPISAM claimed that conservation agreements work for companies interested in sustainable exploitation, not for those who own the land. In general, regional authorities portrayed an image of Indigenous Peoples as opposed to conservation (Interview, San Martin, 9 May 2019). In turn, local environmental NGOs claimed to be concerned about indigenous rights, but they also accused CEPKA of being allied with the oil company to exploit the forests (Interviews, San Martin, 11 November 2019). In contrast, indigenous leaders emphasize that their main goal is self-governance over their ancestral territory, arguing the lack of legitimacy of environmental NGOs to control the area excluding indigenous communities (Interview, San Martin, 25 April 2019). Indigenous leaders also appeal to the benefits of territorial rights to combat illegal interventions: "biodiversity exists here because we have historically protected the forests. We are the best conservationists. The RCA lacks the budget and personnel to protect the area… The only way to stop settlers is by recognizing our land rights" (Interview, 12 November 2019).

The deepest issue at stake in these conflicts is territorial rights, rather than titling or consultation. Indigenous peoples engage with international titling projects or strategic litigation seeking to protect their territories. Titling is problematic because, for those funding the projects, the main goal is conservation; from their perspective, there is no difference between titling property or granting rights to use, and titling within the ACR does not contribute to the goal of reducing deforestation, because this is already ensured, in a way, by protected-area status (Interview, 08.11.2019). This illustrates how titling projects have primarily been used to serve the goal of forest conservation.

This case shows the need to articulate external and internal critiques of conservation. International cooperation efforts appeal to a discourse of Indigenous peoples as forest stewards in instrumental ways to justify titling projects that do not provide real territorial control to Indigenous peoples. International titling projects coexist with oil concessions, forest concessions, and protected areas that disregard ancestral rights. Whereas counting on achieving administrative goals, they legitimize different kinds of extraction on the ground. Illegal extraction by loggers in those areas not properly titled, the potential extraction of oil, the potential extraction of carbon markets, and green funds by sub-national authorities. Internally, the arrangements in place to include indigenous concerns in conservation management deepen the injustices. The lack of recognition of their ancestral territorial rights means that they are intruders in their own territory; they can only participate in a "management committee" with no decision-making power. Internal and external factors are deeply entangled.

4.4.2 Yaguas National Park

The Joint Declaration of Intent (JDI) between Peru, Norway, and Germany is a trilateral REDD+ program that includes amongst its goals "reducing 50 percent of forests without legal definition to avoid land use-change" through both titling and conservation mechanisms. Officials attempt to meet this goal by creating protected areas such as the Yaguas National Park, for which the state reports the protection of 1.5 million ha (JDI Plan of Implementation, 2018). This is a highly biodiverse area that includes peat swamps, which give it one of Peru's highest carbon stocks.

The national government created the Yaguas Reserved Zone in July 2011 in the provinces of Putumayo and Ramon Castilla in the department of Loreto. With the support of international NGOs, SERNANP organized a consultation with indigenous communities between December 2016 and May 2017 to categorize the zone as a national park. No Indigenous People live inside the Park, but many communities alleged that the area is their ancestral territory used for hunting and the collection of forest resources. SERNANP identified twelve communities in the park's area of influence, but during the consultation, other communities asked to be included, and ultimately, twenty-nine participated. Twenty three of them – affiliated with local organizations – agreed to the creation of a Park to shield their resources from mining, coca growing, and logging (Interview, Iquitos, 25 January 2019). In general, state officials, pro-Park communities, and conservation international NGOs saw the Park as a means to maintain order against illegal activities (Interview, Iquitos, 30 May 2019). The result of this process was the agreement by the majority to create the Yaguas National Park on January 11, 2018.

Six communities affiliated with the Regional Organization of Eastern Indigenous Peoples (ORPIO) criticized the process. The national indigenous organization AIDESEP, the International Coordinator of Indigenous Organizations of the Amazon River Basin (COICA), and a national environmental NGO supported ORPIO. Local leaders said that international conservation NGOs controlled SERNANP by "paying all the bills" (Interview, Iquitos, 18 December 2018). They also criticized SERNANP for dividing the movement by including communities unfamiliar with the area, offering them social services to gain their support (Interview, Iquitos, 25 April 2019). The key criticism was about the refusal to classify Yaguas as a communal reserve, allegedly because SERNANP and international NGOs would have an interest in the carbon-capture market (Interview, Iquitos, 25 April 2019). For ORPIO leaders, a model of co-management would ensure both conservation and their ancestral rights. They regret that in the consultation, state officials didn't explain the option of creating a communal reserve and rather imposed the national park. This situation exacerbated opposition in some communities: "They care more about biodiversity than about us… We do not oppose conservation… We are against impositions and divisions" (Interview, Iquitos, 28 September 2019).

Different offices participated in the consultation, but the leading role was of SERNANP. SERNANP authorities said that a communal reserve is technically non-viable because the areas' ecosystems are fragile and cannot withstand frequent resource exploitation (Interview, 7 May 2019). They, rather, along with international conservation NGOs and supportive communities, saw the opposing communities as operators of illegal mining and logging. Park supporters accused a former

COICA President, allegedly allied with those illegal activities, of pressuring for a reserve (Interview, Iquitos, 30 October 2019).

Opposed communities emphasized that they have the right to develop their economies inside the park because it belongs to their ancestral territory, and resource exploitation is crucial for their survival. They also alleged that small-scale exploitation by indigenous communities wouldn't impact the environment significantly and rather would secure biodiversity from external actors (Interview, Iquitos, 25 April 2019). In fact, an ORPIO leader said that state authorities, rather than prohibiting activities, should focus on creating better conditions for sustainable exploitation: "… because of poverty and marginalization, young indigenous people have no alternative but to work in illegal logging" (Interview, Iquitos, 28 September 2019).

This case also illustrates the need to connect external and internal critiques of conservation. Whereas national and international conservation actors proclaim that the Park resembles an alliance between indigenous rights and conservation, the main driver behind the park's creation is the fulfillment of conservation goals, regardless of those groups that demand the recognition of their territorial rights. The exclusion of indigenous economic activities for allegedly being complicit in illegal mining and logging is a way not to fight or govern extractivism, but to distribute it. The Park defines extractive frontiers, indirectly authorizing logging and illegal mining outside its borders. At the same time, it justifies a kind of extractivism pursued by local NGOs and authorities that seek economic and political gains from international green funds. The local institutional mechanism that could deal with these tensions under indigenous knowledge and management, the communal reserve, was a priori excluded as a model of conservation in the area.

4.4.3 Ichigkat Muja-Cordillera del Condor National Park

Awajun and Wampis communities in the Northern Amazon supported the Peruvian army with logistics and knowledge of the area during the Cenepa war against Ecuador, a border conflict for Amazonian territory in 1995 (ODECOFROC, 2009). After the war, indigenous organizations participated in negotiations at the Ministry of Foreign Relations, in which both states agreed to establish protected areas on the borders, respecting indigenous territories. In Peru, the area occupies the districts of Cenepa and Río Santiago, in the Condorcanqui province of Amazonas department (SERNANP, 2020). The zone included river basins that provide water to indigenous communities, but also mining concessions granted since 1993. When Afrodita Mining (holder of 39 concessions) requested authorization for exploration in 2001, the office then in charge of protected areas rejected the petition because of its potential impacts. In March 2004, the local federations Organization for the Development of Border Communities of the Cenepa (ODECOFROC) and the Indigenous Organization for the Development of Alto Comaina Communities (ODECOAC) gave their approval for the creation of the Park as a means of securing their territories against large-scale mining.

An investigation of ODECOFROC (2009) found that Afrodita pressured the protected areas authority to modify its opinion, arguing that large-scale mining was the best way to hold the border. In a second decision, the authority recommended reducing almost half of the Park from 152.873 to 88.477 ha. Then, the government of Alan Garcia created the "Ichigkat Muja-Cordillera del Condor National Park" (Supreme Decree 023-2007-AG) and, the same week, approved mining requests in the zone that had been excluded. For the Awajun and Wampis peoples, the reduction of the Park was offensive because the government transformed an area they meant to protect from mining into a mining zone (ODECOFROC, 2009). When natives protested mining, Afrodita accused them of kidnapping their workers. These tensions exacerbated opposition to government policies for promoting extractive industries and ended with the conflict known as the Baguazo in June 2009, in which 34 people died and hundreds were wounded. Although in the following years, Ollanta Humala's government (2011–2015) enacted pro-indigenous legislation, such as the Consultation Law (2011), tensions continued. In 2016, Afrodita obtained authorization from the Regional Directorate of Mining to begin production, and conflicts escalated in 2017 when people opposed to mining burned part of the company's assets (MINEM, 2020).

The Afrodita CEO, nonetheless, said that they have good relations with the communities and have even created an environmental committee with indigenous participation. From his perspective, mining is the only option for sustainability (Interview, Lima, 21 May 2013). Other corporate actors, such as a former manager of Pacific Rubiales (an oil concession holder close to the area), said that most communities engage in illegal activities (illegal logging; coca harvesting; illegal mining), so "they have no authority to talk about territorial rights or conservation" (Interview, Lima, 23 May 2013). The situation created internal conflicts. As ODECOAC started to support Afrodita, it was accused of dividing the indigenous movement, convincing people in the community of Shain to work as miners. In contrast, the community closest to the Cenepa River basin, Antigua Kanan, completely opposed large-scale mining (Meza, 2019). The chief of Antigua Kanan, Oscar Chigkun (SERVINDI, 2019), accused illegal miners of blackmailing the people from his community: "We want freedom, tranquility, peace, so we beg the state to intervene and help us eradicate illegal mining… our culture is in imminent danger of extinction."

With support from the Human Rights NGO Institute of Legal Defense and national environmental NGOs, communities opposed to industrial mining filed two constitutional complaints. In the first, of 2013, they complained to the Ministry of Energy and Mines and the Geological, Mining and Metallurgical Institute (INGEMMET) for approving mining concessions without consultation. In April 2019, a Court of Justice ruled in favor of the plaintiffs (Wiener, 2019). In the second, of 2017, they complained to SERNANP and the Ministry of Environment for the violation of the agreements reached for creating the Park. In June 2021, the Court of Justice of Lima ordered SERNANP to initiate a consultation process over the extension and categorization of the area. Despite the courts' decisions, indigenous communities accuse Afrodita of continuing operations in alliance with illegal miners (Meza, 2019). However, state responses are ambiguous and depend on power relations in each sector: The Ministry of Energy and Mines promotes large-scale mining and the formalization of illegal miners in the area, whereas the Ministry of Defense, pressured by environmental NGOs and ODECOFROC, has declared the interdiction of the zone, continuously repelling illegal miners (Mongabay, 2019).

In 2024, I attended a roundtable organized by Amazon Watch in Lima about the human rights impacts of five decades of operations of the oil circuit in the Peruvian Amazon. Indigenous leaders updated me about the situation of illegal mining in the Northern Amazon. The situation they reported was tragic. All indigenous organizations in the area would be coopted by illegal miners, and those communities who resist and demand police interventions only obtain ineffective measures. Public forces reach the area, seize some machinery, and later on, miners recover their tools. Journalist reports have denounced the agreements between police forces, illegal miners, and indigenous organizations to continue the activities.

This case illustrates the external and internal problematic dimensions of conservation. The creation of the Park legitimized both legal and illegal mining in the area undesignated for protection, regardless of the impacts on the water basins and indigenous rights. Indigenous peoples seek to appropriate the National Park arrangement under their own terms as a way of territorial defense. However, the exclusion of Indigenous peoples from the process of creating and delimiting the Park and, therefore, from their effective governance, eliminated the possibility of articulating territorial rights and conservation. Moreover, the expansion of illegal mining in the last years, with the support of local and national actors, and international economic supply chains, eliminated any possibility of proper governance of conservation and extraction in the area. Not attending to the international economic dynamics and local arrangements that exclude indigenous rights has impacts on both Indigenous self-determination and conservation.

4.5 The Limitations of Indigenous Conservation in the Amazon

The examination of local cases of conflicts on the creation and management of protected areas in indigenous territories shows the limitations of co-management and participatory mechanisms in conservation. Protected areas are arenas of political contestation. To create, modify, and manage these areas, different social actors engage with different rationales and ontologies, portraying conflicting images of Indigenous Peoples' relationship with nature.

When Indigenous Peoples oppose conservation initiatives advanced by regional and national authorities, state officials tend to portray them as forest exploiters with no ecological concerns. Even though some offices and authorities are sympathetic to indigenous claims and aspirations, those entities directly involved in protected areas' management tend to see opposing communities as security threats that engage in illegal activities. In turn, Indigenous movements frame their struggles under the forest steward identity, but they also appeal to security rationales. Under security arguments, they claim that territorial rights are more effective than protected areas in stopping illegal activities (in Cordillera Escalera and Yaguas) or that the original boundaries of a protected area negotiated with the state ensure the exclusion of illegal mining (in the Cordillera del Condor). International conservation NGOs also use security rationales to defend the creation of protected areas as a buffer against logging and illegal mining. National and international environmental NGOs accept in general, the forest steward identity inasmuch as it doesn't risk their conservation initiatives.

In all the cases, the communities also formulate economic rationales linked to their livelihoods and life projects. For them, the sustainable use and exploitation of their livelihoods ensures their material survival. State actors also advance indirectly on economic grounds. In Cordillera Escalera and Yaguas, regional and national officials see protected areas as an opportunity to gain access to international green funding. In Cordillera del Condor, the economic rationale relates to the reduction in the protected area's size to allow large-scale mining. Although all actors – state, indigenous peoples, conservation NGOs, and pro-indigenous NGOs – claim to be aligned with sustainable development, all of them advance ecological, security, and economic rationales, sometimes highlighting one while concealing another.

The institutions put in place to negotiate these different epistemic frameworks on the environment, the economy, and security are weak or simply serve to justify the government's own decisions. As in the case of Brazil's "hearing of communities" and Colombia's "policy for social participation," the state has the final authority to decide the destiny of the area. In Yaguas, the consultation led by SERNANP included many communities but excluded the possibility of discussing a model of co-management. In Cordillera Escalera, regional authorities recognized land rights for communities as "assignment to use" but denied real dominium over their ancestral land. In Cordillera del Condor, national authorities incorporated communities' concerns to create a Park, but then unilaterally excluded them to reduce the agreed area. The ecological, economic, and security frames serve authorities to limit the political agency of Indigenous Peoples by conceiving them as forest stewards, forest exploiters, or security threats inasmuch as such images justify their own power over those areas.

Indigenous peoples do not renounce the use of conservation institutions but try to appropriate them and extend their scope. They might support a strictly protected area under their own conditions (Cordillera del Condor), they might demand a co-management mechanism such as the communal reserve, although it means a low level of self-determination (Yaguas), or claim the titling of their land rights within a protected area as a means of territorial recognition (Cordillera Escalera). As in the cases of Brazil and Colombia, Indigenous peoples struggle within the system of protected areas, demanding some reforms or a different form of implementation that allows the exercise of sovereignty over their territories and livelihoods.

The strategic use of these institutions by Indigenous Peoples who portray themselves as forest stewards, sustainable economic actors, or security agents deeply expresses the quest for sovereignty over these areas. Indeed, beyond those arguments, they ultimately appeal to their sovereignty: "We are not asking for a favor. We are not beggars. We have a legal right over our territories" (Interview, 12 November 2019). Therefore, the constant tensions around protected areas seem to respond to the lack of recognition of indigenous sovereignty and the *de facto* exercise of this sovereignty. Rather than simply conceiving indigenous communities instrumentally as forest stewards, it is crucial to understand the different rationales behind indigenous claims. Beyond the ecological, economic, and security epistemes advanced, Indigenous peoples are making ontological claims on the sovereign nature of their relationships with their lands and territories. This would need to be institutionalized as a form of "shared sovereignty," where decisions over territories and resources derive from negotiations between the state and Indigenous nations conceived as equal partners in environmental management, not just as participants disempowered in state decision-making processes.

Decolonizing conservation, expressed locally in indigenous forms of conservation, is fundamental to building a framework for shared sovereignty. However, this agenda has many challenges. First, ontological exclusion by national authorities who cannot imagine a different type of sovereignty governing Amazonian territories. Second, institutional and legal limitations. The constitutional framework in Peru and beyond recognizes a weak version of indigenous self-determination and territorial rights, as they might only possess, not own, forest areas, even though they might be ancestral inhabitants. Ultimately, in the cases of Peru, Brazil, and Colombia, the state can grant a conservation status or other rights (mining, infrastructure, oil, agribusiness) over indigenous territories against the will of the people affected. Finally, in all cases, material limitations and power imbalances affect especially indigenous communities that have no option but to engage in illegal activities to survive vis-à-vis the expansion of extractive economies over their territories.

Having indigenous meaningful decision-making power in conservation also requires addressing and dealing with international forces. First, international actors influence the way nation-states localize social and environmental standards to enlarge environmental protection while considering the demands of self-determination and the territorial rights of Indigenous peoples. Second, international actors – transnational corporations, international investors, and multilateral banks – directly or indirectly engage with legal and illegal economies, influencing or conditioning the way national and subnational authorities create and manage protected areas. Therefore, Indigenous conservation requires scaling beyond the governance of conservation sites toward international decision-making spheres that might impact the way states engage with climate goals, indigenous demands, and extractive industries.

4.6 Global Conservation in the Amazon

Conservation is an intrinsic international practice. Beyond the relevance of participatory governance and indigenous rights, different international actors, in contentious ways, influence and impact everyday local conservation governance through their discursive, financial, and political power.

Discursive power means the construction and diffusion of a discourse in which Indigenous peoples are framed as environmental stewards critical for countering climate change and forest degradation. However, the two groups of global actors that advance this discourse, those that primarily fight for social justice for Indigenous peoples and those that primarily promote biodiversity conservation, have diffused this discourse, prioritizing their own agendas. As a result, different interpretations and expressions of it produce different institutional arrangements, such as territorial rights, titling, co-management, and self-determination, which are disarticulated or even opposed, generating policy fragmentation and tensions in implementation. In turn, this discourse allows different norm entrepreneurs at the national and local levels, including indigenous organizations, state officials, and NGOs, to use it strategically to frame and advance the different institutional arrangements under their own goals. The global discourse thus legitimizes disarticulated interventions that trigger conflicts on the ground. On the one hand, Indigenous peoples are accused of demanding communal reserves and property titling to engage in deforestation or to access transnational green funds; and on the other, state authorities and environmental NGOs are accused of using protected areas to gain access to climate funds. As a result, in localizing the discourse, global priorities for indigenous rights and conservation end up in a deadlock where no actor is totally satisfied.

Financial power implies that both global conservation donors and transnational extractive firms influence the interests of national and regional governments to conciliate extractivism and conservation within or near those areas. Ultimately, indigenous territorial rights end up co-existing with conservation initiatives and extractive activities supported, promoted, regulated, or unregulated by the state. In the case of Cordillera del Condor, conservation and industrial gold mining go hand and hand. In the case of Cordillera Escalera, the overlapping of an oil block in the area suggests the potentiality of extractivism since large-scale exploitation has merely been suspended. In the case of Yaguas, the exclusion of commercial logging with the strict protection zone only means that logging might be carried on outside its borders with little or defective supervision and regulation. In all cases, moreover, non-formalized forms of extractivism, illegal mining and logging, are threats or actually exist because there are international circuits that commercialize those commodities. These forces directly impact the governance of the areas and the effectiveness of indigenous rights.

Political power means that those international actors are very influential in setting the rules for the governance of biodiversity conservation and indigenous rights.

Whereas donors, multilateral banks, and conservation and human rights NGOs promote the recognition of participatory rights and land rights in both conservation and extractive industries, international investors and transnational corporations demand flexibility and legal security to develop their economic projects. As a result, Peru in particular, and Amazonian countries in general, have fragmented and disorganized policy regimes in which indigenous knowledge and rights are broadly recognized as critical for conservation, but this recognition falls short of ensuring the actual exercise of their self-determination. In Peru, Colombia, and Brazil, we found common patterns of some recognition of co-management and participation, conflicts for resource use, claims for restructuring the governance of protected areas, and limited decision-making power of Indigenous peoples. The different policy regimens reflect a political struggle that might be found in the international and local spheres, impacting national regulations and local governance.

The critiques provided by connected and extractive conservation have already pointed out how international economic forces impact on in site conservation and, therefore, they suggest going beyond the local level. This is even more relevant if we understand Amazon as a whole ecosystem whose biophysical dynamics are not limited by countries' borders. Illegal logging, illegal mining, oil, and mineral exploitation, and their impacts do not simply affect protected areas. These activities take place in a socio-economic process that encompasses different geographies and reaches demand countries far from the Amazon. Moreover, illegal economies cross the frontiers between Ecuador, Peru, and Brazil without effective national mechanisms of control and enforcement. The ecological impacts that these processes produce affect river basins, extremely biodiverse ecosystems, and endangered animals that are not necessarily the patrimony of a specific nation but live across large segments of the forest. Moreover, the more than 80 Indigenous Peoples in Voluntary Isolation and Initial Contact that live in the basin (Vaz, 2019) know neither nation-state borders. They cross the frontiers between Brazil, Peru, and Colombia, searching for food and shelter. The human–no human dynamics on the whole basin is a living force that cannot be reduced either to protected areas or countries' boundaries. Hence, conservation cannot be limited to some recognition of indigenous knowledge and rights by proclaiming epistemological dialogue and inclusion. It needs to engage with indigenous ontologies of self-determination, and this implies a radical transformation of current national and international institutions.

Conceiving the Amazon as a field of global conservation means, therefore, acknowledging that this space is materially, geopolitically, and geoeconomically international as conservation interacts with transnational economic forces. This also means that the Amazon is a biophysically integrated space whose socio-ecological dynamics cannot be domesticated by state borders. Finally, this means that different international forces impact everyday governance and rights. Given this intrinsic international character, the current fragmented governance of conservation in the Amazon, based on local and national regulations, must be complemented by an international governance that includes indigenous ontological perspectives on territorial rights and sovereignty and the rights of the natural environment, unevenly advanced by conservationists and indigenous organizations.

4.7 Conclusions: Decolonizing Conservation in the Amazon

This chapter has shown the limitations of conventional conservation in the Amazon and how decolonizing conservation can be meaningfully implemented in the region if we are able to close the gap between the internal and external critiques of conservation toward the proposal of a comprehensive, democratic, and multi-scalar project for the governance of conservation. Through a general assessment of conservation governance in the Amazon and the detailed analysis of three cases, this chapter has unveiled the contradictions of conservation arrangements and has assessed the potential of addressing the local and international dimensions of conservation.

The internal critique of conservation focuses on how the concrete governance mechanisms in conservation practice exclude the ancestral knowledge, political agency, and territorial rights of local and indigenous communities. Many protected areas in the Amazon reproduce these dynamics, triggering social conflicts for resource use and demands for transforming governance arrangements. Indigenous conservation seeks to address these problems by advancing protected areas under indigenous management. Whereas this model is still far from being implemented in many countries, Indigenous peoples seek to appropriate current participatory and co-management institutions in conservation to advance their own views of self-determination.

The external critique of conservation focuses on how international forces impact conservation governance and outcomes. This approach also explains how these forces condition the possibility of Indigenous peoples to exert their self-determination and protect their territorial rights, ultimately undermining the very goals and promises of conservation. In the Amazon, protected areas depend to a great extent on the discursive, financial, and political power of international actors, whose diverse agendas produce a fragmented conservation governance that most of the time excludes the concerns and aspirations of indigenous communities.

Decolonizing conservation in the Amazon requires two agendas: a national agenda to extend indigenous sovereignty rights in national legislation through institutional models of indigenous protected areas that recognize not only the different ecological, economic, and security epistemes, but also the ontological basis of indigenous sovereignty; and an international agenda that include indigenous sovereignty in a process to approve standards for governing both extractivism and conservation in the basin. This is the only way to fill the gap between internal/local and external/international critiques of conventional conservation. This gap is a political and policy gap because it refers to how we can govern the internal and external dimensions of conservation. This gap is not located either in the global or the local arena, it is located in a middle-ground in the international space: the regional governance of the whole basin. This means that, rather than relying on global climate summits or polycentric localized initiatives, it is crucial to push for the transformation of regional policymaking and the definition of conditions and governance rules for IPCAs in the basin.

IPCA standards should disrupt policy priorities, imaginaries, and ontologies. Indigenous peoples have been conceived as "participants" in the conception, creation, development, and management of conservation initiatives in their own territories, being at most consulted and/or having membership in non-deliberative "management committees." As Indigenous nations hold sovereignty rights, this process should be the other way around. Indigenous peoples should have territorial rights recognized first, and then the creation of a "management committee" should be the space in which state officials, conservation NGOs, scientific communities, and others would have a voice to support the area's management under indigenous authority. Then, rather than being a window dressing mechanism, these committees would be a space for multi-actor dialogue and deliberation under the lead of Indigenous peoples. These should be spaces for ecological democracy in which the rights of nature (advanced by the different actors), state developmental priorities, and indigenous rights should define the governance of the areas.

CHAPTER 5

Envisioning a Plurinational Governance for the Amazon

5.1 Introduction

The image of the Amazon as a pristine and inhospitable region with nothing more than minerals and forest richness and available spaces for building corridors and expanding extractive projects has legitimized different national and international agendas. These agendas have been linked to sovereignty claims either by imperial powers during colonization or by independent nation-states in the post-colonial era. At the same time, these dynamics have obscured the sovereignty claims of Indigenous nations, who have occupied the Amazon for over 12,000 years, continuously transforming the Amazonian landscape with agro-biological developments embedded in diverse cultural systems (Neves et al., 2021).

The waves of colonization, land grabbing, slavery, deprivation, genocide, and marginalization in the region have not erased the quest for indigenous self-determination. Today, around 410 Indigenous peoples and 2.2 million indigenous persons live in the Amazon (Moutinho et al., 2022). They speak over 300 languages, possess diverse knowledge and cultures, and occupy over 170 million ha of forested area (27 % of the entire region), contributing to the conservation and sustainable management of Amazonian ecosystems (Moutinho et al., 2022).

However, Indigenous nations have many challenges in exerting their territorial governance. Scientists estimate that 48 percent of indigenous territories in the Amazon are under some pressure, with one-third of them facing high stress associated with unsustainable extractive activities and infrastructure development (Moutinho et al., 2022). Extractivist interests have also brought direct violence to these communities with the killing of environmental defenders by illegal loggers, illegal miners, and drug cartels. One in five of the 177 environmentalist killings in the world in 2022 occurred in the Amazon, especially in Colombia (60) and Brazil (34) (Global Witness, 2023). Indigenous peoples also face the climate impacts of large-scale deforestation and GHG emissions outside their borders. Regional drying and warming caused by these factors have intensified fire regimes and altered regional water cycling, driving further forest degradation and affecting the health and livelihoods of Indigenous peoples and local communities (Moutinho et al., 2022).

Despite being the original owners of most of the Amazonian land, being those who suffer the most from environmental deterioration of the basin, and playing a critical role in the conservation of Amazonian ecosystems, Indigenous peoples are not meaningfully participants in the international governance of the Amazon. The Amazonian Cooperation Treaty Organization (ACTO) has not incorporated Indigenous peoples as international actors in the organization and has not advanced a regional strategy for protecting Amazonian ecosystems and indigenous rights. Rather, ACTO has reinforced the power of each basin state to enact its own economic and environmental policies, which often privilege the interests of the most powerful actors, such as mining, oil companies, agribusiness, and construction firms.

What are the prospects for democratizing the international governance of the Amazon through the recognition of indigenous self-determination? Indigenous peoples increasingly engage with international law-making, challenging the state-centric approach to international relations (Carpenter and Riley, 2014). However, few theoretical or empirical examinations explore Indigenous peoples' political agency as peoples or nations on the international level. The literature on indigenous diplomacy has focused on Indigenous peoples located in the Global North, and the literature on the participation of Indigenous peoples in international law-making has focused on global forums, such as climate change summits, or has provided general assessments over legal provisions for participation in some international bodies. Less attention has been paid to the politics of indigenous self-determination in regional international spaces in the Global South for examining the prospects of Indigenous diplomacy. Building on the notions of indigenous self-determination and indigenous diplomacy, this chapter analyzes the role of Indigenous peoples in the international governance of the Amazon. For this aim, it examines the interactions between ACTO and the Coordinator of Indigenous Organizations of the Amazon River Basin (COICA), the world's biggest indigenous organization formed by affiliated organizations from all nine Amazonian countries, including French Guyana.

This chapter argues that the international governance of the Amazon has excluded Indigenous peoples by conceiving them as ethnic groups with no political international agency as nations. Recent policy advances that promise the inclusion of Indigenous peoples within ACTO still rely on a state-centric approach in which these peoples cannot be imagined in the deliberative processes of the organization. The call for decolonizing self-determination in a way that Indigenous peoples are recognized by the international community as collective international actors must be supplemented by decolonizing state sovereignty. This means that with no substantial reforms that tackle ACTO's reliance on the classical sovereignty imaginary,

Indigenous peoples would continue to be excluded from exercising internationally their political agency.

Despite ACTO's political weakness and the different institutional challenges of COICA, Indigenous peoples continuously struggle to decolonize the international governance of the Amazon and enact what would be in practice a plurinational international governance. In this governance, Indigenous nations would be active members of decision-making international bodies. A common space of a decolonized version of nation-state sovereignty and indigenous self-determination in the international governance of the Amazon would democratize international affairs over the basin and could open the opportunity to struggle for more ambitious institutional reforms at the regional level. Since Indigenous peoples live across all Amazonian countries, with recognition of international decision-making power, they could also articulate international support to challenge the unwillingness of ACTO members to enact binding social and environmental standards for the region.

5.2 Indigenous Self-Determination and Diplomacy on the Global Stage

Self-determination is a key principle for both the international indigenous movement and the Amazonian indigenous agenda. Originally, this principle was conceptualized as distinct from state sovereignty. The Universal Declaration of Human Rights, adopted in 1948, did not distinguish between peoples and Member states as holding the right of self-determination; only the rights of sovereignty were exclusive to states (Lightfoot, 2021). However, in the following years, self-determination became a state-centric construction rooted in the Westphalian system of sovereign nation-states, being understood as equivalent to decolonization in the form of independent, sovereign, territorial statehood (Lightfoot, 2021). Thus, the decolonization movement in the 1950s, crystallized in the UN Declaration on the Granting of Independence to Colonial Countries and Peoples of 1960, deemed Indigenous peoples ineligible for the right of self-determination. Under the "Salt Water" or "Blue Water" thesis, only overseas colonies seeking statehood were eligible for self-determination (Henderson, 2007). These developments consolidated a discriminatory version of self-determination, especially for those Indigenous peoples divided by borders, as different state structures, such as citizenship regimes and passports, represented the continuity of colonization and oppression through Westphalian sovereignty (Lightfoot, 2021).

In the next decades, scholars overcame minimalist interpretations that attached self-determination to statehood, excluding Indigenous peoples. Other conceptualizations based on the International Covenant on Civil and Political Rights and the International Covenant on Economic, Social and Cultural Rights portrayed self-determination as a "bundle of social and cultural rights," but this notion de-emphasized the political nature of this right (Lightfoot, 2021). After decades of activism, Indigenous movements finally achieved the explicit recognition of self-determination as a political right in the United Nations Declaration on the Rights of Indigenous Peoples (UNDRIP) of 2007. The UNDRIP conceptualizes self-determination within the boundaries of state unity, namely, as "internal self-determination." This notion entails multiple possibilities for Indigenous–state relationships, from participation in liberal institutions to autonomy and self-government (Lightfoot, 2021). Thus, although for some authors the UNDRIP has limitations as it explicitly relies on a human rights framework rather than a decolonization agenda (Engle, 2011), this Declaration also states that Indigenous peoples have the right to "freely determine their political status" (Article 3). Indigenous peoples thus might engage with the notion of self-determination under decolonial frameworks to reconfigure both sovereignty arrangements at the national level and international sovereign practices and institutions.

5.2.1 Indigenous Diplomacy

In recent years, indigenous international practices and thinking have fed the notion of "indigenous diplomacy," a form of diplomacy in which indigenous politics at the international level express indigenous cosmological commitments, ethics, protocols, and observances (Beier, 2016; Briggs and Graham, 2023). This notion challenges conventional Western understandings of diplomacy attached to the state, which have made invisible ancient ways of conducting diplomacy before the state and alongside the state (Carter and Fry, 2023). For instance, Indigenous peoples in Australia maintained complex systems of transnational networks and regulated trade and dispute resolution before colonization. In North America, the Great Law of Peace of the Haudenosaunee Confederacy regulated two centuries of peaceful interaction among the Mohawk, Cayuga, Onondaga, Oneida, and Seneca, disrupted only by the incursion of European colonial powers (Beier, 2016; Carpenter and Tsykarev, 2021). In South America, the Inca empire achieved geopolitical expansion thanks to the practice of Inca diplomacy that prioritized negotiation and exchange with foreign peoples instead of wars of conquest (Merino, 2025).

Indigenous peoples have also practiced diplomacy with and through the European-imposed international system since the start of colonization (Beier, 2016). Despite colonial violence, they neither abandoned traditional diplomacies nor avoided those of European origin (Carpenter and Tsykarev, 2021). Indigenous cosmologies often allowed the coexistence of those practices without assimilation or conversion under an exclusive sovereign authority. For instance, the Two Row Wampum Treaty of 1613 between the Haudenosaunee and the Dutch newcomers represented the joint agreement that there was room enough on the river for both peoples (Beier, 2016). In South America, after Mapuche leaders swore allegiance to the Crown in exchange for territorial recognition, Spain accepted the Mapuche territory as the southern boundary of its empire. This long-standing agreement only ended after Chile gained independence in 1818 and implemented policies of exclusion and coercive assimilation through military conquest and forced displacement (Schulz, 2019). During the last century, Indigenous Peoples continued engaging with diplomatic practices. For instance, the Maori and Haudenosaunee sent representatives to the League of Nations and the United Nations to campaign for indigenous sovereignty (Carpenter and Tsykarev, 2021).

One aspect of indigenous diplomacy refers to how it contributes to nation-states' foreign policy. In this regard, Briggs and Graham (2023) propose indigenous diplomatic notions of "relationality" as a contribution to Australian foreign policy, instead of conventional approaches to inter-state relations based on a "survivalist" ethos of acquisitiveness, hegemony, maximization of self-interest, and unchecked exploitation of the natural world (Carter and Fry, 2023). In practice, Aotearoa New Zealand has committed to a Maori-inspired foreign policy drawing on the Maori cultural values of reciprocity of goodwill (manaaki), connectedness (whanaunga), shared aspiration (kotahitanga), and stewarding of intergenerational wellbeing (aitiaki) (Carter and Fry, 2023). Indigenous diplomatic principles have also been applied in the negotiation of maritime boundaries between Pacific states, such as Vanuatu and the Solomon Islands (Naupa, 2022).

Another aspect of indigenous diplomacy relates to its contribution to international spaces. Briggs and Graham (2023) propose multipolarity with Aboriginal characteristics based on lateral relations integrally bound by places and histories, and where peoples maintain cross-cutting responsibilities to others, human and non-human. Empirically, this aspect of indigenous diplomacy notes how Indigenous peoples have been "diplomats on the world stage" since they have historically participated in international processes and, in recent decades, they have influenced the creation of UN bodies, such as the UN Permanent Forum on Indigenous Issues, the Special Rapporteur on the Rights of Indigenous Peoples, the Expert Mechanism on the Rights of Indigenous Peoples, the Voluntary Fund for Indigenous Populations, and the Local Communities and Indigenous Peoples Platform (Carpenter and Tsykarev, 2021).

The creation of the UN Permanent Forum in 2000 is considered a milestone in changing international relations based exclusively on state sovereignty (Lindroth, 2006; Tennberg, 2010). This Forum, comprised of eight state-nominated and eight Indigenous-nominated experts, has become an arena for dialogue and alliance-making. However, it primarily provides space for "rhetorical diplomacy," where states and Indigenous Peoples can exchange their views (Carpenter and Tsykarev, 2021). Outside the UN, there are also international experiences of Indigenous peoples' recognition. The Fund for the Development of Indigenous Peoples of Latin America and the Caribbean (FILAC) is an international organization created in 1992 under an agreement signed at the Second Ibero-American Summit. FILAC's supreme organ is the General Assembly, made up of representatives of each of the 22 member states and 18 representatives of Indigenous peoples, one from each of its member states. Decisions are taken by a majority of both member states and indigenous delegates (Jones, 2024). These examples, however, are either soft law in nature (the result of deliberation is not binding) or limited to funding specific development projects. As noted by Jones (2024), the level of indigenous participation is inversely proportional to the power of the body in which Indigenous representatives participate. For Beier (2016) this is exemplified by the fact that Indigenous peoples' delegations to the UN have their seats in the Permanent Forum, not the General Assembly. Therefore, these developments have not substantially challenged decision-making on a global stage.

The key problem is that Indigenous peoples are still excluded from the international distribution of sovereignty and are not fully recognized as nations in the making of international law (Khan, 2019). Although their participation is considered essential, they are not allowed to be represented as "peoples" in most international bodies critical for the realization of indigenous rights (Adeyeye et al., 2019; Belfer et al., 2019) and remain outside deliberative spaces (Zurba and Papadopoulos, 2021; Belfer et al., 2019; Comberti et al., 2019; Garnett et al., 2018). For instance, at the United Nations Framework Convention on Climate Change, indigenous representatives remain on the sidelines of international negotiations and have no role beyond a general consultative position (Khan, 2019). Indigenous peoples can only apply for observer status (Schroeder, 2010) and might be allowed into formal sessions, but are excluded from making interventions other than when specifically invited to do so (Schroeder and Lovell, 2009). They can also hold side events, which are fertile ground for new ideas but have no direct influence on national and global policies. They mostly participate in parallel events that take place outside the official conference venue.

Similarly, the mechanisms of the Convention on Biological Diversity facilitate limited participation through the International Indigenous Forum on Biodiversity as an advisory body (Reimerson, 2013). Although the CBD COP in Cali in 2024 announced for the first time an agreement of the parties to incorporate Indigenous peoples in decision-making, it is still unclear how this would be operationalized in next COPs and, in general, COPs have received much criticism for the inability to reach meaningful agreements to tackle climate change and biodiversity loss.

Authors identify different obstacles to democratizing these spaces, such as the vague recognition of Indigenous peoples as critical actors in environmental governance; a weaker legal standing; a lack of support for their participation by national governments; language barriers; and limited technical and financial capacity in contrast to governments, conservation organizations, and industries (Zurba and Papadopoulos, 2021; Schroeder, 2010). The deepest problem is a depoliticized and rhetorical conception of indigenous self-determination and the preeminence of the classical ideal of state sovereignty in international relations. States have welcomed indigenous self-determination in international governance, whereas, at the same time, they have resisted Indigenous peoples' demands for equal membership in international bodies (Jones, 2024). Rather, for most global institutions, indigenous participation depends on national constituencies. In this view, countries should provide space for Indigenous peoples to be part of national delegations, however, most states do not bring the voice of domestic Indigenous peoples because of continued marginalization and discrimination by the same states (Garnett et al., 2018; Zurba and Papadopoulos, 2021). Besides, indigenous constituencies do not see themselves represented by their national government and do not legitimize them to act on their behalf (Schroeder, 2010). As Carpenter and Tsykarev (2021) argue, many states are only beginning to overcome a historic reluctance to recognize Indigenous Peoples.

5.2.2 The Case of the Arctic Council

The international body that has provided more space for indigenous self-determination is the Arctic Council, an intergovernmental forum that addresses issues faced by the governments and Indigenous peoples of the Arctic.

As with Indigenous peoples in the Amazon, in the Arctic, the Inuit realized early that they needed to address their environmental and cultural concerns beyond national borders (Abele and Rodon, 2007). In 1973, the Inuit overcame geographical and financial obstacles to organize the Arctic Peoples Conference in Copenhagen, which was considered the beginning of modern indigenous internationalism (Abele and Rodon, 2007; Jull, 1999). In 1977, they created the Inuit Circumpolar Council (ICC) to strengthen Inuit unity and promote internationally their rights and interests (Shadian, 2006). They have achieved international recognition and influence on different issues, such as the regulation of chemicals and heavy metals in the Arctic (Tennberg, 2010). In 1992, the Canadian diplomat Walter Slipchenko proposed that in Arctic cross-border settings, Indigenous peoples should be represented as something more than "observers," and introduced the category of "Permanent Participant" to grant participation at all levels of discussion (Wilson, 2018). In December 1996, representatives of the eight Arctic states (Canada; Denmark; Finland; Iceland; Norway; Russia; Sweden; and the United States) and three indigenous organizations as Permanent Participants, the ICC, the Saami Council, and the Russian Arctic Indigenous Peoples of the North (RAIPON), met in Ottawa and signed the Declaration on the Establishment of the Arctic Council. Indigenous permanent participants increased with the inclusion of the Aleut International Association (1998), the Arctic Athabaskan Council (2000), and the Gwich'in Council International (2000) (Wilson, 2018; Shadian, 2017). The Council has also admitted 13 non-Arctic states, 14 inter-governmental institutions, and 13 non-governmental organizations as "observers" between 1996 and 2019 (Knecht, 2020).

The Council is a consensus-based body founded on a political declaration, rather than a legally binding charter. Nonetheless, it has facilitated the making of international binding agreements (Khan, 2019). The six indigenous organizations hold full consultation rights in all aspects of the Council's work (Khan, 2019). Unlike observers, they sit at the negotiating table alongside states and may table proposals. They meet every two years to adopt policy recommendations that emerge from Working Groups and Task Force Meetings (Shadian, 2017). Though indigenous organizations lack full sovereign authority and have no formal voting rights, they exercise extraordinary influence due to the consensus decision-making approach of the Council (Dorough, 2017), holding in practice veto power (Tennberg, 2010; Koivurova and Heinämäki, 2006; Khan, 2019). Scholars argue that the presence of indigenous organizations has been critical in shaping the governance of the Arctic (Wilson, 2021) and constituted a historic shift in international relations by overcoming its traditional state-centric approach (Shadian, 2017; Khan, 2019).

Some scholars, however, problematize the strength of Indigenous peoples in the Council, given their limited participation (Wilson, 2018). Permanent Participants participate more than observers but less than state representatives. Whereas Permanent Participants are always present at ministerial meetings, they participate less in Working Groups (41 % average participation) and task force meetings (34.5 %) (Knecht, 2017). Coote (2016) notes that when Indigenous peoples participate in the Working Groups, they struggle to set the agenda because of capacity limitations. This is important because progress in the Council depends on agenda-setting and evidence-gathering done by the Working Groups. Thus, the eight Arctic states preserve epistemic authority over the Arctic (Knecht, 2020). Wilson (2018) argues that Arctic policies are mostly rooted in the logic of sovereignty and statehood.

In sum, indigenous diplomacies are still diminished by the logic of state sovereignty (Beier, 2016). The challenges for indigenous international political agency are huge, but past and current struggles and their more relevant role in international decision-making suggest that there are real possibilities to change international arrangements for a more plural international governance of critical commons, such as the Amazon.

5.3 ACTO and Indigenous Peoples

In the early 1960s, Amazonian Indigenous peoples created socio-political organizations to give voice to local communities across the basin over issues of territorial loss, human rights abuses, and cultural oppression. The first organizations were the Shuar Federation in Ecuador, the Congress of Amuesha Communities in Peru, and the Regional Indigenous Council of the Cauca in Colombia (Smith, 2003). New indigenous organizations emerged in the 1970s and established alliances with sympathetic Catholic missionaries, human rights organizations, and environmental NGOs (Varese, 2006). On March 14, 1984, indigenous leaders from Ecuador, Bolivia, Colombia, Perú, and Brazil met in Lima for the I Congress of Indigenous Organizations of the Amazonian Basin, as a preparatory meeting before participating in the first Working Group on Indigenous Peoples at the United Nations (Pieck, 2006; Brysk, 2000). In this Congress, the participants created the

Coordinator of Indigenous Organizations of the Amazon Basin (COICA) as a multiethnic and multinational body that articulates all indigenous organizations in the basin (Varese, 2006).

COICA's main body is the Congress, which elects the Directive Council every four years. This Council is formed by the General Coordinator, the Vice-coordinator, and coordinators of seven thematic areas (international relations; territory and natural resources; climate change and biodiversity; gender and family; science and technology; communication and health). Another unit is the Coordination Council, in charge of monitoring the actions executed by the Directive Council and composed of the Presidents of the nine national organizations: COIAB (Brazil), OPIAC (Colombia), CONFENIAE (Ecuador), ORPIA (Venezuela), AIDESEP (Perú), CIDOB (Bolivia), FOAG (Guayana Francesa), APA (Guayana), and OIS (Suriname). COICA is a representative organization. Representation starts with local communities, which elect leaders to represent them in regional federations that are part of national confederations (Nugkuag, 1994). COICA represents 511 Indigenous Peoples across the basin (COICA, n.d.). COICA's purpose is to present a common voice before national governments and the international community on issues of territorial and environmental protection, human rights, and self-determination (Nugkuag, 1994; Varese, 2006).

Nature and creation

ACTO: Intergovernmental organization created in 1998 under the Amazon Cooperation Treaty.

COICA: International indigenous organization created in 1984 in the I Congress of Indigenous Organizations of the Amazonian Basin.

Members

ACTO: Eight Amazonian nation-states, excluding French Guayana.

COICA: National indigenous organizations from all nine Amazonian countries, including French Guayana. These organizations represent over 500 Indigenous Peoples in the basin.

Headquarters

ACTO: Brazilia, Brazil.

COICA: Quito, Ecuador.

Governance

ACTO:

Meeting of Ministers of Foreign Affairs of the Member States (The Meeting). ACTO's supreme body. It elects the General Secretary for three years. It establishes the directives for ACTO work and celebrates biannual summits.

Council of Amazon Cooperation (The Council). Deliberative body integrated by diplomatic representatives of member states. It holds annual meetings and supervises the fulfilment of ACTO goals and decisions.

Coordination Commission of the Amazon Cooperation Council (CCOOR): monitors the planning and budget execution of the organization in quarterly meetings. Formed by high authorities from member countries.

Administrative organization: One Executive Director, Two Administrative Directors, and Seven thematic coordinators (environment, indigenous affairs, health, tourism, infrastructure, science and technology, and transport and infrastructure). Directors and Coordinators are delegates from each member country. They are permanent officials for the period of each administration.
Permanent National Commissions: country teams responsible for implementation of ACTO decisions.

COICA:

COICA Congress: Main body. It elects the Governing Board for four years.
Governing Board: formed by the General Coordinator, the Vice-coordinator, and coordinators of seven thematic areas (international relations; territory and natural resources; climate change and biodiversity; gender and family; science and technology; communication and health).
Coordination Council: monitors the actions executed by the Governing Board. Consists of the Chairs of the nine national organizations:
COIAB (Brazil): Coordinator of the Indigenous Organizations of the Brazilian Amazon.
OPIAC (Colombia): National Organization of the Indigenous Peoples of the Colombian Amazon.
CONFENIAE (Ecuador): Confederation of Indigenous Nationalities of the Ecuadorian Amazon
ORPIA (Venezuela): Regional Organization of the Indigenous Peoples of the Amazon.
AIDESEP (Peru): Interethnic Association for the Development of the Peruvian Rainforest.
CIDOB (Bolivia): Confederation of Indigenous Peoples of Bolivia.
FOAG (French Guiana): Federation of Indigenous Organizations of French Guiana.
APA (Guayana): Amerindian Peoples Association of Guayana.
OIS (Suriname): Indigenous Organizations of Suriname.

Merino, 2025a. Original sources: OTCA (n.d.); COICA (n.d.).

5.3.1 ACTO and COICA Interactions

ACTO and COICA have a long and often unnoticed relationship. Since the mid-80s, COICA not only participated in global forums for indigenous rights, such as UN Work Groups and the meetings toward the enactment of ILO Convention 169 (Fontaine, 2006), but it was also part of the global environmental movement. In 1986, COICA's President, Evaristo Nugkuag, received the Right Livelihood Award, an ecological prize that gave the organization international visibility (Varese, 2006). In 1989, COICA started interactions with the World Bank, the European Community, and global conservation organizations, demanding the recognition of their role in biodiversity conservation (Pieck, 2006; Booth, 1989). In May 1990, in the city of Iquitos, environmental organizations (such as WWF), human rights organizations (OXFAM, Cultural Survival), and COICA created "The Indigenous

Environmentalist Alliance" (Pieck, 2006). COICA was also the founder member of the Climate Alliance of European Cities with Indigenous Rainforest Peoples, along with more than 100 European cities (Smith, 2003; Varese, 2006).

At the regional level, COICA participated in the committees created under the Treaty of Amazonian Cooperation before the creation of ACTO (Varese, 2006; Fontaine, 2006). By 1991, COICA had gained official advisory status with the Indigenous Commission of the Amazon Cooperation Treaty (Varese, 2006). The founder and first President of COICA, Evaristo Nungkuag, narrates his experience in the committees. In the first meeting in Colombia, he was sitting behind the discussion table as an observer. The next day, the organizers gave him 10 minutes to talk. "I said we are indigenous leaders from different countries, we have problems with oil, logging, gold production.... We don't want these problems as if there were no authorities able to solve them; we don't want to appeal to other international instances, but you yourselves must address these issues here under this cooperation treaty. You must make decisions on how to work with us and what you want from us to contribute. We don't want to fight you, we want to discuss diplomatically... We, Amazonian Indigenous peoples, are diplomatic." Nungkuag asserts that after his intervention, COICA started to be officially invited to the commission of indigenous affairs of the Treaty (Interview, Lima, March 5, 2022).

For Nungkuag, "the space within the Treaty of Amazonian Cooperation was already gained." However, the presence of COICA in ACTO did not improve in the following years. Although one of the seven ACTO Coordination Offices is "Indigenous Affairs," these offices are low-level units focused on the everyday implementation of the mandates of the ACTO Secretary and governing bodies. They are not decision-making spaces. Besides, there is no concrete participation of COICA in this office (Figure 5.1).

A former official (Interview, 07.02.2022.) said that in the first years, there was a cooperation agreement between ACTO and COICA, but it was not renewed by the member states. Another official added that the problem was the lack of a unique vision on the type of cooperation member countries wanted with COICA (Interview, ACTO former Director, 23.03.2022). As no legal framework for cooperation exists, ACTO only considers indigenous participation with indirect mechanisms through member states and their national commissions (Interviews, former Director, 23.03.2022; CCOR diplomatic representative, 29.04.2022). The organization of national commissions, however, excludes indigenous participation. In the commissions' statutes, there are no provisions for indigenous representation except for Colombia, in which indigenous communities are "permanently invited" to the meetings. In the rest, no mention exists apart from the participation of state offices in charge of indigenous affairs (ACTO, 2014, National Commission's regulations). However, CCOOR officials and ACTO Directors argued that national governments are responsible for incorporating indigenous demands into national agendas, and only then might they be delivered at ACTO (Interview, Executive Director, 02.03.2022). Only one official (Interview, former coordinator of indigenous issues 12.04.2022) said that there should be an agreement with COICA.

Figure 5.1 Evaristo Nungkuag, 1991. Photo by The Goldman Environmental Prize

As shown in Chapter 2, the cooperation approach of ACTO has meant the proliferation of cooperation projects in which Indigenous peoples are merely conceived as beneficiaries, mostly incorporated in the phase of implementation. This is the case for the two projects exclusively focused on Indigenous Peoples, The Strategic Framework to Develop a Regional Agenda for the Protection of Indigenous Peoples in Voluntary Isolation and Initial Contact, executed between 2011 and 2016, and the Contingency Plans for Health Protection of Highly Vulnerable Indigenous Peoples in Initial Contact, currently in execution. As "stakeholders" and "key informants," Indigenous peoples are invited to workshops to provide information and help in formulating and implementing the projects. They are not conceived as political actors or decision-makers in the phases of planning or design of ACTO interventions.

This approach has been formalized in different ACTO documents. The Strategic Action Plan (AECA, 2010–2018) mentions Indigenous peoples as providers of information so their inputs can facilitate the "exchange of experiences" of country members. In all minutes from the meetings of the different ACTO units, Indigenous peoples are subjects of protection, not political actors. This results in a patronizing approach: "Indigenous populations are an essential element of Amazonia, a source of knowledge and habits that are the basis of culture and local economy, and therefore, they deserve particular attention in the current and future planning of the Amazonian region of each country" (XI Meeting of Ministers of Foreign Affairs, ACTO, 2013). This is an instrumental and paternalistic view of Indigenous peoples as part of the Amazonian landscape.

The announcement of the creation of the Amazonian Regional Platform of Indigenous Peoples and Climate Change at the World Congress of Nature in 2021 (ACTO, 2021) promised a more participative approach. This Platform was proposed as an institutional space to collect and diffuse Indigenous peoples' practices of forest conservation. Another initiative is the Framework Agreement of Cooperation between FILAC and ACTO in October 2020 for six years. The aim is to develop joint actions to promote indigenous rights (ACTO, 2020). The former General Coordinator of COICA, Gregorio Mirabal, said that COICA would monitor this agreement and highlight that it must be executed with the active participation of Indigenous peoples (ACTO, 2020).

However, these indigenous-oriented projects still conceive Indigenous peoples as low-level participants and not as decision-makers. These projects are not ACTO initiatives but derive from the international commitments with the United Nations framework in the fight against climate change (Interview with ACTO Coordinator on indigenous issues, 12.04.2022). Moreover, these projects have not been implemented. During fieldwork in the organization in 2022, no advance was noticed on the proposal of a Regional Platform of Indigenous Peoples and, rather, the only working project was the Regional Amazonian Observatory.

5.3.2 Indigenizing ACTO

Fany Kuiru, the first woman appointed General Coordinator of COICA, participated in the World Economic Forum in Davos in January 2024. In this forum, she emphasized the need to ensure that Indigenous peoples are given a place at the table of international negotiations. During a session, she stressed that Indigenous peoples must have "full and effective participation in decision-making regarding policies affecting the Amazon" (WEF, 2024).

This impetus is shared by indigenous leaders and former COICA officials. They all coincided in having a protagonistic role in ACTO governance. This means that ACTO "should be an instance of representation between Indigenous peoples and states…and COICA should have a voice in ACTO decision-making units" (Interview with a former COICA assessor, 22.04.22). COICA, in this view, should be "a member [of ACTO] but ensuring proper representation of regional leaders" (Interview with a former COICA leader, 21.03.22.). Similarly, a former COICA Coordinator of international relations (Interview, 31.03.22) said, "The role of ACTO could be to facilitate the dialogue directly with the … delegations of each country to reach agreements on issues crucial for the Amazon basin." For a former COICA planning official (Interview, 09.05.2022), it is a necessity that ACTO includes the vision of Indigenous peoples, "How we can talk about cooperation if we have sectors excluded from the conversation?… We suffer the problems, then we should be involved in the solutions… we should be part of an inclusive, effective, and efficient mode in ACTO decisions to improve its activities."

This interest is limited not only by current institutional arrangements at ACTO but also by dominant epistemic and ontological frames that exclude indigenous self-determination. Many ACTO officials believe that Indigenous peoples are not supposed to have a specific role in ACTO governance beyond observership in a future scenario (Interview with CCOOR official, 29.04.2022). Most officials are skeptical about the possibility of having Indigenous peoples at the table of international negotiations. Officials make a parallel with the rejection of the proposals to have France as an observer in the organization (Interview, former ACTO General Secretary, 18.03.2022.): "With this antecedent, just imagine if it is possible to give a seat to indigenous organizations in processes of deliberation." (Interview, 14.03.2022).

It is beyond the scope of this book to discuss the representation of the people from French Guyana in the governance of the Amazon. Nonetheless, we must note that these people share with Indigenous peoples a kind of exclusion embedded in colonization. The key argument to deny Indigenous peoples' actual participation in ACTO governance is that they are not nation-states and cannot have the same prerogatives as sovereign nations (Interview with Council member, 28.04.2022).

Some officials are more optimistic and argue that in the future Indigenous peoples could participate as observers and give opinions (Interview with former ACTO coordinator, 03.03.2022) and even it could be discussed if they can be incorporated into some units (Interview, 14.03.2022). For one official, this should be a space to be heard but with no prerogatives for voting (Interview, 12.04.2022.). One official from the Council (Interview, 29.04.2022) said that their role shouldn't be just observership, but participative, deliberative. Current statutes of the CCOOR and the Council do allow observers from international organizations and non-governmental organizations, but this has never been applied to COICA or another indigenous organization. The statute of the Meeting of Foreign Affairs Ministers only allows observership for international organizations.

Could this scenario change with the Declaration of Belém enacted in 2023 by ACTO state members? This Declaration establishes, as a principle of international cooperation in the Amazon, "the active participation and respect and promotion of the rights of Indigenous peoples." Article 6 of the Declaration also created the "Amazonian Mechanism of Indigenous Peoples" with the aim "to fortify and promote the dialogue between the governments and Amazonian Indigenous peoples on the management and coordination of issues that concern Indigenous Peoples and contribute to ACTO objectives." Whereas this Mechanism is an indicator of some space to push for the international participation of Indigenous peoples in governing the Amazon, it appears to be integrated outside the governing bodies of the organization. If this is the case, it will only be a complement to current coordination offices, or even worse, it could operate as a specific project with no direct influence on ACTO governance. In this way, this Mechanism would only serve to show the apparent commitments of ACTO members to indigenous rights rather than being an opportunity for substantial institutional reform. Nevertheless, Indigenous peoples continue struggling to reform international institutions and reframe sovereign imaginaries to democratize decision-making on the governance of the Amazon.

5.4 Reimagining Amazonian Governance

The previous analysis shows that those communities that suffer the greatest social and environmental impacts in the Amazon currently have no voice in the international governance of the basin. In ACTO units, indigenous demands have been conceived as problems of minority groups to be solved by anti-poverty and development interventions, and not with mechanisms to enhance international political recognition and meaningful participation. The ACTO thus has reproduced the limitations of indigenous participation in international stages (Zurba and Papadopoulos, 2021; Belfer et al., 2019; Comberti et al., 2019; Garnett et al., 2018). First, they were observers at the seminal committees previous to ACTO's creation. Then, with the creation of ACTO, they were supposed to be only indirectly involved through national commissions. This state-centric approach has foreclosed a dialogue between Amazonian states and Indigenous peoples.

The exclusionary and weak nature of ACTO has not avoided the interest of COICA in enlarging the prospects of indigenous diplomacy (Beier, 2016; Briggs and Graham, 2023). Their quest for having more influence in Amazonian affairs and being involved in ACTO initiatives and units explain the recent openness of Amazonian governments to create an Indigenous Mechanism of dialogue within the organization (Declaration of Belém, 2023). However, allowing meaningful international participation of Indigenous peoples has different challenges.

A key problem is that nation-states still rely on a colonial concept of sovereignty that disregards Indigenous peoples as international actors with the foundational right of self-determination. In this regard, the creation of the "Indigenous Mechanism" as a platform within ACTO might be promising, but it does not tackle the colonial nature of international relations based on Westphalian sovereignty. Rather, relying on recognition gestures of Indigenous peoples at the international level might reinforce the innate authority of sovereign power expressed through the state form (Beier, 2016). For Reynolds (2023), this kind of limited recognition is embedded in ossified and racialized international power structures (Brigg and Graham, 2023). If Indigenous peoples are not recognized as peoples or nations, therefore with international political agency in deliberative instances, their participation in regional spaces will be very limited.

Another challenge is that the different cosmological standpoint of indigenous politics is not easily adapted to international epistemic and ontological frameworks (Beier, 2016). As Picq (2017) explains, indigenous politics offer radically different insights into the international because they engage forms of governance articulated outside, and to a large extent before, the modern state. In this regard, Roberto Espinoza, former COICA assessor (Interview, 26.04.2022), explains that the key obstacle to a dialogue between ACTO – COICA is that COICA is autonomous, whereas ACTO depends on the conditions imposed by states dependent on extractive economies. This produces ontological tensions. Nation-states' sovereignty is founded on the absolute dominium of the natural environment within their national frontiers, whereas Indigenous nations portray a kind of sovereignty that coexists with different natural environments, problematizing state territorial projects. Rather than obscuring these differences, the international governance of the Amazon requires embracing these differences in a democratic platform. This would require decolonizing ACTO structures to make space for both indigenous self-determination and state sovereignty at the international level.

A critical point is the institutional capacities of indigenous organizations in international spaces, as has been discussed in the case of the Arctic Council (Knecht, 2017; Coote, 2016; Wilson, 2021). Indeed, COICA has faced problems of cultural differences and linguistic diversity, periods of institutional divisions, precariousness, corruption allegations, and deep reliance on international cooperation (SERVINDI, 2005; Pieck and Moog, 2009). It has also been criticized for having weak representative channels between the community-based units, the regional and national federations, and the central administrative body (Varese, 2006) and for a tendency of autocratic leadership in the central administration (Smith, 2003). Recently, the organization suffered internal conflicts regarding the reelection of the General Coordinator (the members' organizations finally elected Fany Kuiru, from the Colombian Amazon, as the first indigenous woman who led COICA). Despite these problems, COICA has achieved international recognition and reputation. All the informants from global NGOs agree that COICA has been successful in diffusing indigenous demands in international forums and organizations.

A more solid indigenous movement and the acknowledgment of the fairness and importance of its international representation are the premises for decolonizing the international governance of the Amazon. This would result in enacting an international plurinational governance that enlarges the list of legitimate diplomats at the regional stage, including indigenous representatives. COICA would be the natural representative of the Indigenous peoples of the Amazon. In this model, Indigenous peoples are not considered mere beneficiaries of development interventions but sovereign partners in their own right. Therefore, the Meeting of Foreign Affairs Ministers would have to include the COICA President as the indigenous Chancellor representing Indigenous peoples from the nine Amazonian countries. COICA would also have permanent representatives at the other governing bodies of the organization (the Council and CCOOR, see Chapter 2).

To democratize the governance of the Amazon, the idea that only national governments are the legitimate representatives of indigenous interests must be replaced by the respect of self-determination as a collective human right binding both national governments and international organizations. Including Indigenous nations in Amazonian governance might lead, in turn, to putting a voice at the table of negotiation that strongly advocates for harmonizing social and environmental regulations, as Indigenous communities across the region suffer from similar issues and have similar demands. This kind of governance, then, would allow the re-foundation of the ACTO beyond the mere collaboration among countries. It should become a space where democratic processes that include Indigenous nations lead to environmental and socially binding standards to be applied across the region.

5.5 Conclusion

This chapter has developed a theoretical and empirical contribution to the analysis of indigenous diplomacy and indigenous self-determination at international venues by exploring the interactions between ACTO and COICA in the governance of the Amazon. In the early involvement of COICA with the committees of the Treaty of Amazonian Cooperation, Indigenous peoples were treated as mere "observers." With the creation of ACTO, their concerns were approached with top-down developmental interventions and were supposed to be indirectly represented by national commissions. These developments confirm the limitations identified in the literature on indigenous participation in international law and policymaking.

Despite ACTO's political weaknesses and the different institutional challenges to reinforce COICA, COICA leaders imagine another type of international governance for the Amazon. They think that ACTO should be a space where Indigenous peoples' representatives and nation-state officials should negotiate the best standards and policies for the region. Some ACTO officials are also more open to indigenous diplomacy and meaningful participation in regional affairs beyond the mere status of observership. The recent enactment of the Declaration of Belém opens the opportunity to struggle for meaningful international involvement of Indigenous peoples by highlighting the relevance of their international participation and creating an "Indigenous Mechanism" within the organization as an instance for dialogue between states and Indigenous peoples. However, this mechanism is located outside the deliberative bodies of the organization, and most international officials still conceive Indigenous self-determination as a limited prerogative that cannot give them a political voice at the negotiation table with nation-states.

ACTO and the international governance of the Amazon are still embedded in a state-centric and classical sovereign imaginary in which Indigenous peoples are not internationally recognized as nations with political rights. Meaningful international participation of Indigenous peoples requires decolonizing both the limited conception of Indigenous self-determination that conceives it as a prerogative of nation-states and the Westphalian imaginary of state sovereignty that excludes the political agency of non-state actors in the international arena.

This paradigmatic change should lead to decolonizing and democratizing ACTO and enacting a plurinational governance for the Amazon. In this governance, Indigenous nations through COICA would be represented in the deliberative instances of the organization. The democratization of Amazon's international governance would also be an opportunity to push for substantial reforms aimed at enacting international environmental and social standards for the region.

CHAPTER 6

Envisioning a Pluriversal Environmental Governance

Scientific and Indigenous Ontologies in the Amazon

6.1 Introduction

In 2019, an executive director of Andes Amazon Fund, a philanthropic organization in Washington, DC, convened a group of researchers and technology developers in the Amazonian department of Madre de Dios, Peru. His idea was to convert the deep forest into a smart forest that could detect intruders and relay alerts to government authorities and local Indigenous communities. The scientists focused on devices such as microphones and camera systems equipped with artificial intelligence, as well as data from drones and satellites that could be deployed remotely. For the next few years, Indigenous groups have been training to use these devices to patrol their lands and waterways. One of the beneficiaries is the Amarakaeri Communal Reserve, whose Indigenous patrols use smartphones and GPS software to get deforestation alerts (Tollefson, 2022).

Pressures on the forest, however, have continued with the increase of illegal incursions by outsiders and also illegal mining and coca cultivation by some young indigenous groups (Tollefson, 2022). In April 2024, Victorio Dariquebe, leader and wise of the Harakbut People in Madre de Dios and park ranger of the Amarakaeri reserve, was killed allegedly by illegal miners (Santos, 2024). Dariquebe was defending the territory and livelihoods of his people despite the threats from illegal mining and drug trafficking. Although the Indigenous leader had been moved to another ranger post because of these threats, this could not prevent him from being killed when returning to his community (IUCN, 2024).

Satellite monitoring has been crucial to providing valuable data about deforestation trends and justifying the creation of national parks, the implementation of titling projects on indigenous land, and the enactment of coercive mechanisms against illegal groups. However, technological tools are implemented through specific programs that do not challenge the structural drivers of deforestation related to the permanence of extractive – legal and illegal – economies and the endless cycles of extractive endeavors. Moreover, the "technological turn" in conservation has also been blamed for deploying surveilling mechanisms affecting the rights of privacy and data sovereignty of Indigenous peoples while justifying state actions aligned with green colonialism ideals. By generally focusing on quantitative data on large extensions of land, these technologies often neglect local dynamics, justifying discourses that blame small agriculture and local practices for being the main threats to conservation instead of agribusiness, industrial mining, and infrastructure.

These developments raise questions about the relationship between conservation science and Indigenous peoples in the protection and management of the Amazon rainforest. Rather than being one of complementarity, this relationship seems to be predatory. Indigenous peoples are either trainees and users of technological devices or threats that might be addressed by these devices. In this context, Indigenous peoples are discursively portrayed as forest protectors, whereas scientists retain the authority and substantial power to channel their concerns about the forests in national and international spaces. This configures a problem of representation: who are the legitimate political representatives of the natural world? How might scientists and Indigenous peoples represent this world in international governance?

This chapter discusses in what ways international environmental governance might incorporate different ontological standpoints about the protection and management of nature advanced by Indigenous peoples and conservation scientists. Whereas most governance models note that participation of non-state actors in global or regional climate forums, including Indigenous peoples, might shape global environmental politics (Dryzek and Pickering, 2019; Campbell et al., 2014; Corson et al., 2014; Corson et al., 2019), this participation is limited to the epistemological and pre-political level. Indigenous peoples would enrich dialogue in a global public sphere (Bäckstrand, 2006) and would share their ecological knowledge as external providers of information outside decision-making spaces. Some approaches argue that Indigenous ontologies problematize governance structures and call for a pluriversal governance (Querejazu and Tickner, 2020; Torres and Verschoor, 2020), but have not reflected on how the political space must be transformed to contain different ontologies. Normative models based on ecological democracy (Disch, 2016; Dryzek, 2000; Eckersley, 2004) and post-humanism scholarship (Latour, 2017) propose transforming the political space to politically represent non-human beings and address the climate emergency, but Indigenous ontologies are often excluded from these frameworks. These approaches tend to conceive scientists as the legitimate representatives of the interests of the natural world.

This chapter engages with these discussions to problematize how ontological differences are incorporated or excluded in the international environmental governance of the Amazon. It examines the interactions between Indigenous peoples and scientific communities, particularly the Science Panel for the Amazon (SPA), the first scientific organization focused on the Amazon rainforest. It also delves into the prospects of institutionalizing these interactions at the Amazonian Cooperation Treaty

Organization (ACTO). After years of little institutional development and limited participation of scientists and Indigenous peoples, the eight ACTO states approved the Declaration of Belém in 2023. The Declaration announced the creation of the "Intergovernmental Scientific Technical Panel" to be composed of scientists delegated by each member state, aimed at promoting sustainable development and the "exchange of knowledge" with the participation of Indigenous peoples. This chapter examines how this platform might accommodate or exclude ontological differences.

The chapter also provides a comparative analysis of the SPA procedures and reports with the main international scientific platforms dedicated to the environment: the Intergovernmental Panel on Climate Change (IPCC) and the Intergovernmental Science-Policy Platform on Biodiversity and Ecosystem Services (IPBES). The chapter found that Indigenous participation in these panels is not about a "dialogue of knowledges." They participate in "confirming" the systematization of scientific knowledge elaborated by academics embedded in Western universalist ontology. Scientists' claims of being apolitical and neutral experts imply the enactment of a one-world reality that excludes Indigenous plural ontologies. As a result, the outcomes of this process, the assessments or reports, focus on describing the drivers of climate change and biodiversity degradation, predictions if no actions are taken, and the targets to avoid the catastrophe. However, the definition of the concrete means to achieve those targets is left to the political sphere. This is because scientists conceive these panels as pre-political sites to collect, systematize, and diffuse scientific knowledge. Rather, for Indigenous peoples, these are political spaces. From their perspective, these are not sites for symbolic knowledge exchange on the one-world reality; these are spaces for political exchanges on which Indigenous peoples seek to enact their political ontology and the proper ways to protect their world.

Based on these findings, the chapter proposes reimagining scientist platforms and international decision-making forums as spaces for pluriversal governance (see Chapter 1). Scientist platforms must be deliberative spaces in which Indigenous peoples can enact their political ontologies by articulating their views on how to protect their world. This would mean that their concrete proposals should be reflected in specific policy recommendations. More ambitiously, international decision-making forums should be a pluriversal space, in which nation-states, scientists, and Indigenous peoples would share the political stage to negotiate their different worldviews and the authority to represent their own natural worlds. This might trigger ontological clashes, but also the possibility of creating ontological coalitions around the protection of nature and the appropriate means to deal with the climate crisis.

6.2 Nature as a Subject of Rights and as a Political Subject

The "ecocentric turn" in legal theory and practice, expressed in the trend to recognize rights to nature, also supports the idea that Indigenous peoples can be the legitimate representatives of the natural world. This "fastest-growing legal movement of the twenty-first century," as stated by UN Secretary General Antonio Guterres, influenced the incorporation of the rights of nature in a diverse group of legal devices, from municipal ordinances to legislation and constitutional reforms (O'Donnell et al., 2020; Sachs, 2023). In the past decade, over fifty municipalities in the United States enacted ordinances recognizing that nature has the right to "exist" and "flourish," more than a dozen nations have enacted similar legislation, and landmark rulings have granted rights to rivers and other ecosystems. Some advocates argue that this ecocentric approach should replace existing environmental law (Sachs, 2023) since the recognition of the rights of nature is crucial to deal with the complexity of the socio-ecological crisis (Alves et al., 2023).

For many authors, this turn institutionalized the theory of Earth Jurisprudence by Thomas Berry, whose rationale is rooted in the Deep Ecology philosophy in which all living beings have a moral and ethical claim regardless of their utility to humanity (Giacomini, 2022; Alves et al., 2023; O'Donnell et al., 2020). Under this framework, Cormac Cullinan advocated for legal reforms that reflect human dependence on Earth and translate nature's natural laws into human laws. These efforts would have been crystallized in early local ordinances in the United States since the 2000s, constitutional norms in Ecuador in 2008, and national legislation in Bolivia since 2010 that grant rights to whole ecosystems (see Chapter 1). Implementation, however, has been challenging. For some authors, elaborated provisions in the Ecuadorian constitution have not achieved a great difference in environmental outcomes, and judicial rulings based on these provisions have been minimal (Kotzé and Villavicencio, 2017; O'Donnell et al., 2020). In the US, the Courts have consistently declared local ordinances incompatible with state and federal laws responsible for approving development projects (O'Donnell et al., 2020; Sachs, 2023). For Sachs (2023), the ecocentric turn is simply a wrong turn. Because they are nebulous and undefined, the rights of nature create uncertainty about the scope of rights, how judges implement them, and what human activities are prohibited. In this view, this approach would also be ill-equipped to perform essential tasks for environmental protection, such as rulemaking, standard-setting, inspections, investigations, and enforcement. Besides, given its constant judicialization, this movement would lead to the weaponization of these rights by some human organizations, namely, indiscriminate lawsuits against economic activities that modify nature in some way, including farming, fishing, and construction.

Since 2016, these limitations have been addressed with a new strategy aimed at recognizing rivers as legal persons through legislation in New Zealand and the judiciary in India, Colombia, and Bangladesh. The granting of rights has been accompanied by new institutional arrangements, such as the appointment of guardians to act on behalf of the rivers (O'Donnell et al., 2020). For instance, in Colombia, the Constitutional Court on "The Atrato River ruling" in 2016 addressed illegal large-scale mining activities impacting the river and created a guardianship scheme under the lead of local communities (Sierra, 2019). In New Zealand, as a result of Treaty settlement negotiations between the Government and Māori tribal groups, the Parliament enacted the Te Awa Tupua Act in 2017, recognizing the Whanganui River as a subject of rights. This legislation created the Te Pou Tupua office with officials appointed by the government and the Māori, with the task of protecting and promoting the physical and spiritual health of the River (Bosselmann and Williams, 2025). In the United States, since 2017, Indigenous peoples started using strategically "rights of nature" laws to empower tribal authorities to be at the same the custodians of ecosystems and the promoters of a more pluralistic and ontologically diverse interpretation of environmental laws (O'Donnell et al., 2020).

This perspective would be less related to Earth Jurisprudence and closer to Indigenous perspectives and arrangements (O'Donnell et al., 2020; de Salles et al., 2023). Indeed, for some authors, indigenous traditions and jurisprudence have long provided the framework for legalizing the rights of nature (Stilt, 2020) since they would defend the idea that nature has to be considered a living subject that must be protected regardless of human needs (Borras, 2016; Guzmán, 2019). In this view, ecocentric laws and rulings codify Indigenous worldviews in legal terms (Kauffman and Martin, 2021; Cano, 2018) and validate non-Western ontologies (Guzmán, 2019). This conceptual development would potentially ensure both the protection of environmentally and culturally significant natural elements and indigenous rights (Guzmán, 2019). For others, the rights of Nature operate as a cultural bridge that uses Western legal terminology to express Indigenous cultural references, enabling a fruitful hybridization of modernity-based rights language and Indigenous beliefs (Knauβ, 2018), or in the context of New Zealand, it constitutes a bridge between worlds (Geddis and Ruru, 2019; Petel, 2024). In this view, the rights of nature would not have happened or would have been much less effective without the leadership of Indigenous peoples (O'Donnell et al., 2020; de Salles et al., 2023).

There are many concerns about the tendency to assert a universal alignment between the rights of nature and indigenous interests. This trend might represent indigeneity as a singular, unchanging reality, contributing to essentializing indigenous identities (Petel, 2024; Rawson and Mansfield, 2018; Boelens et al., 2024; Viaene, 2022). For instance, the ethnographic work of Viaene (2022) in Guatemala, Peru, Ecuador, and Colombia questions whether the rights of nature have indigenous origins. This explains why the indigenous movements in Ecuador were initially skeptical of including the rights of nature in the constitution and accepted this innovation insofar as it could be used to advance their political agenda (Rzedzian, 2023). Coombes (2020) explains similar reactions in the Whanganui River case in New Zealand, where the Maori people were surprised that their claims were translated into rights of nature, diverting attention from a long history of activism to recover ancestral lands. Scholars explain how the ecocentric approach may compromise everyday local livelihoods and reinforce exclusionary dynamics through the imposition of environmental policies over disenfranchised communities (Boelens et al., 2024; Petel, 2024). For instance, rights of nature institutions such as guardianship reproduce wilderness images that compel Indigenous peoples to adopt specific economic practices aimed at preserving the perceived "integrity" and "pristine" state of ecosystems, disrespecting the autonomy and adaptive capacity of Indigenous communities (Petel, 2024). There are also examples of green colonialism. In 2015, the Ecuadorian government evicted 40 Afro-descendant families from their Isla Trinitaria riverine territory, arguing that their houses occupied the El Salado Mangroves Fauna Production Reserve area. Together, government and private actors interested in building "nature-friendly" golf courses and related eco-business exploitation deployed the rights of nature discourse to legitimize the eviction (Boelens et al., 2024). For Tanasescu (2015), far from being an indigenous creation, these rights have the potential to contravene indigenous practices.

For some (Rawson and Mansfield, 2018), the problem is that the transnational lobbying network of rights of nature is dominated by Global North elites who utilize Western ideas and jurisprudence to promote nature's rights as an indigenous and organic alternative to Western development. This would be an elite proposition in search of a grassroots (Tănăsescu, 2022) that facilitates the appropriation of nature rights by state offices and NGOs and the reproduction of colonial patterns (Petel, 2024). Another problem is the neglect of the underlying political-economic factors that compel certain communities to support extractive industries because of a lack of viable alternative economic opportunities (Petel, 2024). For instance, in the Atrato case, rights of nature and guardianship schemes are limited by ongoing insecurity derived from illegal mining, the lack of financial resources to support community guardians, and structural poverty in the Choco department (Petel, 2024).

These limitations suggest that the key problem is the obscuring of the political struggles around the enactment and implementation of rights of nature. For Pottage (2024), nature rights arrangements do not solve contradictions over the control of resources but project the tensions forward in a form of "hypothecation." For instance, with the world celebrated (and failed) Yasuní-ITT project, the Ecuadorian government sought to leave oil below the Amazon rainforest in exchange for international financing for conservation. Nature acquired a multiple existence in this project: it was the raw resource lying under the national park, with a market value that could be realized as soon as the project failed; the stranded asset which was pledged to the global economy of carbon trading by the Yasuní Guaranty Certificate; and the ecology of indigenous communities. In this context, the constitutional recognition of nature rights obfuscated and deferred the tensions between different modes of appropriation and production. These tensions are solved by a process of "ventriloquization" and "epistemic extractivism" that translates the knowledge of Indigenous peoples into a corroboration of Western assumptions and goals (Pottage, 2024).

Acknowledging the plurality of politics of the rights of nature would involve examining movements that contain different environmentalisms and counter-hegemonies, as in the case of Ecuador, with grassroots firmly positioned against the state and some international activists praising the Ecuadorian state for its ecocentric legal innovations (Rzedzian, 2023). Addressing this complexity would also require "de-centering" the debate to avoid reincorporating human–nature modern dualism in the form of anthropocentrism–ecocentrism (De Lucia, 2017; Giacomini, 2022; Rzedzian, 2023). For some authors (De Lucia, 2017), this requires a biopolitical reading against the imaginary progression from anthropocentrism to ecocentrism and rather a focus on dispositifs of protection and control, conservation, and subjugation used in these narratives. For others (Giacomini, 2022), this is an opportunity to formulate a decolonized version of the rights of nature based on Indigenous philosophies that would be a middle position, not anthropocentric nor ecocentric.

However, rather than seeking a synthesis or middle position and obscuring power relations between human communities (Petel, 2024), it would be important to recognize and embrace the differences and conflicts. In reality, the rights of nature reveal political struggles, confrontations, and negotiations that mark the encounter between Indigenous and Western cosmologies (Boelens et al., 2024). For this reason, the most useful frame for understanding the rights of nature is political, not legal (Tănăsescu, 2022). This relates to political definitions about who has the power to represent nature and how to create new relations through which environmental concerns may be differently expressed.

6.2.1 Indigenous and Scientists' Ontologies in Pluriversal Governance

Whereas in the legal arena, Indigenous peoples are often portrayed as the most adequate representatives of the natural world, in the political sphere, this task is often assigned to scientific communities. The legal arena also restricts nature representation to judicial actions and managerial tasks related to biodiversity conservation (through guardianship schemes), whereas political debates refer to how to reform political systems to incorporate nature as a political actor. These political debates are crucial to rethinking international environmental governance as a pluriversal governance space.

Green deliberative theorists criticize current democratic systems for displacing concerns over ecosystems by not considering harms to nature that do not directly affect human interests. They also criticize how these systems rely on electoral cycles that sacrifice long-term environmental quality for short-term political and economic gains (Eckersley, 2004; Brown, 2018). Beyond environmental agencies that might be seen as authorized by the electorate to protect nonhuman interests, these theorists have proposed the representation of nature in the political arena. In this venue, different actors could adopt the role of nature's trustees, such as experts, activists, or indigenous organizations (Eckersley, 2004; Dryzek, 2000), but most scholars privilege the authority of scientific communities.

Green deliberative proposals have empirical and theoretical challenges. First, conceiving scientists or others as formally authorized representatives of nonhuman nature doesn't eliminate political conflict. The representative's actions might be disputed by other scientists, Indigenous peoples, or activists, who might also argue to have the legitimacy to represent nature (Brown, 2018). Second, as representation is not a matter of dialogue between representatives and constituents, it might reinforce a romantic view of nature and an authoritarian form of representation by those with scientific expertise, local knowledge, or another epistemic resource (Brown, 2018). Third, scientific knowledge might claim objectivity but it is infused by power relationships, which would make nature's representation impossible: if scientists are always infused by different political paradigms, we cannot speak for nature, we can only speak about the nature we humans have discoursively created (Vogel in Eckersley, 2004).

Latour's Politics of Nature (2017) seeks to address these challenges by including different nature representatives in the political space. For Latour, the failure of climate conferences and, more generally, the environmental crisis, responds to deficient political representation (Whiteside, 2013). In this context, nation-states can no longer have the stage to themselves, while scientists, NGOs, and lobbies remain outside, trying to make their voices heard. Unlike green deliberative democrats, for Latour, nature must be represented by a disaggregation of agents with different views and agendas, not by one designated representative. In this new political space, the representatives of human communities would debate on equal terms with those of the other beings that inhabit the planet (De Blic, 2020).

Latour's proposal has been criticized for its dubious empirical viability. Whereas he suggested a classic bicameral Parliament with representatives of humans and those non-human beings able to coexist (De Blic, 2020), it is difficult to imagine rules for the election of too diverse representatives, rules of accountability, and so forth (Whiteside, 2013). For others, Latour's proposal merely seeks to extend Habermas's deliberative democracy, but expanding representation provides no way of creating overarching norms capable of resolving environmental disputes (Whiteside, 2013; Disch, 2016). Decolonial approaches criticized Latour for tending to see the foundational ontological split between nature and culture as universal, rather than critiquing modernity's dogmas and the role of colonialism in their construction (Sundberg, 2014; Mignolo and Tlostanova, 2006). Finally, Ephraim (2018) notes that Latour's late proposals shifted from describing the origins of scientists' agentive positions within actor-networks to prescribing their authority as a new norm for posthumanist politics. In his book *Politics of Nature*, Latour mostly reserves for scientist communities the role of "spokespersons of the nonhumans" (Ephraim, 2018). Latour treats the fact that scientists are already recognizable as qualified to speak for nature as an argument in favor of enshrining this authority as a constitutional right. However, he does not discuss how particular qualifications became recognizable as marks of authority and instead naturalizes this authority, rendering its political origins and sources invisible.

The activist environmental movement that originated in the United Kingdom, Extinction Rebellion (XR), also engages in debates about ecological democracy. XR proposes a different model, "beyond politics," aimed at reinventing democracy and establishing a People's Assembly to address climate change (Berglund and Schmidt, 2020). In this nation-level proposal, assembly members are to be chosen through sortition by lot as a trial jury, in which every eligible citizen has an equal probability of being selected to participate. Extinction Rebellion proposes stratified random sampling based on gender, age, ethnicity, education level, and geography. Unlike jury service, participation would be voluntary, so assembly members are more likely to be motivated in the proceedings (Berglund and Schmidt, 2020). Extinction Rebellion proposes phases of learning, consultation, and deliberation before decision-making. In the first stages, assembly members would receive information from scientists and stakeholders. Then, with this information, they would make informed decisions to address environmental challenges.

This proposal has been criticized for just being an addition to the representative system, drawing on the liberal tradition. "Beyond politics" does not mean transforming the political sphere but is an exception to politics as usual (Berglund and Schmidt, 2020). Moreover, XR may also be overly optimistic in their expectations of the assembly results. A majority of the population might support technocratic authoritarianism with solutions involving unequal adaptation rather than mitigation and a focus on controlling populations rather than controlling production and consumption, namely, neo-Malthusian or ecofascist ideas (Berglund and Schmidt, 2020). In general, XR's proposals seem contradictory as the targets they demand regarding carbon neutrality and emissions reductions are set by the movement itself and not by a larger democratic debate (Berglund and Schmidt, 2020).

In the model of green deliberative democracy, scientists represent the interests of the natural world in national and international governance structures. In Latour's model of global parliament, scientists represent different non-human beings that co-exist with nation-states. In XR's people's assembly, scientists are outside governance structures, but they provide crucial information to a reformed deliberative space to address the climate crisis. In these models, scientists are depoliticized because they are the undisputable representatives of nature who speak an absolute truth from the inside or outside of the political fora. In addition, they reduce political ecology to a problem of different political and epistemological representations of the "one world," disregarding the different ontologies and worlding practices in which different actors engage. By conceiving "one natural world" to be represented and scientists as the most legitimate groups to represent such a world, these frameworks exclude the political ontology of Indigenous peoples.

This double depoliticization is problematic. First of all, scientists also participate in the politics of world-building. They perform embodied practices and create relationships and imaginations to build their own authority. In this way, they enable some agents to speak for others (Ephraim, 2018). Scientists use different world-building strategies. The conventional one is knowledge diffusion. The strength of this strategy is the scientific consensus over specific climate issues and the institutionalization of international advisory bodies, such as the IPCC and IPBES. In this way, scientists are expected to provide information to those actors that hold the legitimacy to perform politics (Castree, 2019). The limitations in convincing others would be overcome by involving more social scientists and "stakeholders" (such as

Indigenous peoples) in scientific assessments (Dryzek and Pickering, 2019; Castree, 2019). Another venue is responsible advocacy through lobbying, petitioning, media interventions, and demonstrations (Recio, 2022). For instance, more than 11,000 scientists declared in a 2020 letter that planet Earth is facing a climate emergency (Ripple et al., 2020). Around two-fifths of IPCC authors have signed petitions calling for action, and a quarter report having participated in demonstrations (Capstick et al., 2022). In recent years, scientists have also engaged in civil disobedience. This entails resisting the law authority with non-violent actions, such as blocking a road or occupying a building, being subjected to arrest by public forces, such as the actions of "Scientist Rebellion" (Gardner and Wordley, 2019; Thackeray et al., 2020). There are also more radical paths deploying insurgent actions under eco-extremist tendencies (Sovacool and Dunlap, 2022).

For Ephraim (2018), being open about the politics of world-building is important to resist climate deniers. This is the case because deniers not only attack science but, more substantially, they attack world-building practices advanced by scientists. If these practices are limited to the technical arena and the mere provision of information, they are more vulnerable to being obscured, appropriated, and deformed. Ephraim (2018) argues that the reality of climate change must be not merely believed but lived, breathed, and acutely felt by the people in their everyday lives. This entails making science more, not less, political to make the reality of the climate emergency into the way of the world.

Therefore, acknowledging and advancing scientists' politics helps in pluralizing the epistemic sphere. This means building the reality of climate change beyond laboratories and scientific assessments. However, it is also crucial to extend the political arena toward ontological questions. The world scientists build, mostly a natural world, is not the only one under attack by the climate emergency and the climate deniers. Indigenous worlds that intersect natural, socio-political, cultural, and spiritual relationships, are on the verge of extinction. International environmental governance should be able to contain these different ontologies, which might be in tension, articulation, or even opposition.

6.2.2 Incommensurable Worlds or Ontological Coalitions in Environmental Governance?

Making the international governance of the environment pluriversal means that states, scientists, and Indigenous peoples should not be conceived as competitors for representing the one natural world. They actually should be able to represent their different worlds. How can different worlds be negotiated in such a political space?

Notions such as "overlapping ontologies" (Ludwig, 2016) and "ontological dialogues" (Yates, 2017) might facilitate this political conversation as they refer to the possibility that social actors might enact relationships respectful of the ontological self-determination of each group (Viveiros de Castro, 2015). The ontologies of Indigenous peoples and scientists, for instance, might overlap in their different conceptions of a lake in the Amazon rainforest. For the Kukama peoples in the Peruvian Amazon, a lake is the expression of their ancestral origins, kinship relationships, and sovereignty power, whereas in the scientist's world, the lake is an ecosystem service important for biodiversity conservation. When these different perspectives overlap over what seems to be the same lake, they are not merely expressing different opinions or knowledge systems over an external reality. From an ontological perspective, they are engaging with completely different worlds in which the lake has a different essence and value. Recognizing this overlapping means recognizing that there are different ontologies. This is a premise to start an ontological dialogue about the proper ways to protect and manage the different lakes these actors engage with.

Ontological dialogues are the most genuine and profound dialogues as they allow the understanding of the deepest differences among groups. This, in turn, is a condition to occupy others' perspectives instead of assuming incommensurable positions or treating differences as "cultural barriers" to be addressed with integration (Ludwig, 2016; Yates et al., 2017). This ability of provisional occupation of others' ontologies should be an open and permanent possibility in these dialogues, not reserved exclusively for experts or scientists, allegedly the most well-equipped to understand different worlds.

For instance, Kohn (2015) reserves for anthropologists the task of "cosmic diplomacy" as they would have the capacity to move among worlds. However, Indigenous peoples might also pertain or have the capacity to engage with different worlds, being able to switch between them and establish connections. For instance, Hirsch (2017) demonstrated how peasant communities in the Peruvian Andes committed to laboring in multiple worlds and tactically combining ontological projects to negotiate investments on their land with mining companies. Schnegg (2021) showed that in Namibia, some Damara people are scientists who observe rainy seasons, engaging with scientists and indigenous worlds.

The fundamental ability of the "diplomacy of the pluriverse" (Conway, 2019) is having concern for contradiction to alleviating the "either/or" of oppositional political thinking. This diplomacy, then, is not primarily concerned with dissolving all antagonisms. It seeks to dispel unnecessary antagonisms so that necessary ones might come to the fore. This idea of diplomatics of the pluriverse as alliance builders (Conway, 2019) is crucial to envisioning how a new political space must facilitate the negotiation and creation of ontological coalitions. This means agreements able to save the different worlds the actors care about in the context of the ecological crisis.

6.3 International Scientific Panels and Indigenous Peoples

International leaders and scientific communities conceive the current climate crisis as one of the greatest existential dangers humanity has ever faced (Glikson, 2021). This "existential threat" (UN Secretary-General Antonio Guterres), "climate endgame" (Kemp et al., 2022; Van der Velden and White, 2021), "climate catastrophe" (Glikson, 2021) or "climate emergency" (Glikson, 2021) can trigger other catastrophic risks, such as international conflict or infectious disease spread (Kemp et al., 2022). To address this danger, concerned scientists claim that we need sustained pressure in politics (Glikson, 2021), so public authorities can quickly implement massive energy efficiency and conservation practices and replace fossil fuels with low-carbon renewables (Ripple et al., 2020). They mainly exert this pressure through the diffusion of the "scientific consensus" on the drivers and consequences of climate change and biological loss, as well as the measures that should be taken to stop these trends. There are, however, many questions about the making and implications of this consensus. Do scientific panels integrate indigenous ontologies in their processes of knowledge-making? How do scientific communities translate the interactions with indigenous communities into the outcomes of knowledge-making (assessments, reports)? How do these outcomes engage with political processes and influence political decisions? The cases of the IPCC, IPBES, and the Science Panel for the Amazon illustrate the complexities in addressing these questions.

6.3.1 The Intergovernmental Panel on Climate Change (IPCC)

Created by the United Nations Environment Programme (UNEP) and the World Meteorological Organization (WMO) in 1988, the IPCC is the leading international body for the assessment of climate change. It aims to facilitate integral evaluations of the state of scientific, socioeconomic, and technical knowledge on climate change. These evaluations delve into the causes and impacts of climate change and provide policy recommendations to address it (IPCC, 2023). The IPCC relies on national representation and the search for internationally negotiated solutions (Beck et al., 2014) and is currently composed of 195 countries. Representatives of IPCC member governments meet one or more times a year in Plenary Sessions. By March 2025, the IPCC enacted six assessment reports.

The way the IPCC systematizes and produces knowledge reinforces a technocratic and universalist perspective on climate change problems and solutions. It positions itself as an inter-state scientific body with a rigorous peer-review process that could only be applied to Western scientific research (Beck et al., 2014; Rashidi and Lyons, 2021). Thus, it has established a complex set of formal rules and procedures, contributing toward greater governance coherence and standardization (Beck et al., 2014). As the agreements must be adopted by unanimity, it follows the rule of "minimum common denominator" to require minimum issues to achieve consensus while excluding a diversity of perspectives on climate change (Van der Sluijs et al., 2010). As a consequence, its global analysis neglects local and regional scales and reinforces bureaucracy and inertia (Beck et al., 2014).

The content of the reports reflects this process. IPCC not only writes about climate change; it also writes the rules by which climate change is conceived and assessed (Hughes, 2024). The IPCC frames climate change as a global risk to be managed by a global policy model in which experts, as politically neutral agents, hold significant power to define policy problems (Miller, 2004). The result is a circular dynamic in which the IPCC exerts power through its reports by legitimizing selective and restrictive policy solutions (Miller, 2004; Reisinger, 2011). The culture of scientific authority thus reproduces and entrenches extractive practices (Hughes, 2024). For instance, although the fifth assessment report called for the inclusion of traditional knowledge, it lacked discussions on the colonial rationale of climate change and expressed little engagement with indigenous knowledge and worldviews. Apart from general mentions in its reports, indigenous ontologies and epistemologies are excluded. This deepens Indigenous peoples' under-representation and legitimizes their utilitarian inclusion as objects of global climate governance (Rashidi and Lyons, 2021).

Moreover, these reports focus on drivers and predictions rather than concrete measures to address the differentiated effects of climate change. For instance, the policy summary of the 2022 IPCC Report focuses on defining the drivers of climate change and explaining the consequences in the short and long terms. The definition of means and targets is framed in very broad terms. The Report calls to "avoid maladaptation" by flexible, multi-sectoral, inclusive, and long-term planning and implementation of adaptation actions, and achieving "enabling conditions," such as political commitment, policies, and instruments with clear goals and priorities, among others. The minimum content of those political commitments, policies, and instruments is not explicitly proposed.

IPCC's inter-governmental nature has been blamed for restricting the policy ambition of its reports. Haas (2015) suggests that the intergovernmental design of the panel makes it difficult to operate and implement independent initiatives to advance collective climate action. Before official approval, the Panel keeps in reserve the report drafts instead of allowing public and transparent discussions. This generates tensions with other scientists who question the IPCC's formal approach. For instance, Scientist Rebellion leaked the drafts of the IPCC Working Group III, complaining about the intergovernmental process of IPCC reports and its policy-neutral position. They appealed to individual scientists to speak the truth without governmental interference (Hartz, 2023). In this perspective, by putting states at the center, the IPCC lacks the independence to criticize governments and fails to respond to the needs and interests of non-state actors (Suliman et al., 2019).

6.3.2 The Intergovernmental Science-Policy Platform on Biodiversity and Ecosystem Services (IPBES)

IPBES was created in April 2012 as an independent intergovernmental body under the auspices of the United Nations Environment Programme (UNEP), the United Nations Educational, Scientific and Cultural Organization (UNESCO), the United Nations Development Programme (UNDP), and the Food and Agriculture Organization of the United Nations (FAO) (IPBES, 2023). Since 2016, IPBES'

Plenary has approved seven general assessment reports and four regional assessment reports. Currently, IPBES has 145 member states and is structured by the Plenary (the decision-making body), a Bureau comprising the Chair and four Vice-Chairs, the Multidisciplinary Expert Panel that provides guidance in the selection of experts nominated by governments, and working groups (IPBES, 2023).

IPBES' process for drafting its reports is more open than the IPCC. It seeks to increase transparency and bridge the gap between science and policy with its three working areas: knowledge production, capacity building, and public policy support (Beck et al., 2014). IPBES also works with a wide range of stakeholders with a multidisciplinary expert approach and is more open to Indigenous knowledge (Beck et al., 2014; Turnhout et al., 2014). It has established a task force for strengthening the quality of Indigenous peoples' participation (Beck et al., 2014). To this aim, IPBES organizes workshops and promotes the participation of indigenous leaders and local communities as "non-scientific actors" to produce inputs that are available for evaluation and consideration by experts (IPBES, 2019a, b, 2021, 2022a, 2023).

Regarding the outcomes of this process, the IPBES generates information at multiple scales (regional, local) and has addressed previous critiques for treating the environment as discrete, quantifiable, and measurable units under neoliberal logic (Turnhout et al., 2014; Beck et al., 2014). For instance, the "Methodological Assessment Report on the Diverse Values and Valuation of Nature" (2022) is a comprehensive compilation of different approaches, concepts, and methods of environmental valuation applied in different regions and contexts, including by Indigenous peoples. The expert authors systematized academic literature, policy documents, and indigenous and local knowledge. This knowledge was validated by three dialogue workshops with knowledge holders and experts. However, the Report acknowledges that academic knowledge is more prominent in the assessment (IPBES, 2022a, b). The reason is that indigenous and local knowledge is more commonly found in grey literature and non-written forms, and scientists often avoid these sources (McElwee et al., 2020). The report framework also conceptualizes nature in epistemic, not ontological terms. Nature is a socially constructed concept whose various understandings are underpinned by knowledge systems, cultural backgrounds, and languages. Therefore, nature is understood as a single "non-human living world" approached through scientific categories and by those categories based on Indigenous peoples and local communities' worldviews. In general, IPBES provides some space to include indigenous concepts, but these spaces are limited to workshops to validate local and indigenous knowledge collected in academic literature.

IPBES reports also formulate some "transformative recommendations" to deal with environmental challenges. However, these recommendations are only nominally transformative. The policy summary of the 2019 IPBES Global Assessment Report, similar to IPCC reports, focuses on the drivers and consequences of biodiversity deterioration. The definition of means and targets is framed in very broad terms. The Report states that nature conservation and sustainable use need "urgent and concerted efforts fostering transformative change" (IPBES, 2019a, b: 16), meaning actions such as capacity-building, cross-sectoral cooperation, environmental law and implementation, among others. Specific measures such as suspending new oil concessions or farm cattle moratoriums in critical biodiverse rainforests are not explicitly proposed.

As in the case of the IPCC, IPBES' intergovernmental nature has been criticized (Wiegleb and Bruns, 2023; Beck et al., 2014). Much like the IPCC, governments participate in the plenary sessions where decisions about the work program, rules, and procedures are made, and reports are accepted, adopted, and approved. The IPBES Plenary provides an important platform for member States to guide the content of the reports (Wiegleb and Bruns, 2023), compromising to some extent the process of report making.

Unlike the IPCC, some stakeholders have been recognized in important aspects of IPBES work, such as the nomination of experts. However, the institutional setting of the UN system does not favor openness (Beck et al., 2014). For instance, the selection of experts for the global assessment reports is led by the Multidisciplinary Expert Panel (MEP), which must work independently of IPBES member States to secure the scientific credibility and quality of IPBES' products. Nonetheless, government representatives are still involved in the selection process following the "80/20 rule," with 80 percent of experts being nominated by governments and 20 percent by other observer organizations such as universities or NGOs (Wiegleb and Bruns, 2023). Power differentials between IPBES member States also express uneven patterns of spatial representation of knowledge, with the majority of experts nominated on behalf of the United States, Australia, and Western Europe (Wiegleb and Bruns, 2023).

Therefore, even if governments are willing to delegate authority to global expert organizations, they still try to safeguard their influence by controlling processes such as the nomination of experts or the drafting of summaries for policymakers (Beck et al., 2014). Governments may utilize such intergovernmental spaces to further their national interests while discussing seemingly policy-neutral knowledge claims (Wiegleb and Bruns, 2023).

6.3.3 The Science Panel for the Amazon (SPA)

Under Jeffrey Sachs' Sustainable Development Solutions Network, the SPA is the world's first-ever international science initiative dedicated to systematizing and diffusing knowledge on the survival of the Amazon. It was created in 2019 as an independent and multidisciplinary community of scientists, in the context of the signing of the Leticia Pact by Amazonian governments to address the wildfire crisis and the challenges for sustainability in the basin. The SPA includes more than 250 scientists who have been involved in the First Amazon Assessment Report of 2021. It has a Scientific Committee in charge of proposing a list of contributors and reviewing the report drafts. It also has a Strategic Committee, a group of leaders in different areas, such as culture, politics, and civil society, who provide advice to the SPA.

The SPA process for drafting the Assessment has been conventional. The Amazon Assessment Report comprises 34 chapters; each one can be read as an independent literature review academic paper. As stated in the preface of each chapter: "These experts came together to debate, analyze, and assemble the accumulated knowledge of the scientific community, Indigenous peoples, and other stakeholders that live and work in the Amazon." Indigenous peoples are considered "stakeholders," and their knowledge is collected by experts, not negotiated with them. There are no specific channels for voicing Indigenous perspectives, and in the long list of scientists associated with the SPA on its website, only three are listed as indigenous scientists.

The leading authors of each chapter decide how they incorporate indigenous knowledge. This might imply workshops in which they diffuse draft papers and receive comments, but there is no homogeneous methodology. Neither is there a "task force," as in the case of IPBES, for including indigenous perspectives. For instance, Chapter 10, "Critical Interconnections between the Cultural and Biological Diversity of Amazonian Peoples and Ecosystems," would have to highlight indigenous perspectives. However, there is no methodological explanation of how these perspectives were integrated into the chapter; rather, it reflects the structure of a conventional literature review research paper authored by a group of academics.

SPA scientists highlight their role as neutral experts. They conceive themselves only as providers of information through responsible advocacy or diffusion of knowledge to the public and influential political actors, including presidential candidates (Interview SPA member, 31.05.2022; Interview SPA member, 15.04.2022). In their view, the Panel's strength would be the authority made by solid scientific consensus; and the role of "allies," such as Indigenous peoples, is helping in diffusing the Panel's messages (Interview SPA member, 05.11.2022). Discussions about concrete policies and responsibilities of each state correspond to the political arena (Interview SPA Strategic Committee member, 17.05.2022).

The Strategic Committee is also insufficient to include diverse voices. This Committee is composed of 24 personalities; only 2 are Indigenous, one is the former General Coordinator of COICA, Gregorio Mirabal, and the other is the young environmental activist Beka Munduruku. This Committee does not intervene in the process of producing the chapters and only brings general orientation to the Panel and helps in "diffusing the SPA messages" (Interview, SPA member, August 2, 2023). For instance, the participation of Mirabal (Interview, August 14, 2024) has been limited to sharing some ideas about the environmental crisis in a Workshop. He has no clarity about the impacts of his contribution or how the Panel would consider the contribution of Indigenous peoples in the future. For different indigenous leaders, in general, the relationship between scientists and Indigenous peoples is tense. For a former COICA leader, not all scientists are allies of the indigenous movement "...most don't do it for the love of the Amazon, but for the love of their study..." (Interview 09.07.2022). Another COICA representative explains that they don't have a great relationship with the academic sector "because many times we have seen that the information that we generate, the data that we have systematized, becomes part of academic repositories but does not revert to us in tangible benefits" (COICA official, Interview 09.07.2022).

Whereas for scientists, the interactions with Indigenous peoples are about collecting and validating data, for Indigenous peoples, these are political interactions. Regarding the invitation to be a member of the SPA Strategic Committee, Gregorio Mirabal (Interview, August 14, 2024) said: "We couldn't say no because we had been claiming for more participation… … We believe we cannot abandon those spaces we have won." Mirabal makes a parallel with indigenous participation in climate conferences: "We should be inside and interact with our governments and the world governments…It is the same with science…." For a COICA representative, some scientific sectors are allies only when they "provide us with data in support for our political proposals." (COICA official, Interview 09.07.2022). Then, from the perspective of SPA scientists, Indigenous peoples are allies to "diffuse the messages" of the Panel related to the drivers and consequences of ecological degradation in the Amazon rainforest. From the perspective of indigenous leaders, scientists are allies insofar as they support their political agenda related to self-determination and territorial rights.

As a result, the inclusion of Indigenous peoples in science panels, either from the perspective of scientists or from the view of indigenous leaders, is not about a "dialogue of knowledges." For a SPA member (Interview, August 23, 2024), this exchange is largely symbolic because of cultural, language, and ontological barriers; the lack of methodologies for such a dialogue, and the fact that within the SPA, there are very conventional scientists. Indigenous leaders also recognize that "inside doors, these spaces still valorize very little oral knowledge and indigenous science," and reject the symbolic nature of these exchanges: "We don't want just appreciation letters and photos" (Gregorio Mirabal, Interview, August 14, 2024). Both indigenous and scientists conceive this space differently. For scientists, this is a neutral space for systematizing and diffusing scientific information. For indigenous leaders, these are opportunities for "actually participating, giving proposals… our solutions of biodiversity, water, food, must be part of the plans of scientific implementation at the level of government… this should be defined in a table of negotiation and agreements." Indigenous peoples have continuously raised their proposals in international spaces. For instance, COICA and the national indigenous organizations of Peru and Ecuador – the upper section of the Amazon basin – formed a coalition called "Amazon Sacred Headwater." They enacted the Indigenous Peoples' Declaration for the Amazon Sacred Headwaters in 2022. This Declaration calls for "stop the expansion of new oil, gas, mining, industrial agriculture, cattle ranching, mega-infrastructure projects, and roads in the Sacred Headwaters."

The exclusion of the political perspectives of Indigenous peoples shapes the outcome of the process. Whereas some of the 34 chapters of the SPA Report have specific recommendations (remarkably, Chapter 20 proposes prohibiting alluvial mining), the Policy Summary of the Report delivered to decision-makers focuses on explaining the drivers of the crisis and predictions. Means for addressing Amazonian degradation are drafted in very general terms, for instance, Message 17 calls for biodiversity and forest conservation strategies, with mechanisms such as "law enforcement inside and outside protected areas, the integration of these areas and sustainable agroecological systems in sustainable supply chains, incentives to restore degraded areas, improvement of management and financial institutions, civil society and social movement engagement, and new forms of environmental and resource governance." Whereas all governments, scientists, and Indigenous peoples might easily agree with those broad terms, establishing specific mechanisms as those proposed by the Amazon Sacred Headwater coalition, is left to the formal political sphere at the national level.

This approach might be institutionalized at ACTO, reproducing the limitations of scientific panels. Among its seven Coordination Offices, the scientific one has not been prominent, and ACTO's cooperation project approach only considers Indigenous peoples as "stakeholders" in specific interventions and scientists as "experts" who provide advice to cooperation initiatives. The Belém Declaration of 2023 has raised some hope for the inclusion and dialogue with these actors. The Declaration created the "Intergovernmental Scientific Technical Panel" as a space of "exchange of knowledge" between scientists delegated by the member states, with the participation of Indigenous peoples.

However, it would be difficult for this Panel to include ontological differences. First, it has not been designed as a decision-making space but as a forum to collect, systematize, and diffuse data, such as the IPCC and IPBES. Second, Indigenous peoples are not active members of the Panel since their participation is conceived as a form of support for the work of the scientists. As in the case of the IPBES and the IPCC, they do not participate in their own right as sovereign nations with ancestral knowledge. They participate to complement scientific work.

When asking scientists and international officials how they envision the implementation of this "Intergovernmental Scientific Technical Panel," they confirm these concerns. They argue that this panel should be an independent and technical space, such as the SPA, under an IPCC model. This means that the participation of Indigenous Peoples could be largely symbolic, only to collect and validate information and not to be part of decision-making processes to reach consensus on concrete proposals to deal with the climate emergency.

6.4 Envisioning a Pluriversal Governance

International science panels are conceived as crucial sites for addressing environmental challenges with the participation of different "stakeholders," including Indigenous peoples. As such, these are important venues for examining how the Western universalist ontology is legitimized, whereas indigenous ontologies are excluded from international environmental governance.

These panels are not directed to co-produce knowledge, but to systematize current scientific knowledge on climate change (IPCC), biodiversity (IPBES), and the Amazon rainforest (SPA), and provide recommendations based on such reviews or assessments. In this process, the participation of Indigenous peoples is mainly through workshops that provide feedback on some sections or chapters of the reports. This is not a "dialogue of knowledges," it is a way to "validate" the assemblages of knowledge formulated by scientific literature reviews, which include scientific research on Indigenous peoples. This process then legitimizes "one-world" ontology in which Indigenous ontologies are reduced to contributions to fighting climate change and biodiversity conservation collected by scientists.

The outcomes of this process are the description of drivers of environmental degradation and the suggestion of policy targets, but not the definition of means to achieve these targets. When formulated, those means are drafted in very general terms, detached from assigning specific responsibilities to nation-states and establishing specific measures to protect what Indigenous peoples consider sacred headwaters and, in general, the rainforest as their natural, cultural, and social world. These issues are left to the political sphere since scientists insist that these Panels are apolitical. However, the exchange that indigenous leaders such as Gregorio Mirabal are looking for in these spaces is a political exchange, not a symbolic knowledge exchange. As for Indigenous peoples, scientific platforms are not pre-political sites but political ones; they expect that their proposals, such as the moratorium of infrastructure projects and the suspension of oil concessions, among others, will be reflected in the outcomes of those processes. Excluding these proposals from these platforms is a form of excluding the political ontology of Indigenous peoples, as through these proposals, they are fighting to enact their own realities.

Whereas the intergovernmental nature of the IPCC and IPBES might explain some limitations of these processes and outcomes, the SPA's similar approach suggests that the key limitation of the policy ambition of these Panels is not their governmental nature but their apolitical culture and, even more, their one-dimensional ontology. The claims of being a-political experts and neutral scientists imply the enactment of a one-world reality that excludes Indigenous plural ontologies (Blaser, 2014). This means that scientists conceive one world and ask for "inputs" from indigenous knowledge holders to help them validate their scientific findings about the environmental challenges of such a world. Indigenous peoples cannot enact their own realities because this space is, a priori, apolitical, and they are mostly seen as contributors to the scientific agenda, detached from their ontological self-determination (Viveiros de Castro, 2015). Whereas the discussions about climate change and biodiversity on the planet and in the Amazon are framed in these terms, Indigenous peoples reclaim politically these spaces to enact their political ontology.

These findings support the need to reimagine those spaces and make normative proposals. As suggested by Ephraim (2018), the science-policy dialogue should pass from the pre-political, informative-only stage to the political ground. Along with a scientific consensus, there should be a political consensus on the establishment of a dialogic process for filling the gap between the gravity of the crisis and the policy means to address this gravity. This should lead to the creation of a plural space for world-making. In this scenario, scientists would have to be more open to engaging with concrete proposals from indigenous organizations that are often transferred to the political sphere. By conceiving scientist platforms as political, not pre-political sites, Indigenous peoples could defend those proposals aimed at saving their own world.

The creation of the "Intergovernmental Scientific Technical Panel" at ACTO risks reproducing the limitations of current international scientific panels. This is the case because the Declaration of Belém seems to incorporate indigenous participation in this Panel as contributors and not as political actors in their own right. This diminishes the potential to become a pluriversal space for negotiating different ontologies. Instead of just collecting and validating indigenous knowledge, this Panel should be designed in a way that allows embracing the proposals advanced by Indigenous peoples. In this way, the Panel would be more respectful of different indigenous ontologies and would be able to formulate strong policy recommendations.

More ambitiously, political ontology should also be incorporated into international decision-making. In this scenario, both scientists and Indigenous peoples would occupy a seat at international negotiations, along with nation-states. This pluriversal governance would be different from how green democratic theory, Latour's political ecology, and XR Peoples Assembly seek to reform governance structures. These models tend to depoliticize scientists' authority to speak for nature, assuming a predominant role. Rather, a pluriversal governance would be a space for negotiating different political ontologies. In these deliberative and decision-making places, there is no one true representative of the natural world, but competing nature-spoken persons under their own cosmological standpoint. In sum, more than models for representing the natural world or specific natural beings, international environmental governance requires the possibility of representing different worlds.

In this pluriversal governance, ontological clashes are unavoidable, but there are also possibilities for an ontological coalition. The notions of cosmic or pluriversal diplomacy and alliance-building are important for the interactions between these different actors. Even though they formulate the notion of alliances with different aims and expectations, the very idea of enacting alliances denotes that whereas each group might have different interests in responding to the natural world they seek to protect, the "diplomats of the pluriverse" (Conway, 2019) might find points of coincidence to reach similar goals. The aim is to create coalitions between indigenous representatives, scientists, and nation-state representatives on actions to reach ambitious targets to save the different worlds they perceive. A dialogue between worlds is something already happening on the ground. One former COICA leader said, "I have always defended ...our identity, culture, spirituality... but we also need science, not to justify or approve our knowledge but to add new knowledge maintaining our indigenous being…" (Interview former COICA leader, 07.26.2022). Some scientists seek not to instrumentalize indigenous knowledge but to formulate actions and targets that might satisfy the needs of their different worlds.

6.5 Conclusions

The emergence of the "eco-centric turn" in laws and policies has raised questions about who is the legitimate political representative of the natural world. Whereas global environmental discourses tend to attach to Indigenous peoples the ecological identity of forest protectors, those who substantially retain the power to articulate nature interests are scientific communities that do not necessarily share the ideals and perspectives of the people on the ground.

Scientists articulate their concern outside political processes. In pre-political stages of scientific panels, they conceive themselves as neutral actors that collect, systematize, and diffuse scientific information with the hope that political actors will consider that information in their political decisions. In these processes, Indigenous peoples are treated as "stakeholders" and their views are used to complement and reaffirm scientific findings. In the post-political stages of implementing concrete cooperation programs and projects, they use drones, GPS, and satellite data to register deforestation trends and justify conservation policies. However, these tools might be used to criminalize local people's use of their livelihoods, and their implementation might imply disrespecting the data sovereignty and self-determination arrangements of these peoples.

Instead of being providers of information in pre-political stages or users and targets of Western science and technology in post-political scenarios, Indigenous peoples demand a different relationship with scientific communities. A relationship that recognizes deep epistemological and ontological differences and allows more transparent and democratic forms to politically represent the natural environment.

In this context, this chapter has examined how ontological differences are excluded or incorporated into the international environmental governance of the Amazon. It has explored the interactions of scientists' panels with Indigenous peoples, and, in particular, it discusses the involvement of indigenous politics and ontology with the Science Panel for the Amazon. Considering that the Declaration of Belém of 2023 announced the creation of the "Intergovernmental Scientific Technical Panel" with the participation of Indigenous peoples, the chapter has reflected on the prospects of this panel for accommodating or excluding ontological differences.

The participation of indigenous representatives in scientists' panels such as the IPCC, IPBES, and the SPA is not about a "dialogue of knowledges." They participate in corroborating the systematization of scientific knowledge elaborated by academics embedded in Western universalist ontology. Scientists' claims of being apolitical and neutral experts imply the enactment of a one-world reality that excludes Indigenous plural ontologies. As a result, the outcomes of this process, the assessments or reports, focus on describing the drivers of climate change and biodiversity degradation, predictions if no actions are taken, and the targets to avoid the catastrophe. However, the definition of the concrete ways to achieve these targets is left to the political sphere. Whereas scientists conceive these spaces as pre-political sites, Indigenous peoples conceive them as political spaces. For them, these are not sites for symbolic knowledge exchange on the one-world reality; these are spaces for political exchanges on which Indigenous peoples seek to enact their political ontology and the proper ways to protect their world.

Based on these findings, the chapter proposes a pluriversal governance to be applied to scientists' platforms and international decision-making spaces. On the one hand, scientific platforms must be deliberative spaces in which Indigenous peoples can enact their political ontologies by articulating their views on how to protect their world. This would mean that their concrete proposals should be reflected in specific policy recommendations. These findings should guide the implementation of the "Intergovernmental Scientific Technical Panel" at the ACTO. On the other hand, international decision-making forums should become a pluriversal space, in which nation-states, scientists, and Indigenous peoples would share the political stage to negotiate their different worldviews and the authority to represent their own natural worlds. This might trigger ontological clashes, but also the possibility of creating ontological coalitions around the protection of nature and the appropriate means to deal with the climate crisis.

CHAPTER 7

Conclusions

Governing the Amazon and Beyond

7.1 Multidimensional Injustices in the International Governance of the Amazon

In 2019, Amazonian governments signed the "Leticia Pact" in the context of what was then the most serious fire crisis ever recorded. They promised coordinated responses to "save the forests." In 2023, they promised the same with "The Belém Declaration." They failed. Forest fires are worsening, and the damage to human health and Amazonian ecosystems is incalculable. Instead, they continue fostering mega-infrastructures and extractive projects across the basin. In 2024, Chinese and Peruvian authorities inaugurated the Chancay Port on the coast of Peru to enhance Asia–Pacific commercial exchange. Some Latin American leaders dream of making this port part of a huge bi-oceanic railway project that would connect the Pacific and the Atlantic oceans through the Amazon of Peru, Brazil, and Bolivia. There are very few concerns among authorities about the possible environmental impacts of this and related projects.

In general, environmental governance responses are weak because national and international priorities are still focused on increasing resource extraction from and through the Amazon. Despite declarations and programs that call, in general, for the sustainability of the basin, high-level meetings within the ACTO and otherwise have no great ambitions in areas other than promoting extractivism. For instance, whereas four Amazonian countries are members of the Andean Community Tribunal, which focuses on enforcing regional trade norms and intellectual property standards, the proposal to create an Environmental Justice Tribunal for the Amazon was rejected at the Belém meeting in 2023.

The problem of forest fires and, in general, environmental degradation in the basin is at the same time global and local. On the one hand, heat waves and droughts are caused by a global history of emissions. The climate crisis is a crisis of inequality.

The most affected are communities that never benefited from the wealth generated by industrialized countries at the expense of pollution. On the other hand, national ruling elites approve regulations favoring the expansion of agricultural, mineral, and oil frontiers. They benefit transnational corporations, national economic champions, state extractive companies, and even illegal groups. These global and local drivers are sustained by institutional, epistemological, and ontological injustices.

Epistemological injustices refer to dominant imaginaries over the basin. The portrayal of the Amazon either as a place of global extractivism, global conservation, or national development justifies extractive interventions in Amazonian territories, disregarding indigenous sovereignty and their ecological imaginaries. For instance, mega-infrastructures in the region served historically the idea of nation-building and, under the IIRSA initiative in the 2000s, mainly served international connectivity to prompt transnational trade. In this extractive imaginary, infrastructures are either a phase in the process of commodity extraction and transport, or it is extraction in itself by speculative practices over Amazonian lands, and by using data and aspirations of the locals in the formulation of infrastructure plans. The conception of the Amazon as a place of global conservation is also problematic, as it justifies a particular kind of extractive mode of intervention in space. Forest and biodiversity are commodified by states, NGOs, and corporate actors seeking access to international green funds and benefitting from carbon markets. Many protected areas in the Amazon depend to a great extent on the discursive, financial, and political power of international actors, whose diverse agendas produce a fragmented conservation governance that most of the time excludes the concerns and aspirations of indigenous communities. ACTO's governance approach, which is based on international cooperation, also reproduces epistemological injustices by empowering national sovereignty and developmental agendas. In this context, no environmental international standard might limit the allure of extraction.

Ontological injustices refer to how more-than-human worlds in the Amazon have been mystified, obscured, and erased. This is not simply the exclusion of a different cultural representation of "the natural world," but the marginalization of the possibility of enacting a completely different interrelation with the natural environment. By conceiving these differences merely as "cultural differences" over how different groups conceive the Amazonian reality, state, corporate, and conservation actors only advance participatory mechanisms to "include" Indigenous peoples in the processes that reproduce the dominant perceptions of the forest and forest governance. As a result, discussions over the international principles of common concern of humankind and the common heritage of humankind reinforce anthropocentric ideals that center all governance efforts on human beings. This is also the case when the participation of Indigenous peoples in scientific platforms is celebrated as a "dialogue of knowledges" or when the forest is conceived as a technology informed by technical instruments and data that are meant to mitigate environmental change with smart technologies (Gabrys, 2020). These perspectives conceive participation as a means to validate the systematization of knowledge elaborated by scientists embedded in Western universalist ontology, irrespective of communities' socio-political engagement with the forest.

Institutional injustices are the formal expression of ontological and epistemological injustices. The anthropocentrism and ethnocentrism of the ideas of sovereignty, conservation, and development support state-centric institutional arrangements that exclude the political representation of Indigenous nations and the natural environment in the international arena. Claims for indigenous sovereignty are reduced to concrete provisions of inclusion and participation in national commissions or international second-level nondeliberative units focused on collecting information. Claims for recognizing the intrinsic value and agency of natural beings are limited to the discursive celebration of the rights of nature in national legislation as a flawed expression of plurality and some environmental sensitivity. The international architecture of the Amazon and the immanent governing principle of polycentricity are the highest expressions of institutional injustices.

7.1.1 Surviving Polycentric Governance

Polycentric governance celebrates diversity, multi-scalar power distribution, local initiatives, and participation, all without challenging the anthropocentrism, ethnocentrism, and state-centrism of international arrangements. By advancing programs and institutions that coexist with or reinforce extractive operations and national developmental goals, polycentricity has fostered regional institutional fragmentation that allows governments to present themselves as engaging with environmental goals and human rights, while legitimizing their nonsustainable policies and actions. In this way, the local initiatives have become symbolic achievements vis-à-vis top-down national arrangements that have instrumentalized Indigenous peoples as mere participants who legitimate different forms of extractivism.

The deepest problem with polycentric governance is treating governing structures as market structures. Deeming different authorities as market players implies assuming that they hold similar prerogatives and limitations in decision-making, but this is simply not the case. Subnational governments, local communities, local organizations, corporations, illegal economies, and state agencies all interact under imbalanced power relations and are embedded in global and national extractive political economies. In this context, praising and supporting local communities in their efforts to enact their own governance and localized environmental initiatives is plausible, but it risks condemning those people to fight alone against extractive threats. Amazonian environmental defenders have achieved the titling of their communities, credits from financial programs, and even compensation for providing environmental services, but they are still killed by illegal logging, illegal miners, land traffickers, and drug cartels.

Certainly, sometimes, local initiatives can be very effective in achieving some wellbeing for their communities, while advancing sustainable forest practices. Sometimes, even these initiatives have the potential to scale and become national programs and policies. But they are strongly limited by the endless transnational forces that extract, transport, and transform Amazonian livelihoods into worldwide commodities. One example is the new wave of international support for "indigenous economies" and "sustainable value chains." After years of efforts with the support of NGOs, a Chapra community in the Peruvian Amazon developed sustainable fish farms with the aim of offering healthy, natural fish to local markets. Although the project was successful for some time, all was lost when an oil spill destroyed the river basins that feed the lakes used ancestrally by the Chapra people. Atomized efforts become meaningless since they continue to be embedded in extractive political economies that ultimately disregard indigenous rights and ecosystems.

The reforms or adjustments to polycentric modes of governance do not address this fundamental tension. For instance, Dehm (2021) explains that to redeem REDD+ from multiple criticisms, such as leakage, commodification, and top-down implementation, authors have shaped it as an expanding and proliferating project that at the same time centralizes forest management under a national approach and incorporates multiple objectives, including poverty reduction, biodiversity, adaptation, and indigenous rights. Some authors have praised these efforts as a "nested approach" and note how this creates a platform where different actors would represent and bring on board competing ideologies, values, and interpretations (Lozano et al., 2024; Gupta et al., 2016; Zelli, 2019).

However, the much-promoted nested approach continues to portray the many flaws of polycentricity as problems of implementation. The assumption is that these problems could be solved by harmonizing decentralized activities within broader subnational jurisdictions and national frameworks, allowing their gradual inclusion in higher management systems (Sikor et al., 2010; West, 2015; Bayrak and Marafa, 2016; Ravikumar et al., 2015; Githiru and Njambuya, 2019). Under this nested system, local and subnational polycentric efforts would have concrete arenas for decision-making shaped by national and global guidelines (van Asselt and McDermott, 2016; Ravikumar, 2015; Sikor et al., 2010). However, rather than being a problem of implementation or lack of political will, REDD+ is embedded in broader governance frameworks and relations of power (Dehm, 2021) that maintain the inherent contradiction of relying on actual or potential forest commodification to legitimate extractive markets (Fletcher et al., 2016).

Thus, whereas some indigenous elements are incorporated into REDD+ projects and policies, such as communal titling in the Peruvian REDD+ national agenda, others are excluded, such as REDD+'s governance structure, its financial mechanisms, and distribution schemes (Lozano et al., 2024). In Ecuador, Colombia, and Brazil, REDD is implemented through national plans that promote territorial ordering and land use planning, seeking to reduce net deforestation by developing green markets and extractive industries under sustainable standards. Indigenous leaders, in contrast, include other worlds and natural and supernatural beings when referring to territorial ordering, and many question market-oriented perspectives (Cifuentes, 2021).

The governance of the Amazon cannot be polycentric simply because the complexity we are dealing with cannot be simplified through the management of decentralized efforts and initiatives, no matter international guidelines and national and subnational coordination. Ecosystems know no borders, nor do fires, oil spills, or illegal economies. Then, we need strong international institutions and measures, and this requires expanding and repoliticizing the political space.

7.1.2 Recentering the Political in Governing the Commons: Redefining Pre-political and Post-Political Stages

Polycentric governance portrays itself as a descriptive and apolitical framework, but actually it reaffirms the power of extractive interests at national and international structures, whereas displacing other forms of nature-society engagements to pre-political and post-political stages. In this operation of political displacement, claims of sovereignty, ontological self-determination, and multi-epistemic dialogues are reduced into requests for participation and appreciation of cultural diversity in depoliticized spaces.

The pre-political stage is the sphere of knowledge production. This sphere is pre-political because different sovereign worldviews, different political ontologies, and multi-epistemic relations are reduced to activism that, at best, might influence public opinion or are conceived as research outputs to be processed in scientific platforms. As seen in Chapter 6, in the pre-political stage, whole indigenous worlds are packed as stakeholders' contributions that serve to corroborate scientific findings. The sole function of the pre-political stage is to provide information to those legitimate diplomats or state representatives with the capacity to negotiate and reach agreements on environmental and social challenges.

Polycentricity not only legitimates the displacement of political tensions – derived from different sovereignties and worldviews- to pre-political stages. It also celebrates this displacement by praising the participation and contributions of Indigenous peoples in pre-political forums, no matter the rhetorical or insubstantial interrelations in this stage. This is also a form of validating the limited ambitions of scientific – indigenous interactions.

The post-political stage is the sphere of policy implementation, which includes the development of mining, oil, and agribusiness with green standards; the creation and management of protected areas; the development of carbon markets and REDD projects, and so forth. This sphere is postpolitical because different sovereignty and ontological questions on territorial rights and the protection and management of nature must be solved within already established national and international regulations and institutions. The sole function of the post-political stage is to apply those regulations approved by diplomats deemed legitimate for representing states' sovereignty and interests.

By displacing the political tensions to post-political spheres, polycentricity ends up reducing sovereignty claims and indigenous worldviews into claims for participating in limited institutional channels of each project or initiative developed under limited frameworks. As in the case of the pre-political stage, polycentricity not only moves those tensions far from political decision-making but also celebrates this operation as a democratic form of participation and diversity.

Polycentricity's call for "embracing complexity" and expanding the power of communities and individuals for self-rule is actually a call for displacing political tensions to pre-political and post-political stages, namely, spaces where communities are disempowered. In this operation, extractive forces are both expanded and liberated from plural forms of regulation and governance. Embracing complexity cannot mean depoliticizing governance. On the contrary, it should mean acknowledging the plurality of politics. Instead of displacing the political tensions to pre-political and post-political stages, the political or the capacity of plural decision-making should be expanded to incorporate different sovereignties and worldviews at the center. This requires creating a new political space that addresses institutional, epistemological, and ontological injustices (Figure 7.1).

7.1.3 Plurinational, Multiepistemic, and Pluriversal Governance

Through these chapters, I have provided arguments for the need to overcome institutional, epistemological, and ontological injustices and their associated state-centrism, ethnocentrism, and anthropocentrism in the current international governance of the Amazon. This would require building a plurinational, multiepistemic, and pluriversal international governance.

A plurinational governance would redefine Westphalian conceptions of sovereignty and self-determination to make a substantial space for indigenous sovereignties in international decision-making. This governance goes beyond conventional venues for the international participation of Indigenous peoples through indirect involvement with national commissions; participation in side or parallel events; or the granting of observer status. It entails rethinking international relations and sovereignty arrangements by conceiving Indigenous nations as legitimate international actors with decision-making power in international bodies and processes relevant to their lives. In a Plurinational Amazon, ACTO would evolve from being a state-centered international organization to becoming a plurinational organization guided under plural conceptions of sovereignty and self-determination. In addition, a Plurinational Amazon must translate plurinational politics in a way that issues of cooptation, bureaucratization, and extractive dependence found in plurinational governments are not reproduced in international arrangements. For this aim, it would be crucial to incorporate the political representation of Amazonian Indigenous nations in the deliberative units of the organization.

Overcoming state-centrism requires then enlarging the meaning of sovereignty to include indigenous sovereignty as a governing principle for managing international commons. In practice, this reformulation should lead to including

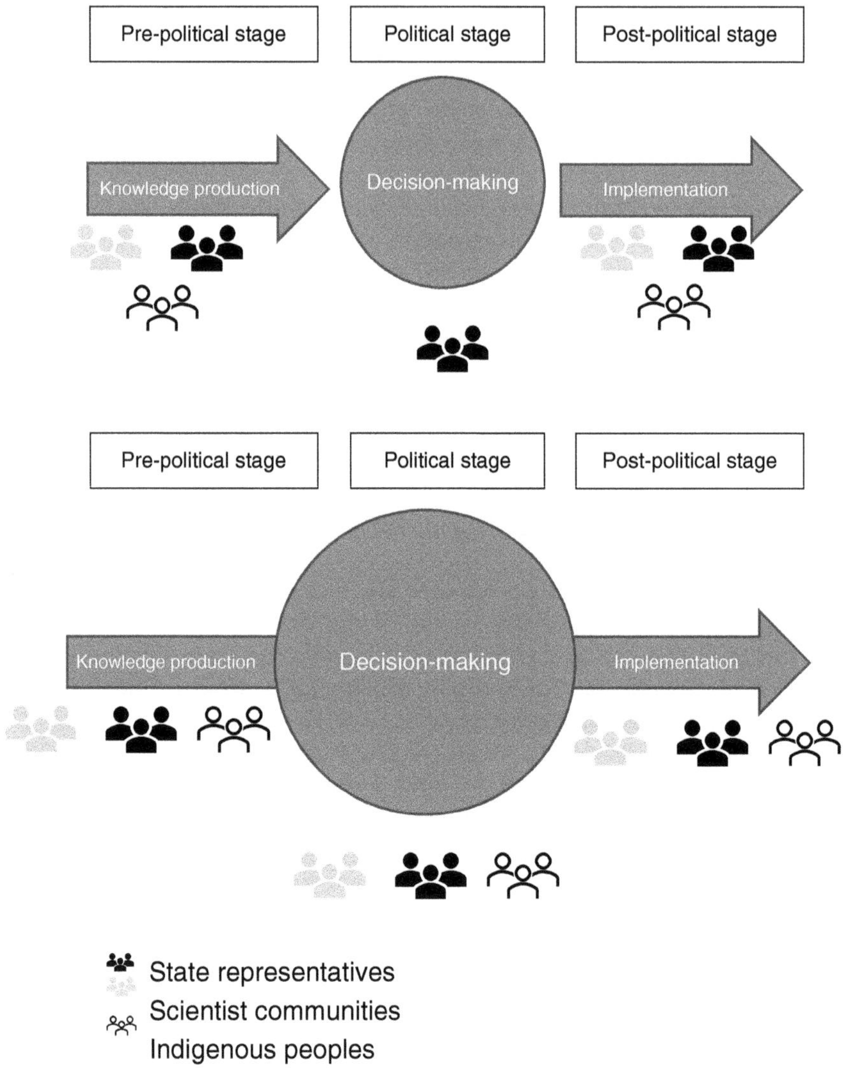

Figure 7.1 Pre-political, political, and post-political stages

Indigenous nations as meaningful participants in the Amazonian governance with the political agency to push for international policies beyond general declarations. Ultimately, this would mean changing the dominant geopolitical imaginary in the region. From conceiving the Amazon as governed under classical state sovereignty and small-scale, project-oriented environmental cooperation, to imagining the basin governed by plural sovereignty and environmental arrangements inspired by indigenous cosmovisions and struggles.

A pluriversal and multi-epistemic governance would open international deliberative forums to negotiate different ontologies and epistemologies. A multi-epistemic governance entails politically discussing varied environmental measures and targets embedded in both indigenous and Western thinking. Namely, more actors are legitimized to be members of the international political table and bring their knowledge to it. A pluriversal governance is something else. It implies discussing the different worldviews on the natural environment. Instead of assuming that state representatives, depoliticized advisory scientist bodies, or indigenous organizations are the only legitimate representatives of the natural world, it would be important to rethink ecological democracy and governance as an instance for negotiating ontological tensions. This pluriversal governance would embrace, rather than avoid, different worldviews emanating from scientist conservationist concerns, indigenous plurinational politics, and state developmental agendas. In this scenario, scientists would have a crucial role along with those people who might coincide with scientists' sense of urgency, but have different views on nature's ontological foundations and propose different means to bring justice to the relationship between ecosystems and communities. In a pluriversal governance, ACTO would have to be transformed from being an anthropocentric and ethnocentric international organization to becoming a pluriversal institutional space. This would mean including independent scientific communities in deliberation processes along with Indigenous nations and nation-states to formulate and negotiate the different ways they portray the representation and protection of the natural environment.

A pluriversal and multi-epistemic international governance might contribute to forging a decolonial form of conservation. This governance could push national agendas to extend indigenous sovereignty rights in national legislation through institutional models of indigenous protected areas that recognize not only the different ecological, economic, and security epistemes, but also the ontological basis of indigenous sovereignty. In international policy-making, this governance would be a more democratic venue to approve standards for governing both extractivism and conservation in the basin.

This governance model can also inspire a transformative path across the world's international forests. These commons suffer similar institutional, epistemological, and ontological injustices.

7.2 International Rainforests: The Congo Basin

With an extent of 2,485,670 km^2 and possessing 29 percent of the planet's tropical peat carbon, the Congo Basin is the second-largest tropical rainforest in the world after the Amazon (Beekmann et al., 2024; Wan, 2009; Livingstone, 2024). It spans six countries in Central Africa (Cameroon, the Central African Republic, the Democratic Republic of Congo, Equatorial Guinea, Gabon, and the Republic of Congo) and has a crucial role in global climate regulation and biodiversity conservation. A study published in Nature, 2017, showed that the Congo Rainforest might store about 30 billion tons of carbon, equivalent to three years of global fossil fuel emissions (Livingstone, 2024). In addition, its remarkable levels of biodiversity include the habitats of critically endangered megafauna such as the African forest elephant (Loxodonta cyclotis), bonobo (Pan paniscus), Western lowland gorilla (Gorilla gorilla gorilla), and Central chimpanzee (Pan troglodytes troglodytes) (IUCN, 2024). The region also provides a livelihood for about 100 million people, including local and Indigenous communities who depend on the forest for their material and cultural survival (Beekmann et al., 2024). In 2021, Congo Basin Environmental Ministers called donors to invest $150 million in research and training, pointing out that this Basin only received 11.5 percent of the international funding toward protecting tropical forests (Livingstone, 2024).

The Congo Basin deforestation rate is low compared to that of other tropical rainforests, however, it reached 12.46 percent between 1990 and 2020, whereas forest intactness decreased from 78 percent in 2000 to 67 percent in 2016 (FAOSTAT, 2022; Shapiro et al., 2021). In general, although the Congo basin's biomass has long-term stability in contrast to a declining trend in the Amazon (Livingstone, 2024; Wan, 2009), it faces multiple threats, including deforestation and forest degradation driven by agriculture, infrastructure development, and extractive industries, as well as illegal wildlife trade (Tyukavina et al., 2018). In the same vein as the Amazon, small-scale agriculture is considered a key driver of deforestation, but large-scale industrial agriculture linked with palm oil, rubber, and sugar production is also a major threat (Shapiro et al., 2023). The impact of extractive industries such as intensive logging or mining is amplified by the construction of roads, which facilitates accessibility and human disturbance in remote areas (Kleinschroth and Healey, 2017).

The conflicts these trends produce on Indigenous peoples also resemble Amazonian dynamics. In the Democratic Republic of Congo (DRC), which holds about 60 percent of the rainforest, the rise of the wild meat trade and demand from the city undermines the Mbuti people's Indigenous food system and exacerbates the poverty in rural communities (Nicolon, 2024). Wildlife and minerals such as gold and diamonds are also attracting mining, farming, and logging operators to the Okapi Wildlife Reserve in the DRC (Nicolon, 2024). Political instability and armed conflicts are also considered key drivers of forest disturbance, with effects on hunting, illegal trade, and forest resource exploitation (Butsic et al., 2015). The DRC, indeed, has a legacy of brutal regional wars in the 1990s and 2000s, which claimed between 1 million and 5 million lives (Livingstone, 2024). Climate change is expected to amplify those threats (Beekmann et al., 2024).

Despite these conflicts, conservation has been critical for national building and governance in the region. Early conservationists believed that colonial wildlife sanctuaries would be lost with independence (Kniewel, 2024). However, the national parks not only survived political turmoil and armed conflict derived from independence processes, but they were also expanded under the subsequent regime of Mobutu Sese Seko (1971–1997). By the early 1970s, Western conservationists lobbied the Congolese regime for an expansion of the national park system and then praised the Congo as an example. The president of the World Wildlife Fund (WWF), Prince Bernhard of the Netherlands, awarded the Congolese autocrat his Order of the Golden Ark for services to nature conservation. In this way, international conservationists propagated authoritarian and militarized practices to deal with conservation threats such as trespassing pastoralists, poaching, or illegal fishing. To legitimize violent actions against "intruders," some conservationists exploited nationalist sentiments and the Mobutu regime's desire for international recognition, suggesting using conservation as a form of securitization. Poachers or pastoralists were not only framed as criminals but as foreigners who violated the country's borders. Although today conservation paradigms have changed, conflicts continue as exemplified by the case of the Kahuzi-Biega National Park (KBNP) (Kniewel, 2024).

The KBNP was created in 1970 and extended in 1975, spanning an area of 600,000 ha located across the Albertine Rift and the Congo Basin (Mangambu-Mokoso et al., 2024). The KBNP is an outstanding habitat for the protection of tropical rainforests and the Eastern Lowland Gorilla. Similar to those conflicts in the Amazon rainforest, the first evictions and violence to create this park produced tense relations with local and indigenous Bantu communities. With the extension of the Park in 1975 and its recognition as a World Heritage Site in 1980, conflicts over land recognition and the control of natural resources reached the Pygmy peoples, who faced arrests, killings, and evictions (Mangambu-Mokoso et al., 2024). The poverty of people living in and around the KBNP, which depends on forest products (firewood, charcoal, bamboo, timber, mushrooms, etc.), exacerbates this situation. During the past few years, some indigenous defenders have launched offensive actions against the Ecoguards to counter governmental measures against illegal logging or the dismantling of militias. With a similar argumentation of authorities opposing communities' self-determination in conservation areas in the Amazon, in the Congo Rainforest, some reports suggest that opposition has been orchestrated by economic interests seeking profit from the exploitation of the Park's resources through the local population. According to the KBNP authorities, the indigenous Pygmy people have destroyed the Park's ecosystems. However, some scholars argue that the Park is opposed by the local people because it encompasses their livelihoods they need to survive (Mangambu-Mokoso et al., 2024).

Pygmy peoples such as the Baka, Bakola, and Bagyéli have ancestrally inhabited this area and are greatly dependent on it for their livelihood (Wan, 2009). To them, land is sacred because it provides food and shelter for the living, and shelter for their ancestors (Mangambu-Mokoso et al., 2024). However, conservation and forest management did not take into account their rights, instead giving preference to industrial forest exploitation and conservation of Gorillas (Wan, 2009). As a consequence of prioritizing these goals, the Pygmy were excluded from nearly two-thirds of their own territory and suffered from lack of arable land, the destruction of the social and cultural fabric, forced recruitment into armed groups, rape, and sexual violence, loss of human life, and increased infant mortality (Mangambu-Mokoso et al., 2024). The multidimensional and complex nature of these conflicts shows that it is urgently needed to have international arrangements to balance the different interests at stake.

7.2.1 Forging an International Architecture

A regional approach for the Congo Rainforest has been weak. The first time the Heads of States of the Congo Rainforest agreed upon a shared long-term vision for the region's forests was the Yaoundé Forest Summit in 1999. In this conference, they enacted the conservation and sustainable development principles of the Yaoundé Declaration and the associated regional action plan, known as the Plan of Convergence. The international consensus reached in these documents asserted the goals of sustainable and joint management by Central African States of both forest resources and the protected areas for their national well-being and to ensure global balance (Wan, 2009). To achieve these objectives, the member states created the Central African Forests Commission (COMIFAC) in 2000 and the Congo Basin Forest Partnership (CBFP) in 2002. The former is an intergovernmental organization, whereas the latter is a nonbinding association of a cooperative nature, originally facilitated by the United States, France, and Germany (Wan, 2009).

Comprised of ten Central African governments, COMIFAC directs, coordinates, and makes decisions on subregional initiatives and actions about the conservation and sustainable management of forest ecosystems. COMIFAC resembles ACTO in its goals, structure, and limitations. It has three organs: the Summits of Heads of State and Government, which envisage policies for the region; a Council of Ministers responsible for decision-making, coordination, and control of implementing policies; and an Executive Secretariat that implements these policies. The Executive Secretariat holds a subregional Forum to involve NGOs, development partners, donors, the private sector, and civil society in monitoring and evaluating policies. As ACTO, COMIFAC is primarily financed by mandatory contributions from member states, but it can also mobilize funds from development partners (Wan, 2009).

Congo Basin countries, through COMIFAC, have participated in international forest-related negotiations to claim financial rewards for deforestation reduction in their territories (Nago and Ongolo, 2021). This approach, however, has not been successful due to their dependence on cooperation agencies and consulting firms, and the weak interests of both African nations and their Northern counterparts in meeting global sustainability goals (Nago and Ongolo, 2021). Moreover, a basic website search shows that the CBFP has been more prominent than the COMIFAC in participating in international forums, engaging with national programs, and promoting cooperation activities. COMIFAC information is outdated and dispersed across different sources, with no official website. CBFP, in contrast, shows consistent and updated information about current programs and activities. This suggests that the region prioritizes an approach based on international cooperation rather than international policy integration.

There is a need to reinforce the regional governance of the Congo rainforests. This requires, first, democratizing this governance. Wan (2009) already alerted about the threats to COMIFAC and CBFP of being dominated by counter-productive forces, be they NGOs, corporations, or some states strongly dependent on external actors. In this view, the Congo Basin forest governance must be reorientated to ensure the engagement of a plurality of voices rather than the privileging of those from above (Wan, 2009). This is crucial because the history of the Congo Rainforest resembles epistemological, ontological, and institutional injustices. The imposition of Western conservation, the aggression over the land and bodies of Indigenous peoples, and the creation of international structures focused on international cooperation, excluding indigenous perspectives and interests beyond simply monitoring and evaluation, all reinforce state-centric, anthropocentric, and ethnocentric forms of governance.

Other global rainforests also lack a regional framework for a just international governance. For instance, the taiga (boreal forest), which lies within the borders of Canada, China, Finland, Japan, Norway, Russia, Sweden, and the United States (IPFRA, 2021), has been absent from global policy agendas on sustainable development and climate change mitigation, although they account for approximately 25 percent of the planet's forest area and contain more than 35 percent of all terrestrial carbon (Burton et al., 2010). Despite being the home to marginalized Indigenous peoples that depend on forest goods and services for their livelihoods and cultural integrity (Chapin et al., 2004), these areas are threatened by timber, oil, and mineral extraction, as well as hydroelectricity (Moen et al., 2014). The unwillingness to engage or build international regional arrangements to govern this forest has resulted in a fragmented governance based on market-driven initiatives such as certification standards dependent on domestic politics (Moen et al., 2014; Teitelbaum et al., 2023). Although some call for creating a new boreal forest policy that considers the socioeconomic needs of local communities and biodiversity conservation under global climate processes (Moen et al., 2014), there is a need to rethink regional arrangements to address the different challenges.

7.2.2 A Plurinational, Multiepistemic, and Pluriversal Governance for Global Rainforests

The unsuccessful efforts to achieve a Global Forest Convention have resulted in leaving the governance of international forests to weak regional cooperative arrangements and national and local initiatives. This resembles the false dichotomy in choosing either global agreements or polycentric governance. The result is that civil society has less interest and resources to struggle for a utopian global agreement whose implementation, in any case, would be very difficult whereas the victorious fragmented governance has only meant the acceleration of extractivism and human rights abuses on forest-dependent peoples.

International forests must be governed by regional arrangements able to balance the different interests at stake as a condition to enact binding standards. This is more achievable since there are already some international structures working on it, such as in the Amazon and the Congo Rainforest. The challenge here is to rebuild those structures in a way to overcome ontological, epistemological, and institutional injustices. This requires building a platform where nation-states that need the forest for national development, Indigenous peoples as sovereign nations that have ancestrally lived in these areas, and conservation scientists with an interest in protecting the forests, all should have a seat in the international governance of each rainforest. In a process of multi-epistemic discussions and with the possibility to enact different ontological standpoints about the relevance of conserving ecosystems, these negotiations should lead to more just and democratic forms of forest governance.

Does the advocacy for regional international arrangements mean that the efforts to develop local initiatives or reach global agreements should be completely rejected? I don't think so. I believe that these efforts should continue as they might contribute to the final goals of global sustainability, national sustainable development, and respecting Indigenous nations. I just believe that we need to give more importance to the middle-ground international level in climate and environmental discussions regarding international commons, such as international rainforests.

Nonetheless, this approach can inspire innovative forms of governance beyond the regional level. Given the current urgency to improve the governance of global commons, I believe that it is also crucial to address institutional, epistemological, and ontological injustices on the global stage. Below, I succinctly address this issue regarding global oceans and outer space.

7.3 Global Oceans

The high seas comprise approximately 62–64 percent of the ocean's surface (Massimi, 2024) and are responsible for almost half of the total ocean's biological productivity (Abegón-Novella, 2024). The high seas and the international seabed area provide important resources, such as seafood, minerals, genetic resources, and environmental services, such as climate regulation, carbon sequestration, air purification, and habitat conservation (Abegón-Novella, 2024). However, given climate change and biodiversity pollution, the open ocean environment and its large marine ecosystems are on the verge of collapse. Fifty percent of all fish stocks in these ecosystems are overexploited, and if current trends continue, more than half of marine species could become extinct by 2100 (Massimi, 2024). Current technologies might accelerate this trend since they have opened up the possibility of accessing and exploiting more resources in these remote areas (Abegón-Novella, 2024).

The legal and institutional frameworks for governing global oceans are fragmented, incomplete, and inadequate (Abegón-Novella, 2024; Radovich, 2023). Two principles have historically governed those areas, the “Freedom of the Seas” on the high seas and the “Common Heritage of Humankind” on the seabed and its mineral resources (Abegón-Novella, 2024). The UN Convention on the Law of the Sea (UNCLOS) of 1982 regulates the “high seas” in Part VII as portions of the ocean that fall outside both territorial seas and the exclusive economic zone (EEZ) of any country or “areas beyond national jurisdiction” (ABNJ) (Massimi, 2024). With UNCLOS, these international waters are still regulated by the “Freedom of the Seas” principle, which goes back to Hugo Grotius’ Mare Liberum (1609). This doctrine states that the High Seas cannot be owned by any person or nation and should be free for anyone to use and exploit, favoring navigation and the interests of maritime powers (Tessnow-von Wysocki and Vadrot, 2022). Under Article 87 of UNCLOS, in the ABNJ, both coastal and landlocked states can enjoy the freedom of navigation, overflight, laying of submarine cables and pipelines, fishing, and scientific research (Li and Xing, 2024; Tessnow-von Wysocki and Vadrot, 2022). In contrast, UNCLOS Part XI, Articles 133 to 150, establishes that the “Area,” namely the deep ocean floor beyond the limits of national jurisdiction and its resources, including “all solid, liquid or gaseous mineral resources” (Art. 133, Part XI, UNCLOS) are “the common heritage of mankind.” During UNCLOS negotiations, Global South governments used this principle to contest the hegemony of traditional sea powers who wished to uphold the Freedom of the High Seas also in the seabed (Tessnow-von Wysocki and Vadrot, 2022).

The Implementation Agreement of Part XI was adopted by the UN in 1994 with the creation of the International Seabed Authority (ISA). The original aim was to allow deep-sea mining to obtain economic benefits and redistribute them fairly among world nations to mitigate poverty and hunger (Massimi, 2024). For this, developing countries under the G-77 (Group of 77) called for creating an international mining company with exclusive exploitation rights, whereas industrialized countries insisted that private companies should also be entitled to mining licenses. The so-called parallel system emerged to reconcile these positions: ISA would run an international public company, “the Enterprise,” and states could request licenses under a site-banking mechanism in which an applicant for an exploration license must name two potential extraction sites of equivalent mineral value. If all requirements are met, an exploration right is granted for one area, while the other is reserved for future exploration and exploitation by the Enterprise or by an entity from a developing country. As a result of this system, more than thirty exploration contracts have been concluded by 2024, with twenty-two contractors (private and state-owned enterprises) having exploration licences (Feichtner and Ginzky, 2024). Whereas African states are demanding the Enterprise’s implementation (it only exists on paper) and to negotiate a benefit-sharing mechanism, some Pacific Island States are sponsoring mining corporations to undertake deep-seabed mining (Feichtner and Ginzky, 2024). The Cook Islands passed a Seabed Minerals

Act in June 2019 to make deep-sea mining part of its economic development strategy (Kung et al., 2021). Nauru sponsored the application of NORI, a subsidiary of the Canadian The Metals Company, to obtain an ISA exploration contract. While UNCLOS assigns sponsoring states the role of guardians of the common heritage, these states hope for economic benefits through taxation of the sponsored entities (Feichtner and Ginzky, 2024).

Deep sea mining, however, has many challenges, including a complex governance. Apart from UNCLOS, there are more than 100 international agreements currently addressing the open ocean (Li and Xing, 2024), and different norms and rules protecting maritime resources are contained in nonsystematic global and regional instruments (Abegón-Novella, 2024). Among them, the UNCLO 1995 Fish Stocks Agreement, the UN Convention on Biological Diversity (CBD), the UNEP Regional Seas Programme, some provisions of the Antarctic Treaty System (ATS), the 1995 Code of Conduct for Responsible Fisheries, and the 1998 International Guidelines for the Management of Deep-sea Fisheries in the High Seas adopted by the Food and Agriculture Organization of the United Nations (FAO). In addition, multiple global and sectoral organizations exercise their mandates over those areas, such as the International Maritime Organization (IMO) concerning shipping, ISA, FAO, and multiple Regional Fisheries Management Organizations. This fragmented and complex governance leads to overlapping mandates, duplication of effort, and inefficiency (Abegón-Novella, 2024).

In this context, scientists and activists alert that mineral exploitation might begin without appropriate governance structures to manage environmental risks (Kung et al., 2021), affecting biodiversity beyond national jurisdictions (BBNJ) and the rights of local and Indigenous peoples impacted by the degradation of oceans' ecosystems. Indeed, the wide-ranging environmental impacts of deep-sea mining might disproportionately affect Indigenous peoples, particularly on islands and coastal areas, as well as those who depend on migratory species, such as salmon (Vierros et al., 2020; Hunter et al., 2018). For this reason, Indigenous Peoples' representatives from the Pacific have long been campaigning for a halt to deep-sea mining. Today, numerous actors are calling for a moratorium, including those states that have an economic interest and whose companies hold ISA exploration contracts. By 2024, the moratorium was supported by more than 800 scientists from 44 states (Feichtner and Ginzky, 2024).

Still, market demand for metals associated with the energy transition is providing new, strong commercial incentives for exploiting these resources (Feichtner and Ginzky, 2024). Three types of mineral formations are found below the surface of the sea: manganese nodules, cobalt-rich ferromanganese crusts, and polymetallic sulfides. All three contain critical metals, such as copper, cobalt, and nickel. This fact has incentivized Norway to be the first country to actively promote deep-sea exploration within its own national boundaries (although the decision was suspended in December 2024), and the current US administration under Trump seems willing to undertake such efforts.

7.3.1 The High Seas Treaty and Indigenous Peoples

The exploitation of biological, nonmineral resources in areas beyond national jurisdiction has also been the subject of growing concern, especially given the lack of an international comprehensive regulation. For this reason, in 2017, UNGA Res. 72/249 established an intergovernmental conference on "biodiversity beyond national jurisdiction" (BBNJ), whose sessions took place from September 2018 to March 2023 (Massimi, 2024; Li and Xing, 2024). The "Agreement under the United Nations Convention on the Law of the Sea on the Conservation and Sustainable Use of Marine Biological Diversity of Areas beyond National Jurisdiction," also known as the BBNJ Agreement, was adopted in June 2023 with 108 signatory states, and by February 2025, 17 states have ratified it. The BBNJ Agreement is formally conceived as the third implementing agreement under the UNCLOS after the 1994 Agreement on Part XI and the 1995 Fish Stock Agreement, in a law-making process considered wide open and inclusive (Abegón-Novella, 2024).

The BBNJ Agreement incorporates the common heritage of humankind as one of its governing principles (Art. 7 b). In this regard, Art. 11.4 establishes that "no State shall claim or exercise sovereignty rights over marine genetic resources of areas beyond national jurisdiction"; Art. 11.6 confirms that "activities with respect to marine genetic resources and digital sequence information on marine genetic resources of areas beyond national jurisdiction are in the interests of all States and for the benefit of all humanity, particularly for the benefit of advancing the scientific knowledge of humanity and promoting the conservation and sustainable use of marine biological diversity, taking into particular consideration the interests and needs of developing States"; and Art. 11.7 determines that such activities "shall be carried out exclusively for peaceful purposes." Indigenous rights and participation are also included as principles of the Agreement, especially, the "use of relevant traditional knowledge of Indigenous Peoples and local communities" and "the respect, promotion and consideration of state obligations relating to the rights of Indigenous Peoples or local communities when taking action to address the conservation and sustainable use of marine biological diversity of areas beyond national jurisdiction" (Art. 7, c, j, k). To build consensus, the text also recognizes the principle of freedom of the high seas (art. 7c) (Abegón-Novella, 2024).

These norms are the result of years of negotiations concentrated on whether marine resources should or should not be governed by the common heritage principle (Massimi, 2024; Abegón-Novella, 2024). The United States, Canada, Russia, and Japan argued that these resources should fall under UNCLOS Part VII concerning the freedom of the high seas. China and the G-77, as well as the Pacific Small Islands Developing States (PSIDS), maintained instead that they should fall under the common heritage principle. Some of the legal arguments for including this principle insisted that since BBNJ implements UNCLOS and Art. 136 of UNCLOS defines "the Area" as a whole as the "common heritage of mankind," nonmineral resources should not be excluded from this definition; in addition, rather than open access, this principle would be better suited for conservation aims (Derrig and Becker Lorca, 2023). In fact, in the past, the common heritage mainly sought fair redistribution, and today, it is also used to safeguard equitable intra- and inter-generational environmental sustainability (Massimi, 2024).

Even though developing countries were successful in incorporating this principle, some authors showed concern about the limited role of local and Indigenous peoples during the Agreement negotiation. In an interconnected ocean crisscrossed by migratory species, island and coastal communities around the world are custodians of globally significant species and ecosystems, and hold traditions, knowledge, and resource use that is important for their management, including subsistence harvest of migratory species, cultural and spiritual practices and beliefs related to such migratory species; and ancestral voyaging and navigation through the high seas (Vierros et al., 2020; Mulalap et al., 2020). Highly migratory species of cultural, social, and economic significance to these peoples include sea turtles, whales and other cetaceans, sharks, fish such as salmon and tunas, seals and other pinnipeds, and seabirds. Some of these species spend part of their lives in coastal habitats and part in the high seas, in the process crossing the jurisdictional boundaries of multiple countries, expressing the ecological connectivity between local and Indigenous peoples with each other and with the high seas (Vierros et al., 2020). For instance, knowledge from Indigenous people of small island states such as Fiji, Vanuatu, and Kiribati, includes the use of indigenous weather pattern monitoring to help in understanding climate change, and indigenous approaches to sustainable harvesting, which have helped maintain a sustainable stock of fish like Salmon (Albar, 2024). This body of knowledge predates the establishment of current national borders and continues to inform access and use of marine areas and resources (Radovich, 2023). For this reason, Vierros et al. (2020) advocated for the substantial involvement of Indigenous peoples and local communities in UN discussions on ABNJ governance.

It might seem that the involvement of Indigenous peoples in the drafting processes was not merely symbolic, as the Agreement mentions thirty-one times the term "Indigenous peoples" in fifteen articles (Albar, 2024). However, some scholars argued that they have been underrepresented in the debates or that their participation was as mere observers or represented by national delegations (Tilot et al., 2021; Albar, 2023; Vierros et al., 2020). Mentions of Indigenous peoples are found in the intervention of state authorities. For instance, on behalf of PSIDS (Intergovernmental Conference no. 1), Nauru emphasized the need to account for regional and subregional characteristics in line with the relevance of traditional knowledge. For the design of a scientific or expert body, Nauru, on behalf of PSIDS (Intergovernmental Conference no. 1), suggested considering traditional navigation alongside the best available science. Micronesia (Intergovernmental Conference no. 2) argued that traditional knowledge about connectivity regarding marine species that migrate between areas within and beyond national jurisdiction and best practices of Indigenous Peoples and local communities could complement science. On behalf of the Alliance of Small Island States

(AOSIS) (Intergovernmental Conference no. 3), Belize reiterated the relevance of traditional knowledge and the connection between coastal waters and areas beyond national jurisdiction (Tessnow-von Wysocki and Vadrot, 2022).

These indirect interventions could have facilitated the inclusion of the term Indigenous peoples in the agreement. However, scholars have noted that it is not clear how the participation of Indigenous peoples will be operationalized through bodies established under the agreement (Tilot et al., 2021). Indigenous peoples continue to be seen as "consultants" who will only be engaged in certain administrative processes like environmental assessment and scientific capacity-building (Albar, 2024). Direct decision-making power from Indigenous peoples was absent in the negotiation process, and no institution has been created to make this possible for the implementation of the agreement.

7.3.2 New Foundations for Governing the Oceans Commons

There are some proposals to improve the governance of the oceans commons. Li and Xing (2024) lamented that the principle of "common concern of humankind" was not included in the BBNJ Agreement and proposed its inclusion in future arrangements. For them, the common heritage principle cannot address ecological problems such as marine plastic pollution, the overexploitation of fish stocks, the extinction of the coral reefs, the loss of marine species, the warming of seawater, and others, because it emphasizes resource redistribution rather than general environmental obligations of the international community. The recognition of the high seas decline as a common concern of humankind would rather help States to address common concerns within their borders, including promoting cooperation and assuming obligations in areas beyond national jurisdiction (Li and Xing, 2024).

The original formulation of the common heritage principle indeed has limitations, as it refers to the redistribution of resources without concerns about global sustainability. However, even if it is reframed in sustainability terms or if we incorporate a "common concern" principle, there remain two crucial problems. Those principles would be inserted into exclusionary governance arrangements that heavily rely on nation-states, and they are infused with anthropocentric and ethnocentric perspectives that neglect indigenous ontological and epistemological standpoints. For this reason, it is important to explore new arrangements beyond those principles in which the ocean commons could be governed under plurinational, pluriversal, and multi-epistemological frames.

New arrangements for governing global oceans could build on indigenous perspectives. For instance, Parsons et al. (2021) note how Indigenous sustainable marine governance and management intersect intergenerational justice by emphasizing how Indigenous people possess obligations to their ancestors (honoring them and their cultural legacies), their families (duties of care to living humans and more-than-human kin), and their descendants (ensuring that future beings can enjoy healthy environments). As Indigenous ontologies and epistemologies frame time, relationships, and environmental justice differently than Western-based theories of justice, Indigenous concerns about future generations are twofold: for nature per se, and the continuation of their unique cultures located in specific places and environments (Parsons et al., 2021). This double objective requires both the recognition of indigenous knowledge, innovations, and practices as beneficial for international policy and science (Vierros et al., 2020), but also of indigenous sovereignty. In this way, Indigenous peoples are political communities in their own right instead of being merely considered as "wardens" of natural resources (Massimi, 2024).

The way to implement indigenous ecologies and sovereignty in the oceans is complex. Epeli Hau'ofa explained that Indigenous peoples from Oceania collectively managed their common ocean spaces for centuries before nineteenth-century imperialism created political boundaries that obstructed these management systems (Tilot et al., 2021). Hence, Hau'ofa (2000) advocated for rebuilding a common identity among Island states to act together as a region and advance their collective interests, including the protection of the ocean for the general good and their own survival. Hau'ofa's argument proposes a regional identity rooted in diversity and connectivity as the political foundation of collective rights to imagine and enact governance over common resources without erasing profound differences between island states, their societies, and cultures. This would mean an alternative mode of governance in which humans act to guarantee a balance between living and nonliving entities, fundamentally coupled in their common heritage and common wellbeing (Bambridge et al., 2021). Based on Hau'ofa (1998), Bambridge et al. (2021) propose the idea of "Oceanian Sovereignty" as a secondary affiliation that does not exclude the sovereignty of Fiji, Tonga, Vanuatu, or other regional states but, rather, complements that narrower sovereignty with broader, region-based sovereignty. A key feature of Oceanian Sovereignty is the way that it appeals to Indigenous futurity: the deep time and place of Oceania's peoples and their culturally rich ecological knowledge and practice include both a relationship to the past and a profound relationship to the future (Bambridge et al., 2021).

The ideal of Oceanian sovereignty might inspire a new political space in which the sovereignty of Indigenous peoples and their deep relationship with the oceans is internationally recognized, along with the agency of the ocean itself. This is because the ocean is not only a subject of law but is a producer of law and a partner in the constitution of this regional sovereignty (Bambridge et al., 2021). This resonates with the proposal to design the governance of BBNJ from a "Rights of Nature perspective" (Abegón-Novella, 2024), based on integral and holistic views on the relationship between oceans and humans (Radovich, 2023). In this view, a nonanthropocentric understanding of BBNJ could encourage progressive interpretations of existing principles and the development of new principles; underpin strict standards for EIAs; encourage the adoption of ambitious management measures; provide a new framework for maritime genetic resources, and foster stronger participation of non-State actors (Abegón-Novella, 2024). In this context, Harden-Davies et al. (2020) proposed the creation of a new body, the "Council of Ocean," which would enable civil society to participate in decision-making along with States; foster greater collective responsibility and long-term management; broader participation in the review of environmental impact assessments; guide the implementation of benefit-sharing measures of maritime resources, among others.

The "Council of Ocean," if conceived as a supranational space for decision-making, and not merely as a consultant and participatory platform, could reflect the plurinational and pluriversal governance of the Oceans Commons. In this council, Indigenous peoples, nation-states, and conservation scientists should bring their epistemological and ontological standpoints to negotiate proper ways of representing ocean beings and governing the global oceans.

7.4 Outer Space

Early concerns about conceiving space exploration as an extension of human colonization (Janssen and Yap, 2024) led to the formulation of the Outer Space Treaty in 1967 as an institutional arrangement aimed at preventing colonial competition (Vidaurri et al., 2020). Article 1 of the Treaty states that "the exploration and use of outer space [...] shall be carried out for the benefit and in the interests of all countries [...] and shall be the province of all [hu] mankind." This provision has been contentious due to growing political and commercial interest in the exploration and exploitation of space resources, including orbital slots, radio frequencies, and minerals (Janssen and Yap, 2024). For some, Article 1 treats outer space as a global commons and its resources as *res communis* subjected to common property, from the edge of the national airspace to the geostationary orbit and onto celestial bodies such as the asteroids, moons, and planets (Johnson, 2024; Janssen and Yap, 2024). Under this interpretation, outer space would be governed by the common heritage of humankind principle (Picq, 2017). For others, outer space and its resources are *res nullius* and subject to open access for anyone to use and exploit. Proponents of this interpretation note that Article 2 prohibits the national appropriation of outer space, the moon, and other celestial bodies, but this would be applied to resources "in place," excluding those that have been removed from their place or are below celestial bodies' surface (Goehring, 2021).

The commons interpretation would be additionally supported by important multilateral instruments, such as the Moon Agreement of 1979 and the 1976 Declaration of the First Meeting of Equatorial Countries (the Bogota Declaration), which incorporate the "common heritage" principle regarding outer space. However, these arrangements lacked broad support and were not recognized by major space countries (Picq, 2017). Apart from some policy documents, such as the Guidelines for the Long-term Sustainability of Outer Space Activities of the Committee on the Peaceful Uses of Outer Space, the European Code of Conduct for Space Debris Mitigation, and the European Space Policy, Picq (2017) found that between 1957 and 2022 hundreds of "space arrangements," including bilateral or multilateral policies, treaties and contracts on outer space, privilege an interpretation of outer space as *terra nullius*.

This trend has been reinforced by private actors and national policies. The US-based network of activists, entrepreneurs, and companies known as "NewSpace" strongly promotes the intensification of space exploration and settlement (Johnson, 2024). They argue that overpopulation and resource depletion caused the ecological crisis, and it is resolvable if the space frontier is colonized and industrialized (Johnson, 2024). In their environmental variant, they propose the exploitation of helium-3, abundant on the Moon, for being a potential element in the technology of controlled fusion reactions and clean energy production (Johnson, 2024). In this view, mining lucrative metals such as cobalt, nickel, platinum, iron, nickel, rare earth elements, and precious metals from asteroids and celestial bodies outside the Earth is seen as a way to mitigate the climate emergency within it (Deberdt and Le Billon, 2023; Janssen and Yap, 2024).

This imaginary is now supported by domestic law and bilateral agreements. In November 2015, the United States approved the Commercial Space Launch Competitiveness Act (CSLCA), entitling US citizens and companies to private property rights over space resources. Luxembourg (2017), the United Arab Emirates (2019), and Japan (2021) introduced similar legislation aimed at granting permits to private companies for the exploration and use of space resources (Johnson, 2024). Deepening this trend, in April 2020, President Trump signed an executive order declaring outer space not to be a global commons and affirmed the right of commercial space mining. In September 2020, the U.S. National Aeronautics and Space Administration (NASA) announced the celebration of bilateral agreements named "the Artemis Accords" to establish guidelines for resource extraction in outer space with countries supporting the U.S. interpretation of international space law. By January 2025, fifty-three nations have signed these Accords with the aim, among others, of allowing commercial exploitation of celestial bodies. The Artemis Accords claim not to conflict with the Outer Space Treaty and reiterate that no private operator or nation has territorial claims in outer space, but they allow operators to remove material from bodies in outer space for commercial purposes (Neilson, 2024a). This has produced doubts about their consistency with international space law (Johnson, 2024).

These legal-institutional structures emerging in anticipation of space mining evoke a deeper historical trajectory of colonialism (Trevino, 2020). For Johnson (2024), these developments resemble the age of maritime colonialism, where spaces and resources that were once open for public use become the private property of powerful actors to the exclusion of others. For Neilson (2024a), the institutional and legal developments of outer space activities have been justified by the same narrative that colonists used to settle the Americas: *terra nullius* and Manifest Destiny. As such, they follow a path of the nineteenth-century Gold Rush, where prospectors took whatever was considered valuable while stealing the land of Indigenous peoples, leaving waste, and harming ecosystems (Neilson, 2024a).

7.4.1 Dark Skies Colonialism

Outer space colonialism is not only a dream ambition, it is a current reality given the societies' dependence on space-based infrastructures for communication, internet services, and monitoring of Earth phenomena ranging from weather and climate to disaster management (Venkatesan et al., 2020; Janssen and Yap, 2024). The impressive growth of the private space industry with the creation of satellite mega-constellations is exemplified by the SpaceX internet satellite project Starlink, which launched 10,000 satellites in a few years; by 2030, it is projected that 100,000 satellites will reach the low Earth orbit (LEO) (Janssen and Yap, 2024; Finnegan, 2022). Given lower entry barriers and limited regulation to rocket launching, this trend would result in more telescope images being interrupted by streaks of light, losing valuable data (Finnegan, 2022; Janssen and Yap, 2024; Neilson, 2024a). The changing night sky with increasing light pollution might also impact the Earth's ecosystems by affecting nocturnal animals that depend on moonlight and starlight to mobilize in search of food, shelter, and partners (Kuthunur, 2023). These developments have also caused increasing concerns among scientists, policymakers, and industry practitioners regarding the long-term sustainability of space infrastructures as a result of increasing space congestion and space debris (Janssen and Yap, 2024). For Venkatesan et al. (2020), the rapid increase in satellite constellations is producing a crisis that soon will reach the point of no return.

As a response, international public and private organizations, such as the United Nations Office of Outer Space Affairs (UNOOSA), the International Astronomical Union (IAU), the National Science Foundation's National Optical-Infrared Astronomy Research Laboratory, the Dark & Quiet Skies for Science and Society, along with dark sky movements such as the International Dark Sky Association (2023), have developed reports and conferences showing their concerns on the impact of the minimally regulated space industry (Neilson, 2024a). The defense of the "right to dark skies" has also unified both professional astronomers and Indigenous Peoples (Finnegan, 2022), although these reports generally treat Indigenous peoples as stakeholders (Neilson, 2024a)

But Indigenous peoples are more than stakeholders. Astronomy is central to their cultural, spiritual, and social practices and ancestral knowledge (Finnegan, 2022). The ancestral connection to their homelands implies holistic relationships with the night sky, the motions of the Moon and the planets, expressed in oral traditions, rituals, calendars, and ethics (Neilson, 2024a). For most Native Americans, ancestral astronomies helped to make sense of life and relationships and reaffirm their belief in the interdependence of all things in an animate and living universe. Concrete practices include the reading of temporal and seasonal changes from the star formations among the Navajo people (Finnegan, 2022). Other people, such as the Polynesians, have practiced seaward voyaging and wayfinding by way of the sky and stars (Finnegan, 2022). In the far north, Inuit peoples use the Flickering Star as a guide for weather prediction (MacDonald and Schledermann, 1998), while in the southern hemisphere, many nations use dark constellations for time-keeping (Urton, 1981). The Mi'kmaw people use the constellation of Muin and the Seven Bird Hunters to produce knowledge about circumpolar stars, hunting ethics, biology, and more (Marschall et al., 2010 in Neilson, 2024a). For this reason, the growth of light pollution around the world has been considered as another form of colonialism and, in the words of Hamacher et al. (2020), cultural genocide.

For Neilson (2024b), not only knowledge and traditions but also indigenous land is affected by launching facilities and the usage of outer space. Contrary to colonial and post-colonial definitions of indigenous lands as material locations, Indigenous peoples include in their definition access to all components that contribute to their ecosystem and culture, such as water, air, the night sky, and outer space (Neilson, 2024a). Based on oral traditions and foundational histories, in which the First Nations refer to themselves as coming from the stars and use the space for a repository of knowledge, Neilson (2024b) argues that celestial objects, such as the Moon, and outer space, itself, are part of the traditional lands of Indigenous peoples (Neilson, 2024b). At the same time, for many Indigenous peoples, the stars, planets, and the Moon are ancestors or living beings and, therefore, express spiritual and kin relations (Neilson, 2024a).

This explains why, as with their superficial land, indigenous connections with the night sky are not extractive, but based on sovereign protocols and treaties that express responsibilities of care (Neilson, 2024a). For instance, in the Mi'kmaw cosmology of six worlds, the Land above Clouds, or outer space, is part of a treaty. Country et al. (2023) note that Sky Country (Space) is to be cared for, not exploited. Ultimately, these treaties express both indigenous sovereignties and duties; the former because outer spaces and celestial bodies are part of their territories, the latter because they also conceive these elements as living beings and/or ancestors. Without necessarily ending any form of space exploration, honoring those sovereignties and responsibilities would avoid pure exploitation (Neilson, 2024a). In this regard, Neilson (2024a) proposes an anti-colonial framework to address outer space, not only including the rights of Indigenous peoples, but also the rights of celestial objects and outer space itself, and thus humanity's responsibilities for engaging in space activities.

Given that the current extractive, *terra nullius* approach to outer space denies Indigenous perspectives, scholars propose using international law to address this exclusion. In this view, the reference to "mankind" in the Outer Space Treaty should include Indigenous peoples (Finnegan, 2022), and policy and industrial developments impacting the night sky should have the consent of these peoples under the UNDRIP (Neilson, 2024b). In addition, under the UNDRIP the current impacts of light pollution and satellite pollution are a violation of Indigenous rights to maintain, use, and live their cultural heritage and knowledge systems (Art. 31.1) and to transmit their knowledges and continue religious and spiritual practices (UDRIP Arts. 12.1 and 13.1) (Neilson, 2024b). The space industry would also affect the rights protected under UNDRIP to use their traditional lands in terms of "traditionally owned, occupied or otherwise used or acquired" (Arts. 26 and 27) (Neilson, 2024b).

The problem with relying on the UNDRIP and general declarations is that there are no international institutions that might enforce them or establish channels to materialize those rights beyond attempts at the courts of justice. For this reason, it is important to think in international governance arrangements to balance the different interests and rights beyond colonial-based institutions, ontologies, and epistemologies.

7.4.2 A Plurinational and Pluriversal Governance for Outer Space

To overcome *terra nullius* in the governance of outer space, scholars propose conceiving it as part of the human environment. This would imply the protection of space bodies and orbits, better debris cleanup technologies, and stricter practices of space mission review (Vidaurri et al., 2020). This perspective also emphasizes the need to protect the space as an "ancestral global commons" that contains the heritage and future of humanity's scientific and cultural practices and as such should be shared by the world community in trust for future generations (Venkatesan et al., 2020). This requires setting up "anti-colonial standards and protocols" to ensure equal and fair participation in space (Vidaurri et al., 2020).

Ideas of environmental protection and global benefit sharing, however, require institutions that are still missing on the global stage. Moreover, despite their calls for an anti-colonial standpoint, these proposals continue to be state-centric and rely too much on ethnocentric ideals, be it preservation or redistribution of benefits among nation-states. For instance, Neilson (2024a) alerts that the ideal to "preserve outer space heritage," also stated by Section 9 of the Artemis Accords, can be colonial since it might reproduce green colonialism practices and mentalities, such as creating National Parks on the Moon under Western interests and perspectives (Neilson, 2024a). Beyond conceiving outer space as an "ancestral commons" under Western conservation or conceiving it as a commodity under the conception of *terra nullius*, a third way would be conceiving space governance under indigenous perspectives.

This is, however, problematic because most authors tend to minimize these perspectives to issues of inclusion, consultation, and cooperation. They acknowledge the relevance of indigenous knowledge about space and highlight the need for participation and inclusion of indigenous communities in space activities (Janssen and Yap, 2024), although within limited procedures and forums. Thus, positive examples of consultations and cooperation are seen in specific activities, such as the Navajo-NASA cooperation program (Milligan, 2023). Finnegan (2022) proposes broadening the understanding of the Space community in organizations such as the IAU and the inclusion of Indigenous voices in the UN Committee on the Peaceful Uses of Outer Space (UNCOPUOS), a state-centric body that could accept recommendations from Indigenous peoples. Neilson (2024a) proposes that international organizations involved in outer space regulation, including the United Nations, "must consult" Indigenous peoples in that work. Although not as mere stakeholders, but as sovereigns, this consultation would be framed under international law standards of FPIC (Neilson, 2024b).

These proposals are very sensitive to epistemological and ontological injustices and call for conceiving relationships with outer space in indigenous terms, in a way that humans operating in space infrastructures are "guests" that respect, give back, and support the nature of outer space, the Moon, and celestial objects (Neilson, 2024a). However, they neglect institutional injustices and, in particular, the sovereignty character of Indigenous views on outer space. Recognizing this sovereignty requires more than inclusion and participation as stakeholders or as honorific sovereign people. This requires making Indigenous peoples part of the political conversation at the international level on equal terms under plurinational and pluriversal arrangements. For this, it is crucial to forge new global institutions and regulations aimed at establishing conditions and duties for space exploration. These institutions should create deliberative spaces in which Indigenous peoples and scientists not only submit recommendations but also engage in decision-making processes.

7.5 Final Thoughts

We are living in one of the most troubling times in history, marked by the rise of far-right, climate-denying, and authoritarian governments advancing extractive agendas. As glaciers melt, forests burn, ecosystems approach critical tipping points, and water scarcity and drought devastate vulnerable populations in rural and impoverished urban areas, world leaders continue to expand the extractive frontier – both on Earth and beyond. In this context, it is imperative to reexamine international governance arrangements that can be both ambitious and achievable, radical and appealing, and above all, that advance justice for those who suffer the most from the climate catastrophe: local and Indigenous communities, as well as the natural environment itself.

Throughout the chapters of this book, I have analyzed the governance of the Amazon over recent decades, shaped by extractive forces, national developmental goals, and conservation initiatives. I have also reflected on the potential to disrupt the current fragmented and narrow governance frameworks. The objective has been to highlight the limitations of the prevailing approach, which celebrates polycentricity as an ideal model for governing this vital rainforest. Rather than continuing to rely on small-scale programs, national policies, or sectoral initiatives that coexist with – or even reinforce – the dominant view of the Amazon as a site of global extractivism, it is essential to reassert the need for comprehensive regulation and shared goals within a framework of plurinational, multi-epistemic, and pluriversal governance.

I argue that achieving this vision requires expanding the political space to include Indigenous peoples and conservation scientists as political subjects alongside nation-states. The goal is to democratize political discourse and international decision-making by incorporating diverse epistemological and ontological perspectives and embracing multiple ways of knowing, valuing, and relating to the natural world.

Ultimately, this book proposes a framework for imagining a new mode of governance for the Amazon – and for other international commons – that addresses institutional, epistemological, and ontological injustices. Rather than expecting global negotiations and agreements to resolve all problems, or relying solely on decentralized and fragmented efforts, it is both crucial and feasible to construct international arrangements at the regional level. Nevertheless, I believe this framework also holds broader relevance, offering a critical lens for rethinking current governance of global commons. While such governance is often framed in terms of participation, conservation, and benefit-sharing, it frequently facilitates extractive interests in practice.

To some, these reflections may appear naïve or utopian. It is true that deepening democratic governance alone does not guarantee just or virtuous outcomes in the face of the climate emergency. Eco-fascist visions of preservation, alongside calls for massive resource extraction under the guise of "saving the planet," may continue to gain traction, furthering human and environmental suffering. However, the rise of fascism and the threat of eco-fascism cannot be countered through a technocratic retreat that leaves political agency solely in the hands of state representatives. I remain convinced of the transformative potential of democratization, collective awareness, and solidarity. This book contributes to the urgent conversation on the necessity and potential for implementing genuinely democratic institutions in international environmental governance.

BIBLIOGRAPHY

Abegón-Novella, M. (2024). Making sense of the agreement on biodiversity beyond national jurisdiction: The road ahead. *Environmental Policy and Law*, 53(5–6), 439–458.

Abele, F., & Rodon, T. (2007). Inuit diplomacy in the global era: The strengths of multilateral internationalism. *Canadian Foreign Policy Journal*, 13(3), 45–63.

Abers, R. N., Oliveira, M. S. D., & Pereira, A. K. (2017). Inclusive development and the asymmetric state: Big projects and local communities in the Brazilian Amazon. *The Journal of Development Studies*, 53(6), 857–872.

Adeyeye, Y., Hardy, J., & Richards, C. (2019). Seeking procedural equity in global environmental governance: Indigenous participation and knowledge politics in forest and landscape restoration debates at the 2016 World Conservation Congress. *Forest Policy and Economics*, 109, 1–14.

Agostinis, G., & Palestini, S. (2021). Transnational governance in motion: Regional development banks, power politics, and the rise and fall of South America's infrastructure integration. *Governance*, 34(3), 765–784. https://doi.org/10.1111/gove.12529

AIDESEP. (2011). *Construyendo REDD Indígena: Adecuación intercultural del REDD+ Perú a los derechos de los pueblos indígenas* (Dalat, Vietnam, 24–25 marzo). Forest Peoples Programme. www.forestpeoples.org/sites/fpp/files/publication/2011/03/aidesepreddindigenasp.pdf

AIDESEP & Forest Peoples Programme. (2014). *Making the invisible visible: Indigenous perspectives on deforestation in the Peruvian Amazon*. AIDESEP.

Akchurin, M. (2015). Constructing the rights of nature: Constitutional reform, mobilization, and environmental protection in Ecuador. *Law and Social Inquiry*, 40(4), 937–968.

Albar, R. (2023). Common heritage of mankind at the expense of indigenous people's rights? BBNJ treaty and beyond. *Harvard Human Rights Journal*. October 25, 2023: https://journals.law.harvard.edu/hrj/2023/10/common-heritage-of-mankind-at-the-expense-of-indigenous-peoples-rights-bbnj-treaty-and-beyond/

Aligica, P. D., & Tarko, V. (2011). Polycentricity: From Polanyi to Ostrom, and beyond. *Governance*, 25(2), 237–262. https://doi.org/10.1111/j.1468-0491.2011.01550.x

Aljazeera (2020). Investors fail to protect the Amazon, conservation group finds. October 1, 2020: www.aljazeera.com/economy/2020/10/1/fuelling-deforestation-big-investors-fall-short-on-amazon-policy

Almeida, A. W. B. de. (2004). Terras tradicionalmente ocupadas: processos de territorialização e movimentos sociais. *Revista Brasileira De Estudos Urbanos E Regionais*, 6(1), 9. https://doi.org/10.22296/2317-1529.2004v6n1p9

Alves, F., Costa, P. M., Novelli, L., & Vidal, D. G. (2023). The rights of nature and the human right to nature: An overview of the European legal system and challenges for the ecological transition. *Frontiers in Environmental Science*, 11, 1175143.

Amazon Sacred Headwaters. (2022). *Declaration for the Protection of the Amazon Sacred Headwaters*. Retrieved from www.sacredheadwaters.org/declaration

Anaya, F. C., & Espírito-Santo, M. M. (2018). Protected areas and territorial exclusion of traditional communities: Analyzing the social impacts of environmental compensation strategies in Brazil. *Ecology and Society*, 23(1), 8.

Anthias, P. (2022). The pluri-extractivist state: Regional autonomy and the limits of indigenous representation in Bolivia's Gran Chaco Province. *Journal of Latin American Studies*, 54(1), 125–154. https://doi.org/10.1017/S0022216X21000997

Aoki Inoue, C. Y. (2018). Worlding the study of global environmental politics in the anthropocene: Indigenous voices from the Amazon. *Global Environmental Politics*, 18(4), 25–42. https://doi.org/10.1162/glep_a_00479

Arnauld de Sartre, X., & Taravella, R. (2009). National sovereignty vs. sustainable development: Lessons from the narrative on the internationalization of the Brazilian Amazon. *Political Geography*, 28(7), 406–415.

Arsel, M., Hogenboom, B., & Pellegrini, L. (2016). The extractive imperative and the boom in environmental conflicts at the end of the progressive cycle in Latin America. *The Extractive Industries and Society*, 3(4), 877–879.

Artaxo, P. (2019). Working together for Amazonia. *Science*, 363, 323. https://doi.org/10.1126/science.aaw6986

Aryal, K., Maraseni, T., Subedi, B. P., Laudari, H. K., Ghimire, P. L., Khanal, S. C., Zhang, H., & Timilsina, R. (2024). REDD+ at risk: Emerging ten questions that REDD+ must answer. *Environmental Science & Policy*, 156, 103744. https://doi.org/10.1016/j.envsci.2024.03.005

Associated Press. (2019). Macron calls Amazon an issue for the whole planet. *AP News*. www.apnews.com/article/brazil-france-emmanuel-macron-iran-nuclear-global-trade-9193fb6a2dc84d55bbc67b16d650b9bc

Atapattu, S., & Gonzalez, C. G. (2015). The North–South divide in international environmental law: Framing the issues. In S. Alam, S. Atapattu, C. G. Gonzalez, & J. Razzaque (Eds.), *International environmental law and the global South* (pp. 1–20). Cambridge University Press.

Atmadja, S. S., Duchelle, A. E., Sy, V. D., Selviana, V., Komalasari, M., Sills, E. O., & Angelsen, A. (2022). How do REDD+ projects contribute to the goals of the Paris Agreement? *Environmental Research Letters*, 17, e044038. https://doi.org/10.1088/1748-9326/ac5669

Augsburger, A. (2021). The plurinational state and Bolivia's formación abigarrada. *Third World Quarterly*, 42(7), 1566–1582. https://doi.org/10.1080/01436597.2021.1899803

Baber, W. F., & Bartlett, R. V. (2015). *Consensus and global environment governance: Deliberative democracy in nature's regime*. The MIT Press.

Bäckstrand, K. (2006). Democratizing global environmental governance? stakeholder democracy after the world summit on sustainable development. *European Journal of International Relations*, 12(4), 467–498. https://doi.org/10.1177/1354066106069321

Balagopal, B., & Chacko, J. (2020). From the tragedy of the commons to sustainable commons: A survey of the theoretical developments on CPR. In M. Pillai, G. Ganapathy-Doré (Eds.), *Global commons: Issues, concerns and estrategies* (1st edn., pp. 2–11). SAGE Publications Pvt Ltd. https://doi.org/10.4135/9789353885724

Barichella, A. (2023). *Can cities, states and regions save our planet? Transatlantic perspectives on multilevel climate governance*. Springer International Publishing. https://doi.org/10.1007/978-3-031-33936-3

Bastos Lima, M. G., Harring, N., Jagers, S. C., Löfgren, Å., Persson, M., Sjöstedt, M., Brülde, B., Langlet, D., Steffen, W., & Alpízar, F. (2021). Large-scale collective action to avoid an Amazon tipping point – key actors and interventions. *Current Research in Environmental Sustainability*, 3, 100048. https://doi.org/10.1016/j.crsust.2021.100048

Bawaka Country, Wright, S., Suchet-Pearson, S., Lloyd, K., Burarrwanga, L., Ganambarr, R., Ganambarr-Stubbs, M., Ganambarr, B., & Maymuru, D. (2016). The politics of ontology and ontological politics. *Dialogues in Human Geography*, 6(1), 23–27. https://doi.org/10.1177/2043820615624053

Bayot, A. B. E. (2019). Free, prior, and informed consent in the Philippines: A Fourth World critique. In I. Feichtner, M. Krajewski, R. Roesch (Eds.), *Human Rights in the Extractive Industries. Interdisciplinary Studies in Human Rights* (vol 3). Cham: Springer. https://doi.org/10.1007/978-3-030-11382-7_11

Bayrak, M. M., & Marafa, L. M. (2016). Ten years of REDD+: A critical review of the impact of REDD+ on forest-dependent communities. *Sustainability*, 8(7), 620. https://doi.org/10.3390/su8070620

Bebbington, A., & Humphreys, D. (2011). An Andean avatar: Post-neoliberal and neoliberal strategies for securing the unobtainable. *New Political Economy*, 16(1), 131–145.

Bebbington, D., Verdum, R., Gamboa, C., & Bebbington, A. (2018). The infrastructure-extractives-resource governance complex in the Pan-Amazon: Roll backs and contestations. *European Review of Latin American and Caribbean Studies*, 106, 183–208.

Beck, S., Esguerra, A., & Borie, M. (2014). Towards a reflexive turn in the governance of global environmental expertise: The cases of the IPCC and the IPBES. *GAIA – Ecological Perspectives for Science and Society*, 23(2), 80–87.

Becker, F. (2022, February 4). Trophy's choice: How the link between trophy hunting and white land ownership challenges notions of community empowerment in Namibia. *Current Conservation*. www.currentconservation.org/trophys-choice-how-the-link-between-trophy-hunting-and-white-land-ownership-challenges-notions-of-community-empowerment-in-namibia/

Bedjaoui, M. (1979). *Towards a new international economic order*. United Nations Educational, Scientific and Cultural Organization.

Beekmann, M., Gallois, S., & Rondinini, C. (2024). Uncertain future for Congo Basin biodiversity: A systematic review of climate change impacts. *Biological Conservation*, 297(1), 110730.

Beier, J. M. (2016). Indigenous diplomacy. In C. Constantinou, P. Kerr, & P. Sharp (Eds.), *The SAGE handbook of diplomacy* (pp. 642–653). Sage Publications Ltd.

Belfer, E., Ford, J. D., & Maillet, M. (2019). Pursuing an Indigenous platform: Exploring opportunities and constraints for Indigenous participation in the UNFCCC. *Global Environmental Politics*, 19(1), 12–33.

Bellinkx, V., Casalin, D., Erdem Türkelli, G., Scholtz, W., & Vandenhole, W. (2022). Addressing climate change through international human rights law: From (extra)territoriality to common concern of humankind. *Transnational Environmental Law*, 11(1), 69–93.

Berglund, O., & Schmidt, D. (2020). *Extinction rebellion and climate change activism: Breaking the law to change the world*. Cham, Switzerland: Springer Nature Switzerland.

Berry, T. (1999). *The great work: Our way into the future*. Harmony/Bell Tower.

Betancur-Santiago, M., & Rubiños-Cea, S. (2021). Colonialidad territorial y conflictividad: Disputas globales-locales en la Amazonía Andina. In N. Nogales (Ed.), *Amazonía y expansión mercantil capitalista* (pp. 315–377). Nueva frontera de recursos en el siglo XXI (CLACSO/CEDLA).

Bhola, N., Klimmek, H., Kingston, N., Burgess, N. D., van Soesbergen, A., Corrigan, C., Harrison, J., & Kok, M. T. J. (2021). Perspectives on area-based conservation and its meaning for future biodiversity policy. *Conservation Biology*, 35(1), 168–178. https://doi.org/10.1111/cobi.13509

Biermann, F. (2014). Global governance and the environment. In M. M. Betsill, K. Hochstetler, & D. Stevis (Eds.), *Advances in International Environmental Politics*. London: Palgrave Macmillan. https://doi.org/10.1057/9781137338976_10

Biermann, F., Pattberg, P., van Asselt, H., & Zelli, F. (2009). The fragmentation of global governance architectures: A framework for analysis. *Global Environmental Politics*, 9(4), 14–40. https://doi.org/10.1162/glep.2009.9.4.14

Blaser, M. (2014). Ontology and indigeneity: On the political ontology of heterogeneous assemblages. *Cultural Geographies*, 21(1), 49–58. https://doi.org/10.1177/1474474012462534

Boczek, B. (1984). Ideology and the law of the sea: The challenge of the new international economic order. *BC International & Comparative Law Review*, 7, 1.

Boelens, R., Hommes, L., & Hoogesteger, J. (2024). Ontological politics in river defence debates: Unpacking fields of contention in eco-centric and non-human turns. *Water Alternatives*, 17(3), 649–668.

Boillat, S., et al. (2010). Protected areas and indigenous peoples in Bolivia and Peru: Dilemmas, conflicts, and ways out. In H. Hurni & U. Wiesmann (Eds.), *Global change and sustainable development: A synthesis of regional experiences from research partnerships* (vol. 5, pp. 501–515). Geographica Bernensia.

Bonifaz Fernández, J. L., & Urrunaga Pasco-Font, R. L. (2012). Acortando brechas en la infraestructura pública. In B. Seminario, C. A. Sanborn, & N. Alva (Eds.), *Cuando despertemos en el 2062: visiones del Perú en 50 años* (1st edn., pp. 237–268). Universidad del Pacífico. www.hdl.handle.net/11354/1565

Boonen, C., Bové, A., Huyse, H., & Vandenhole, W. (2019). Governing as commons or as global public goods: Two tales of power. *International Journal of the Commons*, 13(1), pp. 553–577.

Boonzaier, E. (2011). An "historic victory" for the Basarwa in Botswana? Reading the evidence. *Anthropology Southern Africa*, 34(3–4), 96–103.

Booth, W. (1989, October 19). Amazon area Indians wary of rain forest plans. *The Washington Post*. Retrieved from: www.washingtonpost.com/archive/politics/1989/10/20/amazon-area-indians-wary-of-rain-forest-plans/d64698ff-e9d8-4fee-a087-79e5cbfbace2/

Borrás, S. (2016). New transitions from human rights to the environment to the rights of nature. *Transnational Environmental Law*, 5(1), 113–143.

Borrini-Feyerabend, G., Dudley, N., Jaeger, T., Lassen, B., Pathak Broome, N., Phillips, A., & Sandwith, T. (2013). *Governance of protected areas: From understanding to action* (Best Practice Protected Area Guidelines Series No. 20). International Union for Conservation of Nature.

Bosselmann, K., & Williams, T. (2025, January 29). *The river as a legal person: The case of the Whanganui River in New Zealand*. Heinrich Böll Stiftung. www.boell.de/en/2025/01/29/river-legal-person-case-whanganui-river-new-zealand

Brigg, M., & Graham, M. (2023). Approaching first nations diplomacy from the Australian continent. *Australian Journal of International Affairs*, 77(6), 585–589. https://doi.org/10.1080/10357718.2023.2265849

Brondizio, E. S., & Le Tourneau, F. M. (2016). Environmental governance for all. *Science*, 352(6291), 1272–1273. https://doi.org/10.1126/science.aaf5122

Brown, K. (2014). Global environmental change I: A social turn for resilience? *Progress in Human Geography*, 38(1), 107–117. https://doi.org/10.1177/0309132513498837

Brown, M. (2018). Global environmental governance. *International Studies Review*, 14(1), 125–130.

Brunnée, J. (1996). A conceptual framework for an international forests convention: Customary law and emerging principles. In Canadian Council of International Law (Ed.), *Global forests and international environmental law* (pp. 41–78). Kluwer Law.

Brunnée, J., & Nollkaemper, A. (1996). Between the forests and the trees – An emerging international forest law. *Environmental Conservation*, 23(4), 307–314.

Bruyneel, K. (2007). *The third space of sovereignty: The postcolonial politics of U.S.–Indigenous relations*. University of Minnesota Press. www.muse.jhu.edu/book/27663

Brysk, A. (2000). *From tribal village to global village: Indian rights and international relations in Latin America*. Stanford University Press.

Buchanan, J. M., & Tullock, G. (1962). *The calculus of consent: Logical foundations of constitutional democracy*. University of Michigan Press.

Buck, S. (1998). *The global commons: An introduction*. Routledge.

Bulkeley, H., & Newell, P. (2023). *Governing climate change* (3rd ed.). Routledge.

Bulowski, N. (2022, February 10). "Dene K'éh Didi Ni Sugehin Ma": Indigenous women are blazing a conservation trail. APTN News. www.aptnnews.ca/nationalnews/indigenous-women-climate-change-biodiversity-con

Burdon, P. (2012). A theory of earth jurisprudence. *Australian Journal of Legal Philosophy*, 37, 28–50.

Burow, P. B., Brock, S., & Dove, M. R. (2018). Unsettling the land: Indigeneity, ontology, and hybridity in settler colonialism. *Environment and Society*, 9, 57–74. www.jstor.org/stable/26879578

Büscher, B., & Fletcher, R. (2015). Accumulation by conservation. *New Political Economy*, 20(2), 273–298.

Büscher, B., & Fletcher, R. (2019). Towards convivial conservation. *Conservation & Society*, 17(3), 283–296. www.jstor.org/stable/26677964

Büscher, B., & Fletcher, R. (2020). *The conservation revolution: Radical ideas for saving nature beyond the Anthropocene*. Verso.

Bushley, B. R. (2014). REDD+ policy making in Nepal: Toward state-centric, polycentric, or market-oriented governance? *Ecology and Society*, 19(3), Article 34.

Butler, R. (2020). *The Amazon rainforest: The world's largest rainforest*. Mongabay. Retrieved from www.worldrainforests.com/amazon/

Caldas, B., Thieme, M. L., Shahbol, N., Coelho, M. E., Grill, G., Van Damme, P. A., Aranha, R., Cañas, C., & [others]. (2022, December 14). Identifying the current and future status of freshwater connectivity corridors in the Amazon Basin. *Conservation Science and Practice*, 5(1), e12853. https://doi.org/10.1111/csp2.12853

Campbell, L. M., Corson, C., Gray, N. J., MacDonald, K. I., & Brosius, J. P. (2014). Studying global environmental meetings to understand global environmental governance: Collaborative event ethnography of the 10th Conference of the Parties to the Convention on Biological Diversity. *Global Environmental Politics*, 14(3), 1–20. https://doi.org/10.1162/GLEP_e_00236

Cano Pecharromán, L. (2018). Rights of nature: Rivers that can stand in court. *Resources*, 7(1), Article 13. https://doi.org/10.3390/resources7010013

Cardil, A., De-Miguel, S., Silva, C. A., Reich, P. B., Calkin, D., Brancalion, P. H. S., & Liang, J. (2020). Recent deforestation drove the spike in Amazonian fires. *Environmental Research Letters*, 15. https://doi.org/10.1088/1748-9326/abcac7

Carpenter, K. A., & Riley, A. R. (2014). Indigenous peoples and the jurisgenerative moment in human rights. *California Law Review*, 102(1), 173–234.

Carpenter, K., & Tsykarev, A. (2021). Indigenous peoples and diplomacy on the world stage. *American Journal of International Law*, 115, 118–122.

Carse, A., & Kneas, D. (2019). Unbuilt and unfinished: The temporalities of infrastructure. *Environment and Society*, 10(1), 9–28.

Carter, S. G., & Fry, G. (2023). Australia's indigenous diplomacy and its regional resonance in Oceania. *Australian Journal of International Affairs* 77(6), 1–8.

Carattini, S., Levin, S., & Tavoni, A. (2019). Cooperation in the climate commons. *Review of Environmental Economics and Policy*, 13(2), 227–247.

Carrithers, M., Candea, M., Sykes, K., Holbraad, M., & Venkatesan, S. (2010). Ontology is just another word for culture. *Critique of Anthropology*, 30(2), 152–200.

Castree, N. (2019). An alternative to civil disobedience for concerned scientists. *Nature Ecology and Evolution*, 3(1499). https://doi.org/10.1038/s41559-019-1023-y

Cazala, J. (2020). What international law can teach us about the commons. In M. Pillai, & G. Ganapathy-Doré (Eds.), *Global commons: Issues, concerns and strategies* (1st edn., pp. 2–11). SAGE Publications Pvt Ltd. https://doi.org/10.4135/9789353885724

Chagnon, C., et al. (2022). From extractivism to global extractivism: The evolution of an organizing concept. *Journal of Peasant Studies*, 49(4), 760–792.

Chan, M., & Araujo, A. (2020, February 15). China wants food. Brazil pays the price. The Atlantic. www.theatlantic.com/international/archive/2020/02/china-brazil-amazon-environment-pork/606601/

Chandler, D., & Reid, J. (2019). *Becoming Indigenous: Governing imaginaries in the Anthropocene*. Rowman & Littlefield Publishers.

Chandra, R. (2020). The "moral economy" of cosmopolitan commons. *TWAIL Review*, 1, 51–73.

Che Piu, H., Huamani, S., Valle Riestra, E., & Koc, G. (2016). *¿Un bosque de dinero? Financiamiento para bosques y cambio clim´atico en el Perú*. Lima, Peru: DAR.

Chiavari, J., & Lopes, C. L. (2020). Indigenous land rights in Brazil: Challenges and barriers to land demarcation. In W. Leal Filho, V. King, & I. Borges de Lima (Eds.), *Indigenous Amazonia, regional development and territorial dynamics* (pp. 85–101). The Latin American Studies Book Series: Springer.

Cifuentes, S. (2021). Rethinking climate governance: Amazonian Indigenous climate politics and integral territorial ontologies. *Journal of Latin American Geography*, 20(2), 131–155. https://doi.org/10.1353/lag.2021.0031

Clavé-Mercier, V. (2018). Revisitar la soberanía indígena: Los desafíos de una reivindicación excluida. *Relaciones Internacionales*, 38(38), 99–119. https://doi.org/10.15366/relacionesinternacionales2018.38.005

Clüsener-Godt, M., & Sachs, I. (1995). *Brazilian perspectives on sustainable development of the Amazon region* (Vol. 311, No. 2). United Nations.

Coen, D., Kreienkamp, J., & Pegram, T. (2020). *Global climate governance* (1st ed.). Cambridge University Press. https://doi.org/10.1017/9781108973250

COICA. (2018). *Informe EPU: Vulneraciones a los derechos de los pueblos indígenas en la cuenca amazónica por inversiones chinas.* www.dar.org.pe/archivos/EPUchina_espanol.pdf *(Último acceso: enero de 2024)*

COICA. (n.d.). ¿Quiénes somos? https://coicamazonia.org/quienes-somos/

Collins, Y. A., Maguire-Rajpaul, V., Krauss, J. E., Asiyanbi, A., Jiménez, A., Mabele, M. B., & Alexander-Owen, M. (2021). Plotting the coloniality of conservation. *Journal of Political Ecology*, 28(1), 968–989. https://doi.org/10.2458/jpe.4683

Comberti, C., Thornton, T. F., Wyllie de Echeverria, V., & Patterson, T. (2019). Adaptation and resilience at the margins: Addressing Indigenous peoples' marginalization at international climate negotiations. *Environment: Science and Policy for Sustainable Development*, 61(2), 14–30.

Convention on Biological Diversity (CBD). (2022). *Global Biodiversity Framework.* www.cbd.int/convention/text/

Conversi, D. (2016). Sovereignty in a changing world: From westphalia to food sovereignty. *Globalizations*, 13(4), 484–498.

Conway, P. R. (2019). The folds of coexistence: Towards a diplomatic political ontology, between difference and contradiction. *Theory, Culture & Society*, 37(3), 23–47. https://doi.org/10.1177/0263276419885004

Coombes, B. (2020). Nature's rights as indigenous rights? Mis/recognition through personhood for Te Urewera. *Espace populations sociétés*, 1–2, 3.

Coote, M. L. (2016). Environmental decision-making in the Arctic Council: What is the role of Indigenous peoples? (Doctoral dissertation). University of Calgary.

Corbera, E., Maestre-Andrés, S., Collins, Y. A., Mabele, M. B., & Brockington, D. (2024). Decolonizing biodiversity conservation. *Journal of Political Ecology*, 28(1), 889–903. https://doi.org/10.2458/jpe.5969

Cornejo, E. (2012). El modelo económico peruano: una experiencia exitosa de desarrollo de infraestructura con inclusión social. In *Integración física sudamericana diez años después: impacto e implementación en el Perú* (pp. 25–43). Lima: Universidad del Pacífico; BID-INTAL: CEPEI.

Corson, C., Campbell, L. M., & MacDonald, K. I. (2014). Capturing the personal in politics: Ethnographies of global environmental governance. *Global Environmental Politics*, 14(1), 21–40.

Corson, C., Gray, N. L., Campbell, L. M., & Wilshusen, P. (2019). Assembling global conservation governance. *Geoforum*, 103, 56–65. https://doi.org/10.1016/j.geoforum.2019.03.012

Cortes, A. (2018). *Resguardos Indígenas en la Conservación: territorios en traslape* [Monografía para optar por el Título de especialista en Estudios del Territorio]. Universidad Externado de Colombia. https://bdigital.uexternado.edu.co/entities/publication/2aab17a6-8e21-4111-bdfe-bedc591666a0

COSIPLAN. (2017). *Project Portfolio 2017.* www.iirsa.org/admin_iirsa_web/Uploads/Documents/CARTERA_DIGITAL_INGLES.pdf (Último acceso: enero de 2024)

Costa, F. (2019). *A brief economic history of the Amazon (1720–1970).* Cambridge Scholars Publishing.

Craven, M. (2010). Statehood, self-determination and recognition. In M. Evans (Ed.), *International Law* (3rd ed., pp. 203–251). Oxford University Press.

Craven, M., & Parfitt, R. (2018, June 21). 7. Statehood, Self-determination, and Recognition. In *International Law*. Oxford: Oxford University Press. Retrieved from www.oxfordlawtrove.com/view/10.1093/he/9780198791836.001.0001/he-9780198791836-chapter-7

Cristina, Y. A. I. (2018). Worlding the study of global environmental politics in the anthropocene: Indigenous voices from the Amazon. *Global Environmental Politics*, 18(4), 25–42. https://doi.org/10.1162/glep_a_00479

Cruz Rodríguez, E. (2012). Redefiniendo la nación: luchas indígenas y Estado Plurinacional en Ecuador (1990–2008). *Nómadas: Critical Journal of Social and Juridical Sciences*. Available at: www.redalyc.org/articulo.oa?id=181/18126163021

Cullinan, C. (2002). *Wild law: A manifesto for earth justice*. Siber Ink.

da Costa, I. M., de Andrade, M. O., & Gonçalves, A. F. (2022, September–December). Desacatos; Tlalpan N.º 70, 60–75.

da Silva, C. A., Santos, S. C. D., & Rossetto, O. C. (2024). The paiter suruí indigenous people in defence of their territory: The case of the suruí forest carbon project (PCFS) – Rondonia/Brazil. In A. Penteado, S. P. Chakrabarty, & O. H. Shaikh (Eds.), *Traditional knowledge and climate change*. Singapore: Springer. https://doi.org/10.1007/978-981-99-8830-3_7

Daes, E. (2008). An overview of the history of indigenous peoples: Self-determination and the United Nations. *Cambridge Review of International Affairs*, 21(1), 7–26.

Dalla, V., & Korber, V. (2024). Forests in neoliberal climate governance: An analysis of the Floresta+ Amazônia pilot project. *Ambiente & Sociedade*, 27, Artículo e01341.

Davis, S. (2021). Beyond obstruction: Blockades as productive reorientations. *Antipode*, 53(3), 877–897. https://doi.org/10.1111/anti.12722

Dawson, A., Longo, F., & Survival International. (Eds.). (2023). *Decolonize conservation: Global voices for indigenous self-determination, land, and a world in common*. Commons Notions.

Dawson, N., Coolsaet, B., Sterling, E., Loveridge, R., Nicole, D., Gross-Camp, et al. (2021). The role of Indigenous peoples and local communities in effective and equitable conservation. *Ecology and Society*, 26(3), ehal-03341800. https://doi.org/10.5751/ES-12625-260319

Deberdt, R., & Le Billon, P. (2023). Outer space mining: Exploring techno-utopianism in a time of climate crisis. *Annals of the American Association of Geographers*, 113(8), 1878–1899.

De Blic, D. (2020). Representing nature. *Revue Projet*, 378(5), 56–59.

De Lucia, V. (2017). Beyond anthropocentrism and ecocentrism: A biopolitical reading of environmental law. *Journal of Human Rights and the Environment*, 8(2), 181–202.

De Pourcq, K., Thomas, E., Van Damme, P., & Léon-Sicard, T. (2017). Análisis de los conflictos entre comunidades locales y autoridades de conservación en Colombia: Causas y recomendaciones. *Gestión y Ambiente*, 20, 122–139.

de Salles Cavedon-Capdeville, F., Berros, M. V., Filpi, H., & Villavicencio-Calzadilla, P. (2023). An ecocentric perspective on climate litigation: Lessons from Latin America. *Journal of Human Rights Practice*, 16, 1–18.

de Wit, F. C. A., & Martins de Freitas, P. (2019). Global climate adaptation governance in the Amazon through a polycentricity lens. *Revista Brasileira de Política Internacional*, 62(2), 1–19.

De Wit, F., & Mourato, J. (2022). Governing the diverse forest: Polycentric climate governance in the Amazon. *Global Environmental Change*, 75, 102591. https://doi.org/10.1016/j.worlddev.2022.105955

Dehm, J. (2021). *Reconsidering REDD+: Authority, power and law in the green economy*. Cambridge University Press.

Descola, P. (2004). Las cosmologías indígenas de la Amazonía. In A. Surrallés & P. García (Eds.), *Territorio indígena y percepción del entorno* (pp. 25–36). IWGIA.
Diele-Viegas, L., & Rocha, C. (2020). Why releasing mining on Amazonian Indigenous lands and the advance of agrobusiness is extremely harmful for the mitigation of world's climate change? Comment on Pereira et al. (Environmental Science & Policy 100 (2019) 8–12). *Environmental Science & Policy*, 103, 30–31.
Disch, L. (2016). Ecological democracy and the co-participation of things. *En Mapping Intimacies*. https://doi.org/10.1093/oxfordhb/9780199685271.013.11
Dorough, D. S. (2017). Rough drafts: A personal account of the 25-year struggle to craft the UN Declaration on the Rights of Indigenous Peoples. *World Policy Journal*, 34(4), 46–50.
Dryzek, J. (2000). *Deliberative democracy and beyond: Liberals, critics, contestations*. Oxford University Press. https://doi.org/10.1093/019925043X.001.0001
Dryzek, J. S., & Pickering, J. (2019). *The politics of the Anthropocene*. Oxford University Press. https://doi.org/10.1093/oso/9780198809616.001.0001
Dunlap, A., & Jakobsen, J. (2020). *The violent technologies of extraction*. Palgrave Pivot.
Durand, F. (2019). *La captura del Estado en América Latina. Reflexiones teóricas*. Lima: Oxfam, Fondo Editorial de la Pontificia. Universidad Católica del Perú.
Dürr, J. (2020). A brief economic history of the Amazon (1720–1970). *The Journal of Peasant Studies*, 47(3), 609–612. https://doi.org/10.1080/03066150.2020.1745712
Eckersley, R. (2004). *The green state: Rethinking democracy and sovereignty*. MIT Press. https://doi.org/10.7551/mitpress/3364.001.0001
Eikermann, A. (2015). *Forests in international law: Is there really a need for an international forest convention?* Springer International Publishing.
Engle, K. (2011). On fragile architecture: The UN Declaration on the Rights of Indigenous Peoples in the context of human rights. *European Journal of International Law*, 22(1), 141–163.
Enns, C., & Bersaglio, B. (2020). On the coloniality of "new" mega-infrastructure projects in East Africa. *Antipode*, 52(1), 101–123. https://doi.org/10.1111/anti.12582
Ephraim, L. (2018). *Who speaks for nature? On the politics of science*. University of Pennsylvania Press. www.jstor.org/stable/j.ctv16t6kqj
Eslava, L., et al. (2017). *Bandung, global history, and international law: Critical pasts and pending futures*. Cambridge University Press.
Espinoza Llanos, R., & Feather, C. (2012). *The reality of REDD+ in Peru: Between theory and practice. Indigenous Amazonian Peoples' analyses and alternatives* (Revised edition, febrero). AIDESEP & FPP. www.illegal-logging.info/uploads/realityreddperubetweentheoryandpracticewebsite.pdf
Estrada-Carmona, N., Carmenta, R., Reed, J., & Betemariam, E. (2024). Reconciling conservation and development requires enhanced integration and broader aims: A cross-continental assessment of landscape approaches. *One Earth*, 7(10). https://doi.org/10.1016/j.oneear.2024.08.014
Etchart, L. (2022). *Global governance of the environment, indigenous peoples and the rights of nature: Extractive industries in the Ecuadorian Amazon*. Springer International Publishing.
Falkner, R. (2016). The Paris Agreement and the new logic of international climate politics. *International Affairs*, 92(5), 1107–1125. https://doi.org/10.1111/1468-2346.12708
Fauset, S., et al. (2015). Hyperdominance in Amazonian forest carbon cycling. *Nature Communications*, 6(1), 1–9.

Fearnside, P. M. (2018). Brazil's Amazonian forest carbon: The key to Southern Amazonia's significance for global climate. *Regional Environmental Change*, 18, 47–61. https://doi.org/10.1007/s10113-016-1007-2

Fearnside, P. M. (2023, agosto). The deceptions of the Amazon Summit in Belém (commentary). *Mongabay*. www.researchgate.net/publication/377179793_The_deceptions_of_the_Amazon_Summit_in_Belem_commentary

Fearnside, P., & Figueiredo, A. (2015). China's influence on deforestation in Brazilian Amazonia: A growing force in the state of Mato Grosso (Discussion Paper 2015-3, pp. 1–51). BU – Global Economic Governance Initiative. www.bu.edu/pardeeschool/files/2014/12/Brazil1.pdf

Feichtner, I., & Ginzky, H. (2024). The struggle at the International Seabed Authority over deep sea mineral resources. *npj Ocean Sustainability*, 3(1), 63.

Fernández, C. (2023, September 12). Hundreds of oil spill sites threaten Amazon Indigenous lands, protected areas. *Mongabay*. news.mongabay.com/2023/09/hundreds-of-oil-spill-sites-threaten-amazon-indigenous-lands-protected-areas/

Figueroa, I. (2018). Desplazamientos en virtud del desarrollo: Un estudio de caso del proyecto minero Mirador en Zamora Chinchipe, Ecuador. *Opinión Jurídica*, 17(33), 173–198.

Finnegan, C. (2022). Indigenous interests in outer space: Addressing the conflict of increasing satellite numbers with indigenous astronomy practices. *Laws*, 11(2), 26.

Fischer, F. (2017). *Climate crisis and the democratic prospect: Participatory governance in sustainable communities*. Oxford University Press.

Fitz-Henry, E. (2012). The natural contract: From Lévi-Strauss to the Ecuadorian Constitutional Court. *Oceania Publications*, 82(3), 264.

Fletcher, R., Dressler, W., Büscher, B., & Anderson, Z. R. (2016). Questioning REDD+ and the future of market-based conservation. *Conservation Biology*, 30(3), 673–675. https://doi.org/10.1111/cobi.12648

Fontaine, G. (2006). La globalización de la Amazonía: Una perspectiva andina. *Íconos: Revista de Ciencias Sociales* (25), 25–36. https://doi.org/10.17141/iconos.25.2006.163.

Food & Agriculture Organisation [FAO]. (2010). *The state of world fisheries and aquaculture*. FAO. www.fao.org/3/i1820e/i1820e.pdf

Food & Agriculture Organisation [FAO]. (2022). *FAOSTAT*. www.fao.org/faostat/en/#home

Fowks, J. (2017, febrero). Perú: Negocios ilegales y promesas incumplidas. Nueva Sociedad. nuso.org/articulo/negocios-ilegales-en-la/

Franchini, M. A., & Viola, E. (2019). Myths and images in global climate governance, conceptualization, and the case of Brazil (1989–2019). *Revista Brasileira de Política Internacional*, 62(2), e005.

Fukurai, H. (2018). Fourth World approaches to international law (FWAIL) and Asia's indigenous struggles and quests for recognition under international law. *Asian Journal of Law and Society*, 5(1), 1.

Gabrys, J. (2020). Smart forests and data practices: From the Internet of Trees to planetary governance. *Environmental Humanities*, 12(1), 1–20. https://doi.org/10.1177/2053951720904871

Gago, V., & Mezzadra, S. (2017). A critique of the extractive operations of capital: Toward an expanded concept of extractivism. *Rethinking Marxism*, 29(4), 574–591.

Galeano, E. (1971). *The open veins of Latin America: Five centuries of the pillage of a continent*. Monthly Review Press.

Gallagher, K. P., & Myers, M. (2019). *China-Latin America finance database.* Inter-American Dialogue.

García, B. (2011). *The Amazon from an international law perspective.* Cambridge University Press.

Garcia, B., Rimmer, L., Vieira, L. C., & Mackey, B. (2021). REDD+ and forest protection on indigenous lands in the Amazon. *Review of European, Comparative & International Environmental Law*, 30(1), 1–14. https://doi.org/10.1111/reel.12389

Gardner, C. J., & Wordley, C. F. R. (2019). Scientists must act on our own warnings to humanity. *Nature Ecology & Evolution*, 3(9), 1271–1272. https://doi.org/10.1038/s41559-019-0979-y

Garnett, S. T., Burgess, N. D., Fa, J. E., Fernández-Llamazares, Á., Molnár, Z., Robinson, C. J., Watson, J. E. M., Zander, K. K., Austin, B., Brondizio, E. S., Collier, N. F., Duncan, T., Ellis, E., Geyle, H., Jackson, M. V., Jonas, H., Malmer, P., McGowan, B., Sivongxay, A., & Leiper, I. (2018). A spatial overview of the global importance of Indigenous lands for conservation. *Nature Sustainability*, 1(17), 369–374. https://doi.org/10.1038/s41893-018-0100-6

Garrido, S., Sequeira, T., Santos, M., & Nikuma, D. (2020). Climate change and sustainable development: The case of Amazonia and policy implications. *Environmental Science and Pollution Research*, 27(8), 7745–7756. https://doi.org/10.1007/s11356-020-07725-4

Gathii, J. T. (2019). The agenda of Third World Approaches to International Law (TWAIL). In J. L. Dunoff & M. A. Pollack (Eds.), *International legal theory: Foundations and frontiers* (pp. 153–173). Cambridge University Press.

Geddis, A., & Ruru, J. (2019). Places as persons: Creating a new framework for Māori-Crown relations. In J. Varuhas & S. Wilson Stark (Eds.), *The frontiers of public law.* Hart Publishing.

General Assembly Resolution 626. (1952, December 21). *Resolution on the question of the international status of the Amazon River Basin.* United Nations General Assembly.

Giacomini, G. (2022). *Indigenous peoples and climate justice: A critical analysis of international human rights law and governance.* Springer. https://doi.org/10.1007/978-3-031-09508-5

Githiru, M., & Njambuya, J. W. (2019). Globalization and biodiversity conservation problems: Polycentric REDD+ solutions. *Land*, 8(1), 35.

Glikson, A. Y. (2021). *The event horizon: Homo Prometheus and the climate catastrophe.* Springer.

Global Witness. (2023, September 13). *Almost 2,000 land and environmental defenders killed between 2012 and 2022 for protecting the planet.* www.globalwitness.org/en/press-releases/almost-2000-land-an…onmental-defenders-killed-between-2012-and-2022-protecting-planet/

Godden, L. C., & Tehan, M. (2016). REDD+: Climate justice and indigenous and local community rights in an era of climate disruption. *Journal of Energy & Natural Resources Law*, 34(1), 1–14. https://doi.org/10.1080/02646811.2016.1121620

Goehring, J. S. (2021). Why isn't outer space a global commons? *Journal of National Security Law and Policy*, 11, 573.

Goldman Environmental Prize. (2021). *Three Indigenous leaders protecting the Amazon.* www.goldmanprize.org/blog/three-indigenous-leaders-protecting-the-amazon/

Gonzalez-Vicente, R. (2019). Make development great again? Accumulation regimes, spaces of sovereign exception and the elite development paradigm of China's Belt and Road Initiative. *Business and Politics*, 21(4), 487–513. doi:10.1017/bap.2019.20

Gordon, T., & Webber, J. (2008). Imperialism and resistance: Canadian mining companies in Latin America. *Third World Quarterly*, 29(1), 63–87.

Granja, L., Lacerda Gonçalves, A. L., & Cazalbón, A. (2022). RUNASUR: estudio de caso de la propuesta de Evo Morales de regionalismo plurinacional. *Revista Aportes Para La Integración Latinoamericana*, 47, 45.

Grant, D., Zelinka, D., & Mitova, S. (2021). Reducing CO2 emissions by targeting the world's hyper-polluting power plants. *Environmental Research Letters*, 16(9), 094022. https://doi.org/10.1088/1748-9326/ac13f1

Greenfield, P. (2023, January 18). Revealed: More than 90% of rainforest carbon offsets by biggest certifier are worthless, analysis shows. *The Guardian*. www.theguardian.com/environment/2023/jan/18/revealed-forest-carbon-offsets-biggest-provider-worthlessverra-aoe

Gudynas, E. (2017). Extractivismos y corrupción en América del Sur [Extractivism and corruption in South America]. *RevIISE*, 10(10), 73–87.

Gullison, R. E., & Hardner, J. (2018). Progress and challenges in consolidating the management of Amazonian protected areas and indigenous territories. *Conservation Biology*, 32(5), 1020–1030.

Gupta, A., Pistorius, T., & Vijge, M. J. (2016). Managing fragmentation in global environmental governance: The REDD+ Partnership as bridge organization. *International Environmental Agreements*, 16(3), 355–374. https://doi.org/10.1007/s10784-015-9274-9

Gürçam, S. (2022). The neoliberal initiative of the aviation industry to fight the climate crisis: Greenwashing. *International Journal of Environmental Geoinformatics*, 9(3), 178–186.

Gutiérrez Aguilar, R. (2011). Los ritmos del Pachakuti: Cómo conocemos las luchas de emancipación y su relación con la política de la autonomía. *Desacatos*, 37, 19–32. www.scielo.org.mx/scielo.php?script=sci_arttext&pid=S1607-050X2011000300002

Guzmán, J. J. (2019). Decolonizing law and expanding human rights: Indigenous conceptions and the rights of nature in Ecuador. *Deusto Journal of Human Rights*, 4, 59–86.

Haas, P. (2015). *Epistemic communities, constructivism, and international environmental politics* (1st ed.). Routledge.

Hartz, F. (2023). Leaking the IPCC: A question of responsibility? *WIREs Climate Change*, 14(3), e814. https://doi.org/10.1002/wcc.814

Harvey, D. (2001). Globalization and the "spatial fix." *Geographische Revue*, 8, 23–30.

Harvey, D. (2003). *The new imperialism*. Oxford University Press.

Harvey, P. (2018). Infrastructures in and out of time: The promise of roads in contemporary Peru. In N. Anand, A. Gupta, & H. Appel (Eds.), *The promise of infrastructure*. Duke University Press.

Harvey, P., & Knox, H. (2015). *Roads: An anthropology of infrastructure and expertise*. Cornell University Press.

Hau'Ofa, E. (2000). The ocean in us. *Culture and Sustainable Development in the Pacific*, 32–43.

Hecht, S. B. (2013). *The scramble for the Amazon and the "lost paradise" of Euclides da Cunha*. University of Chicago Press.

Helfer, L. R., Alter, K. J., & Guerzovich, M. F. (2009). Islands of effective international adjudication: Constructing an intellectual property rule of law in the Andean Community. *American Journal of International Law*, 103(1), 1–47.

Henderson, J. (2007). *Indigenous diplomacy and the rights of peoples: Achieving UN recognition*. UBC Press.

Herrera, D. (2019). Geopolítica de la fragmentación y poder infraestructural. El Proyecto "One Belt, One Road" y América Latina. *Geopolítica(s)*, 10(1), 41–68.

Hickmann, T. (2015). *Rethinking authority in global climate governance: How transnational climate initiatives relate to the international climate regime*. Routledge. https://doi.org/10.4324/9781315677071

Hill, D. (2015). Colombian tribe scores 'historic' victory versus Big Gas. The Guardian: www.theguardian.com/environment/andes-to-the-amazon/2015/mar/26/colombian-tribe-scores-historic-victory-versus-big-gas

Hirsch, E. (2017). Investment's rituals: "Grassroots" extractivism and the making of an indigenous gold mine in the Peruvian Andes. *Geoforum*, 82, 259–267. https://doi.org/10.1016/j.geoforum.2016.08.012

Hoffmann, M. (2011). *Climate governance at the crossroads: Experimenting with a global response after Kyoto*. Oxford University Press.

Holst, J. (2016). Colonial histories and decolonial dreams in the Ecuadorean Amazon: Natural resources and the politics of post-neoliberalism. *Latin American Perspectives*, 43(1), 200–220.

Homma, A. (1992). The dynamics of extraction in Amazônia: A historical perspective. *Advances in Economic Botany*, 9, 23–31.

Homma, A. (1995). Modernisation and technological dualism in the extractive economy in Amazonia. In M. Pérez, M. Ruiz, & J. Arnold (Eds.), *Current issues in non-timber forest products research*. CIFOR.

Horn, L. (2015). Climate change and the future role of the concept of the common concern. *Australian Journal of Environmental Law*, 2(1), 24–56.

Houghton, R. A., & Nassikas, A. A. (2017). Global and regional fluxes of carbon from land use and land cover change 1850–2015. *Global Biogeochemical Cycles*, 31(3), 456–472. https://doi.org/10.1002/2016GB005546

Hughes, H. (2024). *The IPCC and the politics of writing climate change* (1st ed.). Cambridge University Press.

Hunter, J., Singh, P., & Aguon, J. (2018, April 16). Broadening common heritage: Addressing gaps in the deep-sea mining regulatory regime. *Harvard Environmental Law Review*, 16. https://journals.law.harvard.edu/elr/2018/04/16/broadening-common-heritage/.

ICCA Consortium. (2012, September 17). *Threats to ICCAs and community responses – facilitating grassroots analyses and the development of a Photo Story* [Online]. ICCA Consortium. www.iccaconsortium.org/wp-content/uploads/2015/08/Photo_story_draft_toolkit_jan_2013.pdf

IIRSA. (2010a). *Cartera de Proyectos 2010*. Planificación Territorial Indicativa. www.iirsa.org/Document/Detail?Id=3353

IIRSA. (2010b). *Metodología de Evaluación Ambiental y Social con Enfoque Estratégico – EASE-IIRSA*. www.iirsa.org/Page/Detail?menuItemId=73

Instituto del Bien Común. (2016). *Tierras comunales: Más que preservar el pasado es asegurar el futuro. El estado de las comunidades indígenas en el Perú – Informe 2016*. Instituto del Bien Común.

Inter-American Development Bank. (IDB). (2024, November). Response by the Inter-American Development Bank (IDB) areas of work relevant to the Permanent Forum on Indigenous Issues: Response: Questionnaire to the UN system agencies. *Funds and Programmes and Intergovernmental Organizations*.

International Union for the Conservation of Nature (IUCN). (2010). *Indigenous and community conserved areas: A bold new frontier for conservation*. IUCN. www.iucn.org/content/indigenous-and-community-conserved-areas-bold-new-frontier-conservation

IPBES. (2019a). *Report of the first ILK dialogue workshop for the IPBES assessment of the diverse conceptualizations of multiple values of nature: Framing the assessment.*

IPBES. (2019b). *Report of the second ILK dialogue workshop for the IPBES assessment of the diverse conceptualizations of multiple values of nature.*

IPBES. (2021). *Report of the third ILK dialogue workshop for the IPBES values assessment: Reviewing the draft summary for policymakers and second order draft of the assessment.*

IPBES. (2022a). *Report of the first indigenous and local knowledge dialogue workshop for the IPBES assessments of the nexus of biodiversity, food, water, and health and transformative change.*

IPBES. (2022b). *The methodological assessment report on the diverse values and valuation of nature* (p. XLIII). www.ipbes.net/the-values-assessment

IPBES. (2023). *Report of the second Indigenous and local knowledge dialogue workshop for the IPBES assessment of the nexus of biodiversity, food, water, and health: Reviewing the first order draft.*

IPCC. (2019). Climate change and land: An IPCC special report on climate change, desertification, land degradation, sustainable land management, food security, and greenhouse gas fluxes in terrestrial ecosystems. In P. R. Shukla, et al. (Eds.), *Intergovernmental Panel on Climate Change (IPCC).* www.ipcc.ch/site/assets/uploads/2019/11/SRCCL-Full-Report-Compiled-191128.pdf

IUCN. (2024, April 25). *Indigenous environmental defender Victorio Dariquebe Gerewa killed in Madre de Dios.* International Union for Conservation of Nature. www.iucn.nl/en/news/indigenous-environmental-defender-victorio-dariquebe-gerewa-killed-in-madre-de-dios/

Janssen, M. A., & Yap, X. S. (2024). Governing outer space as a commons is critical for addressing commons on earth. *International Journal of the Commons*, 18(1), 32–38.

Jasanoff, S. (2015). One. Future imperfect: Science, technology, and the imaginations of modernity. In S. Jasanoff & S. Kim (Eds.), *Dreamscapes of modernity: Sociotechnical imaginaries and the fabrication of power* (pp. 1–33). University of Chicago Press.

Jasanoff, S., & Kim, S.-H. (2009). Containing the atom: Sociotechnical imaginaries and nuclear regulation in the U.S. and South Korea. *Minerva*, 47(2), 119–146.

Jasanoff, S., & Kim, S.-H. (2015). *Dreamscapes of modernity: Sociotechnical imaginaries and the fabrication of power.* University of Chicago Press. https://doi.org/10.7208/chicago/9780226276663.001.0001

Jauregui, J. G. (2020). Latin American countries in the BRI: Challenges and potential implications for economic development. *Asian Education and Development Studies*, 10(3), 348–358.

Johnson, M. (2024). *Property rights in outer space: Mining, techno-utopian imaginaries, and the privatisation of the off-world frontier.* Routledge.

Jones, N. (2024). *Self-determination as voice: The participation of indigenous peoples in international governance.* Cambridge University Press.

Jordan, A., Huitema, D., Van Asselt, H., & Forster, J. (Eds.). (2018). *Governing climate change: Polycentricity in action?* (1st ed.). Cambridge University Press. https://doi.org/10.1017/9781108284646

Jull, P. (1999). Indigenous internationalism: What should we do next? *Indigenous Affairs*, 1, 12–17.

Kanai, J. M., & Schindler, S. (2019). Peri-urban promises of connectivity: Linking project-led polycentrism to the infrastructure scramble. *Environment and Planning A: Economy and Space*, 51(2), 302–322.

Kauffman, C. M., & Martin, P. L. (2016). Can rights of nature make development more sustainable? Why some Ecuadorian lawsuits succeed and others fail. *World Development*, 92, 130–142. https://doi.org/10.1016/j.worlddev.2016.01.005

Kauffman, C. M., & Martin, P. L. (2021). *The politics of rights of nature: Strategies for building a more sustainable future*. The MIT Press. https://doi.org/10.7551/mitpress/13855.001.0001

Kemp, L., Xu, C., Depledge, J., Ebi, K. L., Gibbins, G., Kohler, T. A., Rockström, J., Scheffer, M., Schellnhuber, H. J., Steffen, W., & Lenton, T. M. (2022). Climate endgame: Exploring catastrophic climate change scenarios. *Proceedings of the National Academy of Sciences of the United States of America*, 119(34), e2108146119. https://doi.org/10.1073/pnas.2108146119

Keohane, R. O., & Victor, D. G. (2011). The regime complex for climate change. *Perspectives on Politics*, 9(1), 7–23.

Khan, S. (2019). Rebalancing state and Indigenous sovereignties in international law: An Arctic lens on trajectories for global governance. *Leiden Journal of International Law*, 32(4), 675–693.

Kleinschroth, F., & Healey, J. R. (2017). Impacts of logging roads on tropical forests. *Biotropica*, 49(6), 702–712. https://doi.org/10.1111/btp.12462

Knauß, S. (2018). Conceptualizing human stewardship in the Anthropocene: The rights of nature in Ecuador, New Zealand and India. *Journal of Agricultural and Environmental Ethics*, 31(6), 703–722.

Knecht, S. (2017). The politics of Arctic international cooperation: Introducing a dataset on stakeholder participation in Arctic Council meetings, 1998–2015. *Cooperation and Conflict*, 52(2), 203–223.

Knecht, S. (2020). The Arctic Council, Asian observers, and the role of 'shadow networks' in the science–policy interface. In C. Woon & K. Dodds (Eds.), *Observing the Arctic: Asia in the Arctic Council and Beyond. Edward Elgar Publishing* (pp. 29–53).

Kniewel, J. N. (2024). The responsibility to protect: International conservationists, decolonization and authoritarianism in the dr congo, 1960–75. *Journal of Contemporary History*, 59(3), 553–575.

Kohn, E. (2013). *How forests think: Toward an anthropology beyond the human*. University of California Press.

Kohn, E. (2015). Anthropology of ontologies. *Annual Review of Anthropology*, 44, 311–327. https://doi.org/10.1146/annurev-anthro-102214-014127

Koivurova, T., & Heinämäki, L. (2006). The participation of indigenous peoples in international norm-making in the Arctic. *Polar Record*, 42(2), 101–109.

Kolk, A. (1998). From conflict to cooperation: International policies to protect the Brazilian Amazon. *World Development*, 26(8), 1481–1493.

Kotzé, L., & Villavicencio Calzadilla, P. (2017). Somewhere between rhetoric and reality: Environmental constitutionalism and the rights of nature in Ecuador. *Transnational Environmental Law*, 6(2), 401–433.

Kovič Dine, M. (2019). Consequences of the recognition of forest protection as a common concern of humankind for the Anthropocene. In M. Lim (Ed.), *Charting environmental law futures in the Anthropocene*. Singapore: Springer. https://doi.org/10.1007/978-981-13-9065-4_8

Kramm, M. (2020). When a river becomes a person. *Journal of Human Development and Capabilities*, 21(4), 307–319. https://doi.org/10.1080/19452829.2020.1801610

Kramm, M. (2024). The role of political ontology for Indigenous self-determination. *Critical Review of International Social and Political Philosophy*, 27(5), 714–735. https://doi.org/10.1080/13698230.2021.1997250

Krauss, J. E. (2021). Decolonizing, conviviality and convivial conservation: Towards a convivial SDG 15, life on land? *Journal of Political Ecology*, 28(1), 945–967.

Kurian, A. L., & Vinodan, C. (2020). The global commons and the climate governance regime. In A. L. Kurian & C. Vinodan (Eds.), *Global commons: Issues, concerns and strategies* (pp. 61–84). Pentagon Press.

Kuthunur, S. (2023). Light pollution poses serious threat to astronomy, skywatching and more, study says. *Space.com*. June 15, 2023: www.space.com/light-pollution-serious-threat-astronomy-skywatching

Laing, A. (2015). Resource sovereignties in Bolivia: Re-conceptualising the relationship between indigenous identities and the environment during the TIPNIS conflict. *Bulletin of Latin American Research*, 34(2), 149–166.

Lane, M. B. (2003). Decentralization or privatization of environmental governance? Forest conflict and bioregional assessment in Australia. *Journal of Rural Studies*, 19(3), 283–294. https://doi.org/10.1016/S0743-0167(02)00084-0

Larsen, S. C., & Johnson, J. T. (2016). The agency of place: Toward a more-than-human geographical self. *GeoHumanities*, 2(1), 149–166. https://doi.org/10.1080/2373566X.2016.1157003

Larsen, S. C., Johnson, J. T., & Wildcat, D. R. (2017). Conclusion: Indigenous coexistence in a more than human world. In *Being together in place: Indigenous coexistence in a more than human world* (pp. 184–202). University of Minnesota Press. https://doi.org/10.5749/minnesota/9781517902216.003.0008

Latour, B. (2017). *Facing Gaia: Eight lectures on the new climatic regime*. Wiley.

Law N°. 29763, Forestry and Wildlife Law. (2011, July 22). Peru's Legal Information System. www.spij.minjus.gob.pe/spij-ext-web/#/detallenorma/H1035931

Lawres, N. R., & Sanger, M. C. (2022). Recentering the turn: Bringing Native philosophy into ontological studies. *General Anthropology*, 29(2), 7–10.

Le Billon, P. (2021). Crisis conservation and green extraction: Biodiversity offsets as spaces of double exception. *Journal of Political Ecology*, 28(1), 854–888. https://doi.org/10.2458/jpe.2991

Le Prestre, P. (2017). *Global Ecopolitics Revisited: Towards a complex governance of global environmental problems* (1st ed.). Routledge. https://doi.org/10.4324/9781315563695

Lees, A., Peres, C., Fearnside, P., Schneider, M., & Zuanon, J. (2016). Hydropower and the future of Amazonian biodiversity. *Biodiversity & Conservation*, 25(3), 451–466.

Lenzerini, F. (2006). *Sovereignty revisited: International law and parallel sovereignty of Indigenous peoples*. www.usiena-air.unisi.it/handle/11365/12030

Lesutis, G. (2021). Infrastructural territorialisations: Mega-infrastructures and the (re)making of Kenya. *Political Geography*, 90, 102383.

Li, J., & Xing, W. (2024). A critical appraisal of the BBNJ agreement not to recognise the high seas decline as a common concern of humankind. *Marine Policy*, 163, 106131.

Lightfoot, S. R. (2021). Decolonizing self-determination: Haudenosaunee passports and negotiated sovereignty. *European Journal of International Relations*, 27(4), 971–994. https://doi.org/10.1177/13540661211024713

Lin, J. (2018). *Governing climate change: Global cities and transnational lawmaking* (1st ed.). Cambridge University Press. https://doi.org/10.1017/9781108347907

Lindroth, M. (2006). Indigenous-state relations in the UN: Establishing the indigenous forum. *Polar Record*, 42(3), 239–248.

Little, P. E. (2013). *Megaproyectos en la Amazonia: Un análisis geopolítico y socioambiental con propuestas de mejor gobierno para la Amazonia.* Lima: RAMA/ARA/DAR.

Livingstone, E. (2024). Congo calling. *Science*, 386(6717), 16–19.

Lodge, M. (2021). Enclosure of the oceans versus the common heritage of mankind: The inherent tension between the continental shelf beyond 200 nautical miles and the Area. *International Law Studies*, 97(1), 34–73.

Long, A. (2013). REDD+, adaptation, and sustainable forest management: Toward effective polycentric global forest governance. *Tropical Conservation Science*, 6(3), 384–408. www.tropicalconservationscience.org

López Rivera, A. (2019). Global cooperation in Amazonia: Matters of fact and matters of concern. *Global Cooperation Research*, 1(3), 16–17.

Lord, E. & Sareen, S. (2025). Subjects of injustice: Inequity, misframing and human rights violations in a Tanzanian REDD+ pilot project. *Geoforum*, 161, 104245.

Lozano Flores, L., Delgado Pugley, D., Casas Luna, S., Van den Broeck, P., & Parra, C. (2024). Challenging state authority and hierarchical power: A case study of the engagement of Peru's Amazonian Indigenous Peoples' organizations in the governance of REDD+. *Environmental Policy and Governance*, 34(2), 137–151. https://doi.org/10.1002/eet.2067

Ludwig, D. (2016). Overlapping ontologies and Indigenous knowledge. From integration to ontological self-determination, *Studies in History and Philosophy of Science Part A*, 59, 36–45.

Lyall, A. (2021). Resistencia en retrospectiva: La multitemporalidad del extractivismo en la Amazonía. *Íconos: Revista de Ciencias Sociales*, 69, 17–34.

Magnan, A., & Ribera, T. (2016). Global adaptation after Paris. *Science*, 352(6291), 1280–1282.

Maloney, M., & Siemen, S. (2015). Responding to the Great Work: The role of earth jurisprudence and wild law in the 21st century. *Environmental and Earth Law Journal*, 5(1), 6.

Manestar, M. (2023). Runasur, hacia la integración regional de Nuestra América, desde los pueblos y para los pueblos. *Revista Ecúmene de Ciencias Sociales*, 2, 173–196.

Mangambu-Mokoso, J. D. D., Cakupewa, M. F., Ndetshala, D. A., & Aruna, J. (2024). Conflicts between indigenous Pygmy peoples, the local community and the Kahuzi-Biega National Park in Eastern of the DRC: Conflict management strategies towards perspectives for peaceful cohabitation. *East African Journal of Interdisciplinary Studies*, 7(1), 139–159.

Martín, F. (2017). Reimagining extractivism: Insights from spatial theory. In B. Engels & K. Dietz (Eds.), *Contested extractivism, society and the state: Development, justice and citizenship* (pp. 145–163). Palgrave.

Massimi, M. (2024). The fraught legacy of the common heritage of humankind principle for equitable ocean policy. *Environmental Science & Policy*, 153, 103681.

McCormick, S. (2010). Damming the Amazon: Local movements and transnational struggles over water. *Society and Natural Resources*, 24(1), 34–48.

McDermott, C. L., van Asselt, H., Streck, C., Assembe-Mvondo, S., Duchelle, A. E., Haug, C., Humphreys, D., Mulyani, M., Shekhar Silori, C., Suzuki, R., Zelli, F., Frick, S., Lentini, M., Luintel, H., & Salimon, C. (2012). Governance for REDD+, Forest management and biodiversity: Existing approaches and future options. In J. A. Parrotta, C. Wildburger, & S. Mansourian (Eds.), *Understanding relationships between biodiversity, carbon, forests and people: The key to achieving redd+ objectives.* A Global Assessment Report. (pp. 115). International Union of Forest Research Organisations (IUFRO).

McElwee, P., Fernández-Llamazares, Á., Aumeeruddy-Thomas, Y., Babai, D., Bates, P., Galvin, K., ... Brondízio, E. S. (2020). Working with Indigenous and local knowledge (ILK) in large-scale ecological assessments: Reviewing the experience of the IPBES Global Assessment. *Journal of Applied Ecology*, 57(9), 1666–1676.

McGahan, A., & Pongeluppe, L. S. (2021). There is no Planet B: Polycentric governance in the Amazon rainforest. *Academy of Management Proceedings*, 2021(1), 49.

McGinnis, M. D. (Ed.). (1999). *Polycentric governance and development: Readings from the Workshop in Political Theory and Policy Analysis*. University of Michigan Press.

McGinnis, M., & Walker, J. (2010). Foundations of the Ostrom workshop: Institutional analysis, polycentricity, and self-governance of the commons. *Public Choice*, 143(3), 293–301. https://doi.org/10.1007/s11127-010-9626-5

McNeish, J.-A., & Shapiro, J. (2021). Introduction. Our extractive age: Expressions of violence and resistance. In J.-A. McNeish & J. Shapiro (Eds.), *Our extractive age: Expressions of violence and resistance* (pp. 1–15). Routledge.

Medeiros da Costa, I. V., de Andrade, M. O., & Gonçalves, A. F. (2022). Conflictos socioambientales en áreas de conservación y tierras indígenas en el Nordeste brasileño: Racionalidades confrontadas. *Desacatos. Revista de Ciencias Sociales*, 70, 60–75. www.desacatos.ciesas.edu.mx/index.php/Desacatos/article/view/2576

Merino, R. (2016). An alternative to "alternative development"? Buen vivir and human development in Andean countries. *Oxford Development Studies*, 44(3), 271–286.

Merino, R. (2020). The geopolitics of food security and food sovereignty in Latin America: Harmonizing competing visions or reinforcing extractive agriculture? *Geopolitics*, 27(3), 898–920.

Merino, R. (2022). The politics of localizing human rights: Chinese policies and corporate practices in Latin America. *Business and Human Rights Journal*, 7(3), 439–460. https://doi.org/10.1017/bhj.2022.23

Merino, R. (2025). Governing international commons: Re-examining environmental and sovereignty imaginaries in the Amazon. *Transnational Environmental Law*, 1(1), 1–27. https://doi.org/10.1017/S2047102524000414

Merino, R. (2025, September 23). Peru and the making of international law. In L. O. Tarazona, and others (Eds.), *The Oxford handbook of international law and the Americas* (online ed.) Oxford Academic, 23 February 2023, https://doi.org/10.1093/oxfordhb/9780197661062.013.47.

Merino, R. (forthcoming). Peru, global extractivism and the making of international law. In O. Tarazona, L. Betancur-Restrepo, J. M. Amaya Castro, & D. R. Quiroga-Villamarín (Eds.), *The Oxford handbook of international law and the Americas*. Oxford University Press. https://doi.org/10.1093/oxfordhb/9780197661062.001.0001

Meza, R. (2019, July 31). *Cuenca del Cenepa: la nueva Madre de Dios* [Online]. IDL. www.idl.org.pe/cuenca-del-cenepa-la-nueva-madre-de-dios/

Mgbeoji, I. (2003). Beyond rhetoric: State sovereignty, common concern, and the inapplicability of the common heritage concept to plant genetic resources. *Leiden Journal of International Law*, 16(4), 821–837. https://doi.org/10.1017/S0922156503001412

Mickelson, K. (1996). Seeing the forest, the trees and the people: Coming to terms with developing country perspectives on the proposed global forests convention. In Canadian Council of International Law (Ed.), *Global forests and international environmental law* (pp. 239–264). Kluwer Law.

Mickelson, K. (2014). The maps of international law: Perceptions of nature in the classification of territory. *Leiden Journal of International Law*, 27(3), 621–639.

Mignolo, W., & Tlostanova, M. (2006). Theorizing from the borders: Shifting to geo- and body-politics of knowledge. *European Journal of Social Theory*, 9(2), 205–221. https://doi.org/10.1177/1368431006063333

Milhorance, F., Hirota, R., Bispo, F., Ponce, I., Paz y Miño, E., Puentes, P., & Castro, A. (2025, April 1). *The Amazon rainforest emerges as the new global oil frontier*. Infoamazonia.

Miller, G. (2004). *Sustaining the earth* (6th ed.). Thompson Learning.

MINAM. (2015). *Estrategia nacional sobre bosques y cambio climático* (pp. 1–112). Ministry of Environment.

MINEM. (2020, January 10). *Proyecto Minero Afrodita* [Online]. Ministerio de Energía y Minas. www.minem.gob.pe/minem/archivos/file/Minera%20Afrodita_enero%202019.pdf

Mistry, J., & Berardi, A. (2016). Bridging indigenous and scientific knowledge. *Science*, 352(6291), 1274–1275.

Mondardo, M. (2022). In defense of indigenous territories in Brazil: Rights, demarcations and land retake. *Geousp*, 26(1), e-176224. Available in: www.revistas.usp.br/geousp/article/view/176224. https://doi.org/10.11606/issn.2179-0892.geousp.2022.176224

Mongabay. (2019, October 17). Cordillera del Cóndor: policías y militares ingresan a zona tomada por mineros ilegales. *Mongabay*. www.es.mongabay.com/2019/10/cordillera-del-condor-policias-y-militares-ingresan-a-zona-tomada-por-mineros-ilegales/

Monjane, B., Land, C., de Carvalho, D. T., Samuel, E., Prawiranegara, I., Cabello, J., & the WRM Secretariat. (2022). *15 years of REDD: A mechanism rotten at the core*. World Rainforest Movement (WRM).

Monsalve, J. E., & Vargas, M. C. E. (2018). Conflictos de uso del territorio y áreas protegidas en Colombia: Aproximaciones para su análisis. *Administración & Desarrollo*, 48(2), 76–106.

Moore, J. W. (2017). The Capitalocene, Part I: On the nature and origins of our ecological crisis. *The Journal of Peasant Studies*, 44(3), 594–630.

Moore, J. W. (2022). Anthropocene, capitalocene & the flight from world history: Dialectical universalism & the geographies of class power in the capitalist world-ecology, 1492–2022. *Nordia Geographical Publications*, 51(2), 123–146. https://doi.org/10.30671/nordia.116148

Morales Chocano, D. (2000). Las poblaciones prehistóricas amazónicas. *Investigaciones Sociales*, 4(6), 1–22.

Moreton-Robinson, Aileen (2021). Incommensurable sovereignties: Indigenous ontology matters. In B. Hokowhitu, A. Moreton-Robinson, L. Tuhiwai-Smith, C. Andersen, & S. Larkin (Eds.), *Routledge handbook of critical indigenous studies* (pp. 257–268). Routledge. https://doi.org/10.4324/9780429440229-23

Mosweunyane, D. (2017). Brutal development agenda by political panjandrums in Botswana: How CKGR evictions massacred the native citizens (Basarwa) through HIV/AIDS. *African Educational Research Journal*, 5(1), 75–90.

Moutinho, P., Leite, I., Baniwa, A., Mirabal, G., Josse, C., Macedo, M., Alencar, A., Salinas, N., & Ramos, A. (2022). *The role of Amazonian Indigenous peoples in fighting the climate crisis. Science Panel for the Amazon, Policy Brief.* https://files.unsdsn.org/PB-Indigenous-en.pdf

Müller, F. (2020). Can the subaltern protect forests? REDD+ compliance, depoliticization and Indigenous subjectivities. *Journal of Political Ecology*, 27(1), 419–435. https://doi.org/10.2458/v27i1.23198

Myers, M. (2018). China's Belt and Road Initiative: What role for Latin America? *Journal of Latin American Geography*, 17(2), 239–243.

Nabais, M. (2000). The internationalization of the Amazon. *Sustainable Development Law & Policy*, 1(1), 17.

Nago, M., & Ongolo, S. (2021). Inside forest diplomacy: A case study of the congo basin under global environmental governance. *Forests*, 12(5), 525.

Naupa, A. (2022). *Sealed with kava and betel nut: Lessons in oceanic diplomacy from the Mota Lava treaty*. Australian National University. https://doi.org/10.25911/2SGH-D402

Neilson, H. (2024a). Indigenous knowledges and kinship as a model for our future in outer space. *arXiv preprint* arXiv:2412.06669.

Neilson, H. (2024b). Overview of Indigenous rights and outer space for the IAU-CPS Policy Hub. *arXiv preprint* arXiv:2412.06675.

Neves, E. G., Furquim, L. P., Levis, C., Rocha, B. C., Watling, J. G., Almeida, F. O., Betancourt, C. J., Junqueira, A. B., Moraes, C. P., Morcote-Rios, G., Shock, M. P., & Tamanaha, E. K. (2021). Chapter 8: Peoples of the Amazon before European colonization. In C. Nobre et al. (Eds.), *Amazon Assessment Report 2021*. New York: United Nations Sustainable Development Solutions Network. www.theamazonwewant.org/spa-reports/ https://doi.org/10.55161/LXIT5573

Nicolon, T. (2024). *Protecting wildlife and indigenous peoples' livelihoods in the Democratic Republic of the Congo*. European Commission. https://international-partnerships.ec.europa.eu/news-and-events/stories/protecting-wildlife-and-indigenous-peoples-livelihoods-democratic-republic-congo_en

Nielsen, T. D. (2014). The role of discourses in governing forests to combat climate change. *International Environmental Agreements*, 14, 265–280. https://doi.org/10.1007/s10784-013-9223-4

Nobre, C. A., Sampaio, G., Borma, L. S., Castilla-Rubio, J. C., Silva, J. S., & Cardoso, M. (2016). The fate of the Amazon forests: Land-use and climate change risks and the need of a novel sustainable development paradigm. *Proceedings of the National Academy of Sciences of the United States of America*, 113(39), 10759–10768.

Norman, M., & Nakhooda, S. (2014). *The state of REDD+ finance (Working Paper 378)*. Center for Global Development.

Nuesiri, E. O. (Ed.). (2018). *Global forest governance and climate change*. Springer International Publishing. https://doi.org/10.1007/978-3-319-71946-7

Nugkuag, E. (1994). El desarrollo indígena autónomo en la Amazonía luego de 500 años. *Caravelle (1988-)*, 63, 195–208.

O'Donnell, E., Poelina, A., Pelizzon, A., & Clark, C. (2020). Stop burying the lede: The essential role of Indigenous law(s) in creating rights of nature. *Environmental Politics*, 29(7), 1–23.

ODECOFROC. (2009). *Crónica de un engaño. Los intentos de enajenación del territorio fronterizo Awajun en la Cordillera del Cóndor a favor de la minería* (Informe 5). Perú: A Chronicle of Deception.

Oliveira, E. (2023, March 7). Brazil's indigenous groups demand a voice in new soybean railway project. *Mongabay*. www.news.mongabay.com/2023/03/brazils-indigenous-groups-demand-a-voice-in-new-soybean-railway-project/

Olson, M. (1965). *The logic of collective action: Public goods and the theory of groups*. Harvard University Press.

Olson, M. (2002). *The logic of collective action: Public goods and the theory of groups* (20th printing). Harvard University Press.

Orihuela, J. C. (2014). La gobernanza de los recursos y el ambiente en la Amazonía peruana: Delineando una agenda de investigación desde el institucionalismo económico. In G. Damonte & G. Vila (Eds.), *Agenda de investigación en temas socioambientales en el Perú: Una aproximación desde las ciencias sociales* (pp. 47–73). PUCP.

Orihuela, J. C. (2019). Embedded countermovements: The forging of protected areas and native communities in the Peruvian Amazon. *New Political Economy*, 25(2), 1–16. https://doi.org/10.1080/13563467.2019.1570101

Osborne, T., Cifuentes, S., Dev, L. et al. (2024). Climate justice, forests, and Indigenous peoples: Toward an alternative to REDD + for the Amazon. *Climatic Change*, 177(128). https://doi.org/10.1007/s10584-024-03774-7

Ostrom, E. (1998). A behavioural approach to the rational choice theory of collective action. *American Political Science Review*, 92(1), 1–22.

Ostrom, E. (2010). Polycentric systems for coping with collective action and global environmental change. *Global Environmental Change*, 20(4), 550–557. https://doi.org/10.1016/j.gloenvcha.2010.07.004

Ostrom, E. (2011). Honoring James Buchanan. *Journal of Economic Behavior & Organization*, 80(2), 370–373.

Ostrom, V., Tiebout, C. M., & Warren, R. (1961). The organization of government in metropolitan areas: A theoretical inquiry. *American Political Science Review*, 55: 831–842.

OTCA. (2020, October 14). *Framework Agreement of Collaboration between OTCA and FILAC.* Retrieved from www.otca.org/acuerdo-marco-de-colaboracion-entre-la-otca-y-filac-pone-derelieve-los-derechos-de-los-pueblos-indigenas-de-lacuenca-amazonica/

OTCA. (2021, September 8). World Conservation Congress: ACTO announces the creation of the Amazon Regional Platform for Indigenous Peoples and Climate Change. www.otca.org/en/world-conservation-congress-acto-announces-the-creation-of-the-amazon-regional-platform-for-indigenous-peoples-and-climate-change/

OTCA. (2023). Declaration of Belém. Organización del Tratado de Cooperación Amazónica. www.otca.org/en/wp-content/uploads/2023/10/Declaration-of-Belem.pdf

OTCA. (n.d.). ¿Quiénes somos? https://otca.org/quienes-somos/

Paim, M. A. (2021). Zero deforestation in the Amazon: The Soy Moratorium and global forest governance. *Review of European, Comparative and International Environmental Law*, 30(2), 220–232. https://doi.org/10.1111/reel.12408

Palacio, G. (2011). Suelo, subsuelo y vuelo. Los previsibles desafíos ecopolíticos para la región amazónica colombiana. In H. Alimonda (Ed.), *La naturaleza colonizada. Ecología política y minería en América Latina* (pp. 85–104). CLACSO.

Palacio, G. (2012). An eco-political vision for an environmental history: Toward a Latin American and North American research partnership. *Environmental History*, 17(4), 725–743. www.jstor.org/stable/41721443

Palacios Llaque, D., & Sarmiento Barletti, J. P. (2021). The meeting of multiple governmentalities and technologies of participation in protected areas: The case of the Amarakaeri Communal Reserve (Peruvian Amazon). *International Forestry Review*, 23(S1). www.ingentaconnect.com/content/cfa/ifr/pre-prints/content-ifrb

Parfitt, R., & Craven, M. (2018). Statehood, self-determination and recognition. In M. D. Evans (Ed.), *International law* (pp. 177–226). Oxford University Press.

Peralta, C. (2021). Intensificación de los extractivismos en la Amazonía boliviana. *Aurora Voces Jesuitas en tiempos de pandemia*, 17, 32–35.

Pereira, J., & Viola, E. (2020). Close to a tipping point? The Amazon and the challenge of sustainable development under growing climate pressures. *Journal of Latin American Studies*, 52(3), 467–494.

Perreault, T., & Valdivia, G. (2010). Hydrocarbons, popular protest and national imaginaries: Ecuador and Bolivia in comparative context. *Geoforum*, 41, 689–699.

Petel, M. (2024). The illusion of harmony: Power, politics, and distributive implications of rights of nature. *Transnational Environmental Law*, 13(1), 12–34. https://doi.org/10.1017/S2047102523000262

Phelps, J., Webb, E. L., & Agrawal, A. (2010). Does REDD+ threaten to recentralize forest governance? *Science*, 328(5976), 312–313.

Phillips, D. (2019, July 19). Bolsonaro declares "the Amazon is ours" and calls deforestation data 'lies'. *The Guardian*. www.theguardian.com/world/2019/jul/19/jair-bolsonaro-brazil-amazon-rainforest-deforestation

Picq, M. L. (2017). Situating the Amazon in world politics. In C. Tan & J. Faundez (Eds.), *Natural resources and sustainable development: International economic law perspectives*. Edward Elgar Publishing Ltd.

Pieck, S. K. (2006). Opportunities for transnational indigenous eco-politics: The changing landscape in the new millennium. *Global Networks*, 6(3), 309–329.

Pieck, S. K., & Moog, S. (2009). Competing entanglements in the struggle to save the Amazon: The shifting terrain of transnational civil society. *Political Geography*, 28(7), 416–429.

Pio, R. (2020). *La Organización del Tratado de Cooperación Amazónica (OTCA): Un análisis crítico de su funcionamiento* [Memoria del Máster en Estudios Internacionales]. Universitat de Barcelona.

Pokorny, B., Sotirov, M., Kleinschmit, D., & Kanowski, P. (2019). *Forests as a global commons: International governance and the role of Germany*. Report to the Science Platform Sustainability 2030. Universität Freiburg.

Polanyi, M. (1951). *The logic of liberty*. University of Chicago Press.

Popkin, G. (2015, December 2). Indigenous people could be key to storing carbon in tropical forests, new report concludes. *Science*. www.science.org/content/article/indigenous-people-could-be-key-storing-carbon-tropical-forests-new-report-concludes

Porro, R. (2005). Palms, pastures, and swidden fields: The grounded political ecology of "agro-extractive/shifting-cultivator peasants" in Maranhão, Brazil. *Human Ecology*, 33(1), 17–56.

Postero, N. (2017). *The Indigenous State: Race, politics, and performance in plurinational Bolivia*. University of California Press. https://doi.org/10.1525/luminos.31

Pottage, A. (2024). Why nature has no rights. In A. Alvarez-Nakagawa & C. Douzinas (Eds.), *Non-Human Rights* (pp. 39–65). Edward Elgar Publishing.

Povinelli, E. (2015). *Geontologies: A requiem to late liberalism*. Duke University Press.

Premauer, J. M., & Berkes, F. (2015). A pluralistic approach to protected area governance: Indigenous peoples and Makuira National Park, Colombia. *Ethnobiology and Conservation*, 4(4), 1–16. https://doi.org/10.15451/ec2015-5-4.4-1-16

Querejazu Escobari, A., & Tickner, A. B. (2020). The rights of Mother Earth: A pluriversal reading of climate change governance. In T.-A. Teo (Ed.), *Postcolonial governmentalities: Rationalities, violences and contestations* (Kilombo: International Relations and Colonial Questions). Rowman & Littlefield.

Quijano, A. (2000). Colonialidad del poder y clasificación social. *Journal of World-Systems Research*, 2, 342–386.

Quijano, P., Veit, P., Tipula, P., & Reytar, K. (2020). *Undermining rights: Indigenous lands and mining in the Amazon*. World Resources Institute and RAISG. https://files.wri.org/d8/s3fs-public/Report_Indigenous_Lands_and_Mining_in_the_Amazon_web_1.pdf?_gl=1*1biggt*_gcl_au*OTUxMzUwNzU0LjE3NjA3MzYxMTA

Radhuber, I. M., & Radcliffe, S. A. (2023). Contested sovereignties: Indigenous disputes over plurinational resource governance. *Environment and Planning E: Nature and Space*, 6(1), 556–577. https://doi.org/10.1177/25148486211068476

RAISG. (2022). Pasado y futuro de la deforestación en la Amazonía: Pérdida de bosque ocurrida entre 2001–2020 y escenarios predictivos al año 2025. Septiembre 2022.

Ranta, E. (2023). Nascent activism in times of disillusionment: Struggles between Indigenous self-determination and state co-optation in plurinational Bolivia. *AlterNative: An International Journal of Indigenous Peoples*, 19(4), 841–851.

Rashidi, P., & Lyons, K. (2021). Democratizing global climate governance? the case of indigenous representation in the intergovernmental panel on climate change (IPCC). *Globalizations*, 20(8), 1312–1327. https://doi.org/10.1080/14747731.2021.1979718

Rashidi, P., & Lyons, K. (2022). Democratizing global climate governance? The case of indigenous representation in the Intergovernmental Panel on Climate Change (IPCC). In B. Gill, & J. Morgan (Eds.), *Economics and climate emergency* (1st ed., pp. 284–299). Routledge.

Ravikumar, A., Larson, A. M., Duchelle, A. E., Myers, R., & Gonzales Tovar, J. (2015). Multilevel governance challenges in transitioning towards a national approach for REDD+: Evidence from 23 subnational REDD+ initiatives. *International Journal of the Commons*, 9(2), 909–931.

Rawson, A., & Mansfield, B. (2018). Producing juridical knowledge: "Rights of nature" or the naturalization of rights? *Environment and Planning E: Nature and Space*, 1(1–2), 99–119.

Recio, M. E. (2022). Shaping REDD+: Interactions between bilateral and multilateral rule-making. *Journal of Environmental Law*, 34(1), 83–106. https://doi.org/10.1093/jel/eqab022

Red Amazónica de Información Socioambiental Georreferenciada (RAISG). (2015). *Amazonia 2015: Protected natural areas and indigenous territories*. RAISG. www.amazoniasocioambiental.org/es/mapas/

Reimerson, E. (2013). Between nature and culture: Exploring space for indigenous agency in the Convention on Biological Diversity. *Environmental Politics*, 22(6), 992–1009.

Reisinger, A., Meinshausen, M., & Manning, M. (2011). Future changes in global warming potentials under representative concentration pathways. *Environmental Research Letters*, 6(2) 1–8.

Rengifo, H. (2010). *GEI [Gases efecto invernadero] o mercado carbono? Construyendo un REDD+ indígena* (27 de octubre). Bank Information Center. www.bicusa.org/en/Document.102796.pdf

Reynolds, H. (2023). Racialised foreign policy and the prospects for Indigenous diplomacy. *Australian Journal of International Affairs*, 77(6), 632–636.

Ribot, J. C., Agrawal, A., & Larson, A. M. (2006). Recentralizing while decentralizing: How national governments reappropriate forest resources. *World Development*, 34(11), 1864–1886. https://doi.org/10.1016/j.worlddev.2005.11.020

Riofrancos, T. (2017). Extractivismo unearthed: A genealogy of a radical discourse. *Cultural Studies*, 31(2–3), 277–306.

Ripple, W., Wolf, C., Newsome, T., Barnard, P., & Moomaw, W. (2020). World scientists' warning of a climate emergency. *BioScience*, 70(1), 8–12. https://doi.org/10.1093/biosci/biz088

Rival, L. (2016). *Huaorani transformations in 21st century Ecuador. Treks into the future of time.* University of Arizona Press.

Rivera Cusicanqui, S. (2012). Ch'ixinakax utxiwa: A reflection on the practices and discourses of decolonization. *South Atlantic Quarterly*, 111(1), 95–109.

Rocha, I., et al. (2015). *Manual de Direito Agrário e Constitucional: Lições de Direito Agroambiental.* Fórum.

Rubiños Cea, S., & Betancout-Santiago, M. (2021). Colonialidad territorial: Disputas globales-locales en la Amazonía Andina (Colombia, Ecuador, Perú y Bolivia). In N. Nogales (Ed.), *Amazonía y expansión mercantil capitalista: Nueva frontera de recursos en el siglo XXI.* CLACSO. (pp. 315–376).

Rueda-Saiz, P. (2017). Indigenous autonomy in Colombia: State-building processes and multiculturalism. *Global Constitutionalism*, 6(2), 265–297. https://doi.org/10.1017/S2045381717000144

Rühs, N., & Jones, A. (2016). The implementation of earth jurisprudence through substantive constitutional rights of nature. *Sustainability*, 8(2), 174.

Runde, D. F., Bandura, R., & McKeown, S. (2020). *Sustainable infrastructure in the Amazon: Connecting environmental preservation with governance, security, and economic development* (pp. 43–50). Center for Strategic and International Studies (CSIS). https://csis-website-prod.s3.amazonaws.com/s3fs-public/publication/201022_Bandura_Sustainable_Infrastructure_Amazon_Brazil.pdf

Rzedzian, S. (2023). Divergent environmentalisms, conflicting counter-hegemonies: Lessons from the rights of nature movement. *EPE: Nature and Space*, 6(4), 2557–2575.

Sabel, C. F., & Zeitlin, J. (2012). Experimentalism in the EU: Common ground and persistent differences. *Regulation & Governance*, 6(3), 410–426. https://doi.org/10.1111/j.1748-5991.2012.01157.x

Sachs, N. (2023). A wrong turn with the rights of nature movement. *Georgetown Environmental Law Review*, 36, 1–25.

Santos, B. S. (2010). La difícil construcción de la plurinacionalidad. In Secretaría Nacional de Planificación y Desarrollo (Ed.), *Los nuevos retos de América Latina: Socialismo y Sumak Kawsay.* SENPLADES.

Santos, G. (2024, April 23). Perú: asesinan a guardaparque de la Reserva Comunal Amarakaeri. *Mongabay.* www.es.mongabay.com/2024/04/asesinan-a-guardaparque-de-la-reserva-comunal-amarakaeri/

Santos-Granero, F. (2009). *Vital enemies: Slavery, predation, and the Amerindian political economy of life.* Austin: University of Texas Press.

Santos-Granero, F., & Barclay, F. (2010). Bultos, selladores y gringos alados: Percepciones indígenas de la violencia capitalista en la Amazonía peruana. *Anthropologica*, 28, 21–52. www.researchgate.net/publication/285805403_Bultos_selladores_y_gringos_alados_percepciones_indigenas_de_la_violencia_capitalista_en_la_Amazonia_peruana

Sarmiento Barletti, J. P., & Rolando, G. (2024). Between co-management and responsibilisation: Comparative perspectives from two Reservas Comunales in the Peruvian Amazon. *Bulletin of Latin American Research*, 43(2), 104–119. https://doi.org/10.1111/blar.13539

Sauvêtre, P. (2018). Forget Ostrom: From the development commons to the common as social sovereignty. In S. Cogolati & J. Wouters (Eds.), *Introduction: Democratic, institutional and legal implications of the commons for global governance* (pp. 78–100). Edward Elgar Publishing.

Schaeffer, A. (2017). *The CERN model, United Nations and global public goods: Addressing global challenges. Report on the symposium that took place on 2 November 2015 at the Palais des Nations, Geneva.* UNOG: https://cds.cern.ch/record/2271745/files/Report_TheCERNmodel_theUN_andGlobalPublicGoods_Final_20.04.2017.pdf

Schelly, C., Gagnon, V., Arola, K., Fiss, A., Schaefer, M., & Halvorsen, K. E. (2021). Cultural imaginaries or incommensurable ontologies? Relationality and sovereignty as worldviews in socio-technological system transitions. *Energy Research & Social Science*, 80, 102242. https://doi.org/10.1016/j.erss.2021.102242

Schillmoller, M., & Pelizzon, A. (2013). Mapping the terrain of earth jurisprudence: Landscape, thresholds and horizons. *Environmental and Earth Law Journal*, 3(1), 1.

Schnegg, M. (2021). Ontologies of climate change: Reconciling indigenous and scientific explanations for the lack of rain in Namibia. *American Ethnologist*, 48(3), 260–273. https://doi.org/10.1111/amet.13028

Schneider, L. (2023). Decolonizing conservation? Indigenous resurgence and buffalo restoration in the American West. *Environment and Planning E: Nature and Space*, 6(2), 801–821. https://doi.org/10.1177/25148486221119158

Schoenefeld, J. J. (2023). *The evaluation of polycentric climate governance* (1st ed.). Cambridge University Press. https://doi.org/10.1017/9781009049658

Schroeder, H. (2010). Agency in international climate negotiations: The case of indigenous peoples and avoided deforestation. *International Environmental Agreements*, 10, 317–332.

Schroeder, H., & González, N. C. (2019). Bridging knowledge divides: The case of indigenous ontologies of territoriality and REDD+. *Forest Policy and Economics*, 100, 198–206.

Schroeder, H., & Lovell, H. (2009). The role of side events in the UNFCCC climate negotiations. In Amsterdam (Ed.), *Conference on the Human Dimensions of Global Environmental Change*, Amsterdam.

Schulz, C.-A. (2019). Territorial sovereignty and the end of inter-cultural diplomacy along the "Southern frontier." *European Journal of International Relations*, 25(3), 878–903.

Schuster, R., Germain, R. R., Bennett, J. R., Reo, N. J., & Arcese, P. (2019). Vertebrate biodiversity on indigenous-managed lands in Australia, Brazil, and Canada equals that in protected areas. *Environmental Science & Policy*, 101, 1–6.

Science Panel for the Amazon [SPA]. (2021). *Executive summary of the Amazon assessment report 2021* (C. Nobre et al., Eds.). United Nations Sustainable Development Solutions Network. www.theamazonwewant.org/wp-content/uploads/2022/06/220717-SPA-Executive-Summary 2021 EN.pdf

Science Panel for the Amazon. (2021). *Amazon assessment report 2021: Executive summary*. www.theamazonwewant.org/wp-content/uploads/2022/06/220717-SPA-Executive-Summary-2021-EN.pdf

Sempértegui, A., & Báez, M. (2024). Ontological conflicts in the plurinational state: The case of Indigenous resistance against the Mirador mega-mining project in Ecuador. *Society & Natural Resources*, 37(5), 660–677.

Sène, A. L. (2023). Justice in nature conservation: Limits and possibilities under global capitalism. *Climate and Development*, 16(9), 838–847.

SERNANP. (2020, March 3). *Listado de Áreas Naturales Protegidas por el Estado Peruano* [PDF]. SERNANP.

SERVINDI. (2005). *Servicio de Información Indígena. N° 63 Año 2005 – Edición de Julio.* www.servindi.org/pdf/Serv_63_Coica.pdf

SERVINDI. (2019, January 12). *Dramático llamado para frenar minería en Cordillera del Cóndor* [online]. Servindi. www.servindi.org/actualidad-noticias/12/01/2019/dramatico-llamado-para-frenar-invasion-minera-ecuatoriana-en#:~:text=Servindi%2C%2012%20de%20enero%2C%202019,la%20supervivencia%20de%20su%20pueblo

Shadian, J. M. (2006). *Reconceptualizing sovereignty through Indigenous autonomy: A case study of Arctic governance and the Inuit circumpolar conference* [Doctoral dissertation, University of Delaware].

Shadian, J. M. (2017). Reimagining political space: The limits of Arctic Indigenous self-determination in international governance? In K. Keil, & S. Knecht (Eds.), *Governing Arctic Change: Global Perspectives* (pp. 43–57). Palgrave Macmillan.

Shapiro, A., et al. (2023). Small scale agriculture continues to drive deforestation and degradation in fragmented forests in the Congo Basin (2015–2020). *Land Use Policy*, 119, 106922. https://doi.org/10.1016/j.landusepol.2023.106922

Shapiro, A., Grantham, H., Aguilar-Amuchastegui, N., & Murray, N. J. (2021). Forest condition in the Congo Basin for the assessment of ecosystem conservation status. *Ecological Indicators*, 122, 107268.

Shelton, D. (2009a). Common concern of humanity. *Environmental Law and Policy*, 39(2), 83–93.

Shelton, D. (2009b). Common concern of humanity. *Iustum Aequum Salutare*, 5(1), 33–40.

Siegel, K. M. (2017). *Regional environmental cooperation in South America*. Palgrave Macmillan.

Sierra, X. (2019). The ecocentric turn of environmental justice in Colombia. *King's Law Journal*. https://doi.org/10.1080/09615768.2019.1645433

Sikor, T., et al. (2010). REDD-plus, forest people's rights and nested climate governance. *Global Environmental Change*, 20, 423–425.

Silva-Junior, C. H. L., Silva, F. B., Arisi, B. M., Mataveli, G., Pessôa, A. C. M., Carvalho, N. S., Reis, J. B. C., Silva Júnior, A. R., Motta, N. A. C. S., Moreira e Silva, P. V., Ribeiro, F. D., Siqueira-Gay, J., Alencar, A., Saatchi, S., Aragão, L. E. O. C., Anderson, L. O., & Melo, M. (2023). Brazilian Amazon indigenous territories under deforestation pressure. *Scientific Reports*, 13, 5851. https://doi.org/10.1038/s41598-023-32746-7

Silveira Junior, W. J., Mariano, R. F., de Souza, C. R., & Moura, C. (2021). Conservation conflicts and their drivers in different protected area management groups: A case study in Brazil. *Biodiversity and Conservation*, 30(4), 1–14. https://doi.org/10.1007/s10531-021-02308-2

Simpson, A. (2014). *Mohawk interruptus: Political life across the borders of settler states*. Duke University Press.

Smith, R. C. (2003). Lo transnacional, instrumento y desafío para los pueblos indígenas. In F. Morin y R. Santana (Eds.), *Los indígenas amazónicos suben al escenario internacional: Reflexiones sobre el accidentado camino recorrido*. Quito.

Smouts, M. (2003). *Tropical forests, international jungle: The underside of global ecopolitics*. Palgrave.

Sovacool, B. K., & Dunlap, A. (2022). Anarchy, war, or revolt? Radical perspectives for climate protection, insurgency and civil disobedience in a low-carbon era. *Energy Research & Social Science*, 86, 102416. https://doi.org/10.1016/j.erss.2022.102416

SPA. (2022). SPA at COP27. *The Amazon We Want*. www.theamazonwewant.org/science-panel-for-the-amazon-at-cop27/

Stein, S., Ahenakew, C., Oliveira da Silva Huni Kui, S., Bowness, E., Mendes, W., & Evans, S. (2023). Towards settler responsibility in conservation. *ACME*, 22(2), 894–920.

Stevenson, H. (2017). *Global environmental politics: Problems, policy and practice* (1st ed.). Cambridge University Press. https://doi.org/10.1017/9781316344354

Stilt, K. (2020). Rights of nature, rights of animals. *Harvard Law Review Forum*, 134, 276. www.harvardlawreview.org/forum/vol-134/rights-of-nature-rights-of-animals/

Stone, C. (1972). Should trees have standing? Towards legal rights for natural objects. *Southern California Law Review*, 45, 450.

Streck, C. (2021). How voluntary carbon markets can drive climate ambition. *Journal of Energy & Natural Resources Law*, 39(3), 367–374. https://doi.org/10.1080/02646811.2021.1881275

Suliman, S., Farbotko, C., Ransan-Cooper, H., McNamara, E., Thornton, F., McMichael, C., & Kitara, T. (2019). Indigenous (im)mobilities in the Anthropocene. *Mobilities*, 14(3), 298–318. https://doi.org/10.1080/17450101.2019.1601828

Sullivan, S. (2022). "Hunting Africa": Trophy hunting, neocolonialism and land. *The Land Magazine.* www.thelandmagazine.org.uk/articles/hunting-africa-trophy-hunting-neocolonialism-and-land

Sundberg, J. (2014). Decolonizing posthumanist geographies. *Cultural Geographies*, 21(1), 33–47. https://doi.org/10.1177/1474474013486067

Sunderlin, W. D., Sills, E. O., Duchelle, A. E., Ekaputri, A. D., Kweka, D., Toniolo, A., Ball, S., Doggart, N., Pratama, C. D., Padilla, J. T., Enright, A., & Otsyina, R. M. (2015). REDD+ at a critical juncture: Assessing the limits of polycentric governance for achieving climate change mitigation. *International Forestry Review*, 17(4), 400–413. https://doi.org/10.1505/146554815817476468

Svampa, M. (2015). Commodities consensus: Neoextractivism and enclosure of the commons in Latin America. *South Atlantic Quarterly*, 114(1), 65–82.

Tanasescu, M. (2015). Nature advocacy and the indigenous symbol. *Environmental Values*, 24(1), 105–122.

Tanasescu, M. (2022). *Ecocene politics*. Open Book Publishers.

Tauli-Corpuz, V., Alcorn, J., Molnar, A., Healy, C., & Barrow, E. (2020). Cornered by PAs: Adopting rights-based approaches to enable cost-effective conservation and climate action. *World Development*, 130, 104923.

Te Awa Tupua Act (2017). *Te Awa Tupua (Whanganui River Claims Settlement) Act 2017*. New Zealand Government. Retrieved from www.legislation.govt.nz/act/public/2017/0040/latest/whole.html

Tennberg, M. (2010). Indigenous peoples as international political actors: A summary. *Polar Record*, 46(3), 264–270.

Tessnow-von Wysocki, I., & Vadrot, A. B. (2022). Governing a divided ocean: The transformative power of ecological connectivity in the BBNJ negotiations. *Politics and Governance*, 10(3), 14–28.

Thackeray, S. J., et al. (2020). Civil disobedience movements such as School Strike for the Climate are raising public awareness of the climate change emergency. *Global Change Biology*, 26(3), 1042–1044. https://doi.org/10.1111/gcb.14978

Thiel, A., & Moser-Priewich, C. (2019). Foundational aspects of polycentric governance: Overarching rules, social-problem characteristics and heterogeneity. In A. Thiel, W. A. Blomquist, & D. E. Garrick (Eds.), *Governing complexity: Analysing and applying polycentricity* (pp. 65–90). Cambridge University Press.

Tickner, A. B., & Querejazu, A. (2020). The rights of Mother Earth: A pluriversal reading of climate change governance. In A. Teo & E. Wynne-Hughes (Eds.), *Postcolonial governmentalities: Rationalities, violences and contestations* (pp. 217–238). Rowman and Littlefield Publishers, Inc.

Tigre, M. A. (2017). *Regional cooperation in Amazonia: A comparative environmental law analysis.* Brill.

Tilot, V. C., Guilloux, B., Willaert, K., Mulalap, C. Y., Bambridge, T., D'Arcy, P., … & Dahl, A. (2021). The concept of oceanian sovereignty in the context of deep sea mining in the Pacific region. *Frontiers in Marine Science*, 8, 756072.

Tockman, J., & Cameron, J. (2014). Indigenous autonomy and the contradictions of plurinationalism in Bolivia. *Latin American Politics and Society*, 56(3), 46–69.

Tollefson, J. (2022, October 6). The last stand. *Nature*, 610, 22.

Torres, C., & Verschoor, G. (2020). Re-imagining environmental governance: Gold dredge mining vs. territorial health in the Colombian Amazon. *Geoforum*, 117, 124–133.

Trevino, N. B. (2020). The Cosmos Is Not Finished. PhD thesis, The University of Western Ontario (Canada), 2020.

Turnheim, B., Kivimaa, P., & Berkhout, F. (Eds.). (2018). *Innovating climate governance: Moving beyond experiments* (1st ed.). Cambridge University Press. https://doi.org/10.1017/9781108277679

Turnhout, E., Neves, K., & de Lijster, E. (2014). "Measurementality" in biodiversity governance: Knowledge, transparency, and the Intergovernmental Science-Policy Platform on Biodiversity and Ecosystem Services (IPBES). *Environment and Planning A*, 46(3), 581–597.

Tyukavina, A., et al. (2018, November 7). Congo Basin forest loss dominated by increasing smallholder clearing. *Science Advances*, 4(11), 1–12.

United Nations. (1960). *Declaration on the Granting of Independence to Colonial Countries and Peoples* (General Assembly Resolution 1514 (XV)).

United Nations. (1992). *Rio Declaration on Environment and Development.* United Nations Conference on Environment and Development.

United Nations. (1994). *Agreement relating to the implementation of Part XI of the United Nations Convention on the Law of the Sea.*

Urpelainen, J. (2022). *Global environmental politics: The transformative role of emerging economies.* Columbia University Press.

Valdivia, G., & Lyall, A. (2018). The oil complex in Latin America: Politics, frontiers, and habits of oil rule. In J. Cupples, M. Palomino, & M. Prieto (Eds.), *The Routledge handbook of Latin American development.* Routledge.

Valladares, C., & Boelens, R. (2017). Extractivism and the rights of nature: Governmentality, "convenient communities" and epistemic pacts in Ecuador. *Environmental Politics*, 26(6), 1015–1034. https://doi.org/10.1080/09644016.2017.1338384

van Asselt, H., & McDermott, C. (2016). The institutional complex for REDD: A "benevolent jigsaw"? In C. Voigt (Ed.), *Research handbook on REDD+ and international law* (pp. 63–88). Edward Elgar.

Van der Sluijs, J., Van Est, R., & Riphagen, M. (2010). Beyond consensus: Reflections from a democratic perspective on the interaction between climate politics and science. *Current Opinion in Environmental Sustainability*, 2(5–6), 409–415. https://doi.org/10.1016/j.cosust.2010.10.003

van der Velden, J. & White, R. (2021). *The extinction curve: Growth and globalisation in the climate endgame.* London: Emerald Publications.

Varese, S. (2006). *Witness to sovereignty: Essays on the Indian movement in Latin America.* IWGIA document, 117.

Vásquez, S., & Cojtí, A. (2020, December 7). Apropiación cultural, otra forma de extractivismo en las comunidades indígenas. *Cultural Survival*. www.culturalsurvival.org/news/apropiacion-cultural-otra-forma-de-extractivismo-en-las-comunidades-indigenas

Venkatesan, A., Lowenthal, J., Prem, P., & Vidaurri, M. (2020). The impact of satellite constellations on space as an ancestral global commons. *Nature Astronomy*, 4(11), 1043–1048.

Viaene, L. (2022). Can rights of nature save us from the Anthropocene catastrophe? Some critical reflections from the field. *Asian Journal of Law and Society*, 9(2), 187–206.

Vidaurri, M., Wofford, A., Brande, J., Black-Planas, G., Domagal-Goldman, S., & Haqq-Misra, J. (2020). Absolute prioritization of planetary protection, safety, and avoiding imperialism in all future science missions: A policy perspective. *Space Policy*, 51, 101345.

Vincent, G., Hocking, M., & Ervin, J. (2004). Assessing the management of protected areas: The work of the World Parks Congress before and after Durban. *Journal of International Wildlife Law and Policy*, 7(1–2), 31–42.

Viveiros de Castro, E. (2004). Exchanging perspectives: The transformation of objects into subjects in Amerindian ontologies. *Common Knowledge*, 10(3), 463–465.

Viveiros de Castro, E. (2015). *The relative native: Essays on indigenous conceptual worlds*. HAU Books.

Viveiros de Castro, E., & Skafish, P. (2015). *Cannibal metaphysics*. University of Minnesota Press.

Vogler, J. (2012). Global commons revisited. *Global Policy*, 3(1), 61–71.

Walker, R., & Simmons, C. (2018). Endangered Amazon: An indigenous tribe fights back against hydropower development in the Tapajós Valley. *Environment: Science and Policy for Sustainable Development*, 60(2), 4–15.

Walker, X. J., et al. (2019). Increasing wildfires threaten historic carbon sink of boreal forest soils. *Nature*, 572, 520–523.

Wall, D. (2014). *The sustainable economics of Elinor Ostrom: Commons, contestation and craft*. Routledge.

Wan, K. (2009). Global sustainable development – from above|| and local injustice below||: The governance challenge facing the Congo basin rainforest. *Law. Social Justice & Global Development Journal (LGD)*, 2009(1), 2. www.go.warwick.ac.uk/elj/lgd/2009_1/wan.

Watson Jimenez, A., & Davidsen, C. (2022). Conservation and Indigenous resistance: Protected areas and extractive agendas in the Peruvian Amazon. *Debates en Sociología*, 54, 77–113.

Wegner, R. C., & Pereira, M. (2018). The Amazon and the internationalisation of Chinese companies. *Contexto Internacional*, 40(2), 361–385.

Weiss, E. (2012). The coming water crisis: A common concern of humankind. *Transnational Environmental Law*, 1(1), 153–168.

West, T. (2015). Indigenous community benefits from a decentralized approach to REDD+ in Brazil. *Climate Policy*. https://doi.org/10.1080/14693062.2015.1058238

West, T. A. P., Rausch, L., Munger, J., & Gibbs, H. K. (2022). Protected areas still used to produce Brazil's cattle. *Conservation Letters*, 15, e12916. https://doi.org/10.1111/conl.12916

Weston, B. H., & Bollier, D. (2013). *Green governance: Ecological survival, human rights, and the law of the commons*. Cambridge University Press.

Wheatley, S. (2014). Conceptualizing the authority of the sovereign state over indigenous peoples. *Leiden Journal of International Law*, 27(2), 371–396. https://doi.org/10.1017/S092215651300037X

White, D. (2014). A perfect storm? Indigenous rights within a national REDD+ readiness process in Peru. *Mitigation and Adaptation Strategies for Global Change*, 19(5), 657–676. https://doi.org/10.1007/s11027-013-9523-6

Whiteside, K. (2013). A representative politics of nature? Bruno Latour on collectives and constitutions. *Contemporary Political Theory*, 12, 185–205.

Whitington, J. (2016). Carbon as a metric of the human. *PoLAR*, 39, 46–63. https://doi.org/10.1111/plar.12130

Wiegleb, V., & Bruns, A. (2023). Working the boundary: Science–policy interactions and uneven knowledge politics in IPBES. *Sustainability Science*, 18(5), 1069–1084.

Wiener, L. (2019, May 21). La consulta previa en debate: Sentencia del Parque Ichigkat Muja. *CooperAcción Opina*. www.cooperaccion.org.pe/la-consulta-previa-en-debate-sentencia-del-parque-ichigkat-muja/

Wijkman, P. (1982). Managing the global commons. *International Organization*, 36(3), 511–536.

Wilson Rowe, E. (2018). *Arctic governance. Power in cross-border cooperation*. Manchester: Manchester University Press.

Wilson, R. E. (2021). Ecosystemic politics: Analyzing the consequences of speaking for adjacent nature on the global stage. *Political Geography*, 91, 1–13.

Wit, A., & Freitas, M. (2019). Global climate adaptation governance in the Amazon through a polycentricity lens. *Revista Brasileira de Política Internacional*, 62(2), 1–19.

Witter, R., & Satterfield, T. (2019). The ebb and flow of Indigenous rights recognitions in conservation policy. *Development and Change*, 50(4), 1083–1108. https://doi.org/10.1111/dech.12456

World Economic Forum. (2024, January). Indigenous leaders bringing their knowledge to Davos 2024. *World Economic Forum*. www.weforum.org/agenda/2024/01/indigenous-leaders-knowledge-davos-2024/

Yates, A., Dombroski, K., & Dionisio, R. (2023). Dialogues for wellbeing in an ecological emergency: Wellbeing-led governance frameworks and transformative Indigenous tools. *Dialogues in Human Geography*, 13(2), 268–287.

Yates, J. S., Harris, L. M., & Wilson, N. J. (2017). Multiple ontologies of water: Politics, conflict and implications for governance. *Environment and Planning D: Society and Space*, 35(5), 797–815. https://doi.org/10.1177/0263775817700395

Ybarra, M. (2017). *Green wars: Conservation and decolonization in the Maya Forest*. University of California Press. https://doi.org/10.1525/9780520968035

Ye, J., van der Ploeg, J. D., Schneider, S., & Shanin, T. (2019). The incursions of extractivism: Moving from dispersed places to global capitalism. *The Journal of Peasant Studies*, 47(8), 1–29.

Youatt, R. (2017). Personhood and the rights of nature: The new subjects of contemporary earth politics. *International Political Sociology*, 11(1), 39.

Youdelis, M., Townsend, J., Bhattacharyya, J., & Moola, F. M. (2021). Decolonial conservation: Establishing Indigenous protected areas for future generations in the face of extractive capitalism. *Journal of Political Ecology*, 28(1), 633–658. https://doi.org/10.2458/jpe.4716

Young, M. (2021). A quiet revolution: The exclusivity of exclusive economic zones. In K. Rubenstein (Ed.), *Traversing the divide: Honouring Deborah Cass's contributions to public and international law*. ANU Press.

Zárate, C. G., & Motta, J. A. (2020). Las fronteras amazónicas: un mundo desconocido. *Nueva Sociedad*, 289, 126–137.

Zeitlin, J. (Ed.). (2015). *Extending experimentalist governance? The European Union and transnational regulation.* Oxford University Press. https://doi.org/10.1093/acprof:oso/9780198724506.001.0001

Zelli, F., Bäckstrand, K., Nasiritousi, N., Skovgaard, J., & Widerberg, O. (2020). Introduction: Governing the climate-energy nexus. In F. Zelli, K. Bäckstrand, N. Nasiritousi, J. Skovgaard, & O. Widerberg (Eds.), *Governing the climate-energy nexus: Institutional complexity and its challenges to effectiveness and legitimacy* (pp. 1–18). Cambridge: Cambridge University Press.

Zelli, F., Nielsen, T., & Dubber, W. (2019). Seeing the forest for the trees: Identifying discursive convergence and dominance in complex REDD+ governance. *Ecology and Society*, 24(1), Article 10. https://doi.org/10.5751/ES-10632-240110

Zubrow, E. B. W. Meidinger, E., & Connolly, K. D. (2019). In the vortex of the thaw. In K. D. Connolly, E. Meidinger & E. B. W. Zubrow (Eds.), *The Big Thaw: Policy, Governance, and Climate Change in the Circumpolar North.* Albany: State University of New York Press. https://dx.doi.org/10.1353/book.100021.

Zurba, M., & Papadopoulos, A. (2021). Indigenous participation and the incorporation of Indigenous knowledge and perspectives in global environmental governance forums: A systematic review. *Environmental Management*, 67(1), 35–51.

Zurba, M., Beazley, K. F., English, E., & Buchmann-Duck, J. (2019). Indigenous Protected and Conserved Areas (IPCAs), Aichi Target 11 and Canada's pathway to Target 1: Focusing conservation on reconciliation. *Land*, 8(1), Article 10. https://doi.org/10.3390/land8010010

INDEX

For EU product safety concerns, contact us at Calle de José Abascal, 56–1°, 28003 Madrid, Spain or eugpsr@cambridge.org.

www.ingramcontent.com/pod-product-compliance
Ingram Content Group UK Ltd.
Pitfield, Milton Keynes, MK11 3LW, UK
UKHW050108290926
475880UK00030BA/191
* 9 7 8 1 0 0 9 6 8 9 0 4 5 *